# The Military Intellectuals in Britain:
## 1918-1939

*By the same author*

*Britain's Imperial Air Routes, 1918-1939* (1960)
*The British Rigid Airship, 1908-1931: A Study in Weapons Policy* (1961)
*Armed Forces in Peacetime: Britain 1918-1939* (1963)

*With David H. Zook, Jr.*
*A Short History of Warfare* (1966)

ROBIN HIGHAM

# The Military Intellectuals in Britain: 1918-1939

*Rutgers University Press*

*New Brunswick, New Jersey*

To my fellow charter founders of the
Duke-University of North Carolina National Security Seminar,
stimulating friends, and for Barbara, Susan, Martha, and Carol,
my patient family

# Preface

This work contains the first systematic bringing together of the lives, ideas, and work of Richmond, Fuller, and Liddell Hart. But more than this, its special contribution is to show the development of British thought about the strategic air offensive and the hostile and then unfortunately decisive role that Marshal of the R.A.F. Lord Trenchard played in its creation. In part the book becomes then a contrast between the independent pundits on the one hand and the official thinkers on the other. The former were composed of the advocates of seapower and of landpower, while the latter were mostly in the field of airpower. Moreover, the materials for this study were also divided. The independents left the traditional materials—books, articles, and comments—whereas the airpower school's papers are still covered by the Fifty Year Rule, and most material has had to be gathered from memoirs and official histories as well as from history itself.

The approach, which will not satisfy every critic, is in terms of men rather than of ideas, especially in connection with the problems facing British defence in the interwar years. If there is repetition, it is in part because the writers often repeated themselves in their didacticism.

The origins of the work were two: the first, Captain Liddell Hart's remark in 1934 that students of intellectual history almost never examine the work of the men who have had an immediate life-or-death influence upon society—the military theorists; the second, the kind suggestion of Jon Hassell of G. T. Foulis and Co. Ltd., my London publishers, who, after reading the completed manuscript of my *Armed Forces in Peacetime: Britain 1918-1940* (1963), suggested that the long chapter on the theorists be removed and made the basis for a companion volume.

Since this manuscript was completed in the spring of 1962, new works in the field have included Major William P. Snyder's *The Politics of British Defence* (Columbus, Ohio, 1965); the important volume by Jay Luvaas, *The Education of an Army: British Military Thought, 1815-1940* (Chicago, 1964), which deals only with writers from the Army; Donald M. Schurman, *The Education of a Navy: The Development of British Naval Strategic Thought, 1867-1914* (Chicago, 1965); B. H. Liddell Hart's *Memoirs, 1895-1938* (New York, 1966), and the *festschrift* to him edited by Michael Howard, *The Theory and Practice of War* (London, 1965; New York, 1966).

I wish to thank for their support of the original research the Social Science Research Council of New York and the Faculty Research Council of the University of North Carolina.

A number of friends have been good enough to read the manuscript and offer their wise suggestions: Professors Andrew McKay Scott and Robert Voitle of the University of North Carolina, Captains David H. Zook, Jr., and Alfred Hurley (then of the U.S.A.F. Academy), Dr. Douglas H. Robinson of Pennington, New Jersey, and my father, David Higham of London. To all of them I express my thanks. Errors and opinions are still my own.

R. D. S. H.

Manhattan, Kansas, and
Lake Ariel, Pennsylvania
January 1966

### NOTE

All books cited were published in London, unless otherwise noted.

I am grateful to the Controller of Her Britannic Majesty's Stationery Office for permission to quote from official materials.

# Contents

# The Military Intellectuals in Britain:
1918-1939

# Chapter I — Introduction

This book is about a little band of military men who have, as a group, been dangerously neglected.* Yet they were an important segment of the British ruling class and their influence was of a life-and-death nature within their own lifetimes.

The principals were Vice-Admiral Sir Herbert Richmond, Major-General J. F. C. Fuller, Captain B. H. Liddell Hart, Major-General Sir Frederick Sykes, and Marshal of the R.A.F. Viscount Trenchard. They provide the title for this book—*The Military Intellectuals in Britain*. A few of them never rose much above being successful within their own Service; others became writers whose scholarship and intelligent analyses rank high. They were supported by some lesser lights. With the possible exception of Richmond, all made their greatest contributions in the interwar years. With the exception of Liddell Hart, who was twenty-three in 1918, all were in their forties when the First World War ended. The audience they attempted to influence was divided between the small group of their supporters within and without the armed forces who had a common desire to prevent a repetition of the near-disaster that occurred in the years 1914-18, and a much larger agglomeration of individuals who were more interested in their own affairs than in the central theme of national defence until 1940. When the blitzkrieg hit, the latter group laid the blame upon the military intellectuals rather than upon themselves.

* Though Fuller and Liddell Hart did their most effective writing in the interwar years, 1918-39, it was not until 31 October 1963 that they were awarded the Royal United Service Institution's Chesney Memorial Medal (*The Times*, 1 November 1963) and not until 12 December 1964 that Oxford University recognized Liddell Hart's work with an honourary Doctor of Letters (*The Oxford Times*, 20 November 1964). The Government conferred a Knighthood upon Liddell Hart in the New Year's Honours, 1966.

*3*

These men held varying positions of power and influence, but none reached the summit achieved by Chief of the Air Staff Lord Trenchard, whose fifteen years of control over the infant Royal Air Force was so significant. Trenchard and the airpower exponents show the dangers into which any theoretical programme can fall when its directors and planners do not periodically face realities, when criticism is stifled, and when they are beset with all the problems of creating a new Service. Airpower theory was forced to logical conclusions for political reasons, but the technical equipment to make it practical was not pursued.

These military intellectuals all had moments of influence. For most of them these were periods of only a few months in which they had the ear of decision-makers. Trenchard was the exception. He enjoyed power for nearly fifteen years as General Officer Commanding the Royal Flying Corps in France and then as Chief of the Air Staff. Second to him came Liddell Hart with his memoranda and his period as adviser to the Secretary of State for War, Leslie Hore-Belisha, in the late thirties. Apart from Trenchard, Richmond was nominated for First Sea Lord, Fuller was seriously suggested for Chief of the Imperial General Staff * and Liddell Hart for Secretary of the Committee of Imperial Defence.

That this group desired to make changes was the result not so much of their individual backgrounds as of their feeling that the First World War had shown the military incapable of meeting the challenge of the Industrial Revolution in a rational way. They lived in the postwar depression years in Britain, when it became obvious that there was something more to war than victory in the field. They wanted to avoid, then, both the inefficiency of the sort displayed in action in the late war and to see that in any future conflict a decision would be reached, as effectively and in as short a time as possible, that would decide the issue and leave the world free to revive trade and prosperity.

In order to achieve this goal, they fitted themselves into the mainstream of intellectual history by becoming humanitarians, psychologists, economists, political scientists. They were interested in the lot of the citizen at war, whether he was on the fighting or on the home front. They studied the conditions under which the soldier

---

* In a letter to the author of 20 October 1965, General Fuller said that on the outbreak of war in 1939 General Ironside asked for Fuller as his Deputy, but that his request was turned down on the grounds of Fuller's political leanings.

had to fight and the psychological approaches that might help him. They sought to educate everyone, from privates, able-seamen, and airmen, to Cabinet Ministers. They analysed society to see how it functioned and how money could best be spent to give the greatest results.

These military intellectuals do not as a group fit into any type or any pattern, except the broad one found in studying any group of intellectuals. Their breadth of view and their vision seem to have been in inverse ratio to the rank they achieved. This may be due to the fact that the end of a major war found them at various ranks and, in the ensuing stagnation and career-consciousness of peacetime, the older men saw more future in the Service, while the younger saw more outside it. Nevertheless, it was true that life in the Services had not been such as to encourage research, writing, and the expression of individual and controversial opinions. But whether within or without the Services, they suffered much as other pundits and prophets have, from neglect by their colleagues and attention to their ideas by their nation's enemies. And like other intellectuals, they had their blind spots. There were areas into which they never looked or about which they could not speak. If they were closely associated with policy-making, or had been secretly briefed, they could not speak. Moreover, more than others, especially during re-armament, they had to bear in mind the national interest, owing to the fact that they might have an influence that would harm Britain. In fact, they all strove severely and at personal cost to alert the country to the truth as they saw it. If they made mistakes and sometimes supported the unsuccessful weapon, so have many others made similar mistakes.

All their work might have been in vain if they had not been able to catch the attention of at least some persons of influence. That they were able to do this is not only to their credit as writers, but also to that of the editors and publishers who were willing to publish them. This gave them a wider following and influence than they might have had if they had merely written for select Service audiences composed largely of friends. Like others, they had a message, but theirs was not so unrealistic: War would remain as an instrument of national policy because men were not yet perfect, but that was no reason why war should be any more inefficient than any other human activity, even if it had to be more brutal. Moreover, they were principally concerned with preventing war in the first place by making their democratic nation strong enough to deter any agressor from taking a hostile course of action toward it.

Though these men thought of themselves as modern, they had many ties with the past, and their story is not dissimilar, in some of its concern with education and in natural laws, to that of the *philosophes* of the eighteenth century from which sprang the gods of military theory, Jomini and Clausewitz.

# Chapter II — Background

In studying the British military intellectuals of the interwar years one cannot help but be impressed with two facts: on the one hand that the moderates, Richmond, Fuller, and Liddell Hart, proved correct by the Second World War, were denied sufficient influence to prevent the Higher Direction (the phrase is Kingston-McCloughry's) stumbling unprepared into war in 1939; on the other hand, that the extremely long tenure of power of a Chief of Staff doggedly committed to his own prejudices (Trenchard) can lead to disaster. In order to avoid these possibilities, it is vital that many ideas, orthodox or not, be analysed and tested. To every challenge there is a response. But whether the riposte is clumsy massive retaliation or a more sophisticated, less expensive, and sometimes more practicable answer, depends to a large extent on who is allowed to find a countermeasure and under what circumstances. Economy of force is just as much a principle of action as is concentration.

It is essential, therefore, that not only should the Government sponsor civilian research such as that undertaken in the United States by the RAND Corporation and other semiprivate bodies, by Senator Henry M. Jackson's subcommittee on national security policy of the Senate Committee on Government Organization, and by Senator (now Vice-President) Hubert Humphrey's subcommittee of the Senate Small Business Committee, but that the Services themselves make room for the very small group of talented thinkers, marking them in the junior ranks and providing them with the time and the means with which to develop their own breadth and ideas.* Perhaps because there was a very considerable lack of this sort of thing

* For a full expansion of this point, see my article in *The Navy Times* (Washington, D.C.), 3 September 1960, pp. 13, 54, pleading for a Mahan Institute for junior officers.

in Britain in the interwar years, and even after World War II, the best military thinking was done by a handful of outsiders. It is ironic that the Institute for Strategic Studies in London should have been established in 1958 by Ford Foundation money. And yet, despite this, as *The Times Literary Supplement* commented, the bulk of the works on strategy are still coming from Americans.*

Another danger that this book reveals is that of defining in logical and immutable terms the role or mission of a Service. This tends to create an insularity within the Service that may result in the means having no relation to the ends or to realities. But from British experience, it can also be said that when the political leadership, the Higher Direction, fails to define the strategic purposes or even to take an interest in the Services, then an equally disastrous situation can arise.

The vexing question as to why the leaders in Britain failed to pay more attention to the armed forces is one that will continue to puzzle scholars, especially those unwilling to consider the contributions of military historians towards an understanding of this problem. There can, of course, be no simple answer, but increasingly studies seem to show that the ruling class on the Tory side could be perfectly bloodthirsty and brutal about foxes and pheasants, but shrink from the same ruthlessness in dealing with world problems. In fact, the Tories seem to have shrunk once again since 1951 from dealing with Continentals and to have put their trust in the Navy and the Channel and to a lesser extent in the Royal Air Force, without, however, making sure that these protectors of private gain are able to deal with the threats rising on the other side of the moat. Liberals were politically powerless voices crying in the wilderness, while Labour politicians, until Clement Attlee demanded differently in 1935, misunderstood the realities of disarmament, the League of Nations, and the place of war.

Critics raise the question of Churchill's record at this point. It must be said in his defence that in the decade after the First World War in which he held office, he acted as a normal, proper British politician. He sought to reduce costs. At the same time, the Cabinet had laid down in August 1919 that no major war was to be expected

---

* Lawrence W. Martin, "The Market for Strategic Ideas in Britain," *The American Political Science Review*, LVI, No. 1 (March 1962), 23-41. *The Times Literary Supplement*, 14 November 1963, pp. 917-918.

for ten years, and that period did not come to an end until the later years of his days at the Exchequer. Even then, when he proposed that the Ten Year Rule be placed on a moving annual basis, Britain had no enemies. But in the thirties, when he was an outsider not bound by party responsibility and regarded as a has-been, he spoke as events demanded. It is a mistake to confuse the Churchill of 1919-30 with the Winston of 1931-39.

A further danger, other than from Tories, Liberals, and Labourites, assailed Britain in the interwar years. Her military leaders showed a surprising complacency and lack of interest in foreign armies, navies, and air forces. Thus comparisons were not made (until very late) that would have revealed to the Cabinet the many weaknesses that existed. Even worse, relatively little work was undertaken to ascertain the weak points in the economies of potential opponents. It could be argued that there were no enemies since France, Japan, and the United States were all former allies. But as Machiavelli long ago pointed out, the friend of today may be the enemy of tomorrow, and the Second World War certainly proved the point.

In our own day in the United States, the opposite danger seems to have arisen. Not only is there a hypnotic fascination with Russia, now a traditional enemy, but in an influential part of the community an almost hero-worship of academic theorists and war-gamers and of the computer.* These people are in danger of expecting ordinary military men to act in war situations just as calmly and rationally as they will at peacetime games, but with live troops who may or may not be able to carry out their orders. The history of the R.A.F. bomber offensive of 1939-45 shows only too well what happens when the civilian soldier is sent to battle. Yet another danger has been spotlighted by one of the leading operational scientists—that the military will expect scientists to make their decisions for them.† Furthermore, history also shows that scientists are themselves human beings with prejudices that may affect their judgments and the history of their nations, as witness Lord Cherwell's (Prof. F. A. Linde-

* See the counterblast by Irving Louis Horowitz, *The War Game: Studies of the New Civilian Militarists* (New York, 1963); and Sidney Hook's review of Anatole Rappaport's *Strategy and Conscience* in *The New York Times Book Review,* 19 July 1964, pp. 6, 25.

† Sir Solly Zuckerman, "Judgment and Control in Modern Warfare," *Foreign Affairs,* XL, No. 2 (January 1962), 196-212.

mann's) hostility to radar and the Oppenheimer-Teller quarrel over the hydrogen bomb.*

Basically, what is offered in this book is a historical study showing that despite the antiwar attitude that existed in England, despite the attempts to return to the Victorian era (which succeeded almost too well in the case of the two older Services), there was in Britain a fountainhead of military thought whose influence, ironically, was far greater amongst future enemies than amongst Englishmen themselves. At the same time, the one Service that was compelled to listen to a new doctrine preached by its own Chief of Staff was led down almost the same path as that trod by the French naval radicals of the *jeune école* in the late nineteenth century. Why?

### THE CLIMATE OF OPINION

The British had been on the winning side in the First World War. In the last two years their armies had borne the brunt of the fighting, and their morale had not cracked. The Empire had not only been preserved but enlarged with mandates. They could, therefore, return to business as usual, to a reduction of State expenditure, and to an idealistic reduction of armaments. Since the Services had the poorest political lobbies, and were the best-disciplined part of society, they were a natural target for reductions as the 1931 financial crisis demonstrated. In the climate of opinion that prevailed, why should anyone listen to a minute band of militarists who said that another war might occur and who said it before even "the Last War," "the War to End All Wars," had been paid for. The subject of war, therefore, became one that simply was not to be mentioned.

In France, where the armies had mutinied after the bloodbath at Verdun in 1916 and had but barely been kept from deserting, war was feared. Germany had to be kept in her place. Despite some belief in a new war opening with a massive aerial blow, the emphasis was upon a 1916-style defence against a German invasion, which culminated in the construction of the Maginot Line, trench

---

* C. P. Snow, *Science and Government* (the 1963 New American Library edition contains the revisions that the original Harvard edition does not), and *Life,* 13 December 1963, pp. 87A-110. Another side of this story is contained in Fletcher Knebel and Charles A. Bailey, Jr., *No High Ground* (New York, 1960), supplemented by their article in *Look,* 13 August 1963, pp. 19-23.

warfare in comfort sufficient to prevent cowardice.\* The one light in this darkness was a young officer named Charles de Gaulle, who wrote a series of works in the manner of Fuller and Liddell Hart, but whose fame, rather like that of Sir Winston Churchill, now rests largely on his actions during and since the Second World War.† The French Army was strong during the twenties and so was the Air Force, but both suffered from involvement in politics in the thirties, when the Navy was being rebuilt to meet the Italian menace in the Mediterranean.

In Italy the early take-over by Mussolini allowed the Italian armed forces to advance fairly rapidly. The national preoccupation with showing-off resulted in a rapid acceptance of mechanization and of the Douhetian doctrines of a massive aerial blow against a neighbouring enemy while the Army held the Alpine passes. Mechanical speed became the symbol of modern dictatorship. The problem for the Italians was that as a people they loved life too well to fight effectively, as Caporetto in 1917 and the Second World War proved. Nor did they have the vital natural resources, especially oil.

In the United States isolationism prevailed. The return to an Indian-fighting Army without any Indians to fight was as complete as the return to the Northwest Frontier force was in the British Army. Politically isolationism was the order of the day far into the end of the thirties. But complete stagnation was avoided because of a number of things. First, Billy Mitchell and his flyers fought for an independent Air Force and, not content with fighting their own Army brass, they aroused the Navy by sinking battleships and claiming, like Trenchard's R.A.F., the ability to defeat invasion far out at sea. Though the claim was unsound, to say the least, in the then current state of the art, it did have the magnificent side effect of reviving the Navy's air-consciousness and thus impelling it along the road to the development of the carrier task forces that played such

---

\* Sir Basil Liddell Hart has kindly called my attention to the view now gaining ground that the Maginot Line was originally intended as an offensive shield to guard the flank of an offensive French thrust through Belgium. This may have been the first intention; it was not how it worked out, since the aggressiveness of the French Army was sapped in the thirties.

† Charles de Gaulle, *La discorde chez l'énnemi* (1924), *Le fils de l'Epée* (1932), *Vers l'Armée de Metier* (1934), *France et son Armée* (1938, English edition 1945). See also the Harvard dissertation on French military doctrine between the wars by Alvin D. Coox (1950) and Paul de la Gorce, *The French Army in Politics* (New York, 1962).

a vital part in the Pacific war, 1941-45.* To this may be added the American interest in things mechanical. Third, the British writers, particularly Liddell Hart, wrote upon the one subject that Americans could not ignore—the Civil War. Having read *Sherman,* men like "Blood and Guts" Patton sought out Liddell Hart's other works. But the American Army was slow to accept armoured forces until after the 1940 German blitzkrieg in France; fortunately, the American Army had time to recover before being committed to action in North Africa in late 1942.† In the meantime, in 1935 the U.S. Army Air Corps (created by Congress in 1926) thought it had the weapon with which it could undertake a strategic bombing campaign, the Boeing B-17. But the United States Army Air Corps was to be proved optimistic as it was later forced to admit.‡

In the interwar years Japan built both on her own experiences and with an eye upon others. Her Navy was given excellent training in the early twenties by a group of Royal Naval Air Service veterans. But how much her military development was influenced by European or American ideas is not known generally though we gather that they were familiar with the United States Navy's work.§ What the 1941-45 war did show was that the Japanese had worked out a successful carrier doctrine based upon tactics employed with other forces during the Russo-Japanese War. But like Germany in the Second World War, Japan suffered from the economic inability to conduct a long-drawn-out war when faced with the industrial potential of the United States.

The last of the major Allies of the First World War was Russia. There, as in Italy, a totalitarian dictatorship took over with mech-

* The story is told in Walter Millis, *Arms and Men* (New York, 1956); Archibald D. Turnbull and Clifford L. Lord, *History of United States Naval Aviation* (New Haven, 1949); S. E. Morison, *U.S. Naval Operations in World War II* (Boston, 1947-63).

† Outside of the voluminous series on the U.S. Army in World War II being issued by the Office of the Chief of Military History in Washington, about the only account of the development of American armoured forces is in Mildred Harmer Gillie's *Forging the Thunderbolt* (Harrisburg, 1947).

‡ H. H. Arnold, *Global Mission* (New York, 1949); W. F. Craven and James L. Cate, *The Army Air Forces in World War II* (Chicago, 1948-54).

§ The article in E. M. Earle (ed.), *The Makers of Modern Strategy* (Princeton, 1943) needs serious revision. Otherwise the above statement is based on the search of the Library of Congress Catalogue subject headings on World War II that I undertook as adviser to the Eisenhower Library during 1963-64. My check did not include works in Japanese.

anization as a symbol of modernization. The sheer necessity of fighting for its life in 1917-22 compelled the Communist Government to
develop its armed forces. Moreover, the stigma of tsarist defeats
moved the new military hierarchy to seek means of avoiding a
repetition of the 1914-18 debacle. Though little was done with the
Navy, the Red Army was modernized as part of the third Five Year
Plan. Its leaders not only read but pirated the works of outsiders on
military theory. And the more the threat of war with Germany became apparent and the lessons of Spain sank in, the harder the
Russians strove to build an army that could stand up to the *panzers*.
The Russian Air Force was also created and turned primarily into a
tactical vehicle, which, in the last analysis, was probably its best
role, since the strategic targets that it might have reached were few.

The power that most avidly sought to avoid another stalemate
and another defeat was Germany, the sole member of the Central
Powers to survive as a potential aggressor. Helped by the "stab in
the back" myth, the German armed forces were allowed by their
government to develop by themselves despite the Versailles restrictions. The result was that though Germany possessed no colonies in
which to gain experience, German military men did. They went to
Russia and Colombia, Spain and Holland, where they trained soldiers, ran schools and airlines, and designed and developed tanks,
aircraft, and submarines. Because the Army had been beaten in part
by the tank and because younger officers rebelled against the uselessness of trench warfare, German Army Officers became avid disciples of Fuller and Liddell Hart.* And, owing to the special German geographic position, much thought was given to defence along
the lines of a holding action *à la* Schlieffen. This meant that defensive
actions were not relegated to the realm of the unmilitary the way
they were officially in the British Army. In the German Navy the
Versailles limitations, coupled with the successes of raiders and
U-boats, encouraged an active pursuit of these weapons in contrast
to a High Seas Fleet composed of forbidden and probably useless
battleships. The Air Force gained considerably from its enforced
concentration on civilian operations and emerged with surprising
speed in Hitler's day from chrysalis to venomous tactical moth rather
than strategic hornet. In 1940 two things, apart from British morale,

---

* See Friedrich von Mellinthin, *Panzer Battles* (Norman, Okla., 1955) and
Heinz Guderian, *Panzer Leader* (New York, 1956).

prevented the Germans from defeating Britain: the lack of range in fighters and bombers, and insufficient seapower.

In all these countries people argued about *war*.

## WAR

War is gaining by force what cannot be obtained by threat or negotiation. The objective is a better position.

As Clausewitz noted, wars are fought for two main purposes: limited wars to obtain small gains along the frontiers and major ones to force an opponent to bend to your will.*

One of the major distortions of the nineteenth century was to convert Clausewitz's concept of success in the field sufficient to obtain the goal of war into an overall destructive victory. This confusion was further nurtured in such conflicts as the Second World War by the need to hold coalitions together. It should be clearly noted that Clausewitz pointed out both that wars might be won by a long defensive (the strategy of exhaustion) followed by a counterstroke and by indirect action that achieved the desired end without fighting. The Napoleonic Wars repeated the difficulty of the Thirty Years' War in bringing onto the field once again ideological differences that in themselves tended to spawn mass armies content to live off the opponent's land. The French Revolution added the *levée en masse*, the conscript army, thus enabling the generalissimo (Napoleon) to command vast forces endowed with burning zeal. The First World War produced a logical extension of this concept of nations at war when the idea of naval bombardments was converted into strategic air attacks upon enemy capitals and civilians, for these were thought to be the weakest part of the will to fight. Despite the lessons of Napoleon's fall, caused by the inevitable coalition against one-power domination of the continent of

* Karl von Clausewitz, *On War* (New York, 1943). This Modern Library translation, the first American edition, contains an interesting introduction by Colonel Joseph I. Greene, then editor of *The Infantry Journal,* which in itself reveals much of the American military mind. Clausewitz, however, wrote as a Prussian who had served both Napoleon and the Russians. His work was regarded as the bible of military thought and like the greater Gospel is not only open to many interpretations, but reflects its national background. So, too, has it been more often quoted than read. The piece on Clausewitz together with the other essays in E. M. Earle (ed.), *Makers of Modern Strategy*, needs to be read with great care.

Europe, and of Bismarck's superb campaign for German unification, civilian lack of understanding combined with military cupidity and nationalism pushed Europe towards the stalemate of 1914-18. In that cauldron grand strategy, strategy, and tactics became bogged. In part this was because almost everybody was fighting a defensive war. And having lost face by not achieving a victory in short order, no one, understandably, wanted to stop until the advantage was on his side. War without an objective or the means to achieve one could not but become a bloody, senseless struggle of exhaustion versus survival.

Grand strategy requires a clear objective in which war is but a drastic means to an end. What role the nation's military, diplomatic, and economic forces must play and for what purpose are questions that the Higher Direction, focused in the Cabinet and the Chiefs of Staff, is called upon to answer. Until this has been done, taking due account of likely moves by enemy and neutral powers during the same period and the countermoves needed to offset these, nothing can really be accomplished by strategies designed to bring the military forces into play. Moreover, grand strategy, and even strategy, must be exercised as much in peacetime as in war. In fact, until the Cold War, there was a delusion in the twentieth century that these were topics that only needed to be pursued in wartime. Yet military conflict is but an inconstant and occasional interlude in a continuous struggle for survival.

Britain entered the Second World War with a somewhat clearer grand strategy, the containment of Hitler, than she had the First.* The objective soon came to be the defeat of Hitler, and at the Casablanca Conference early in 1943 it was coupled to "unconditional surrender," a policy designed to hold together the alliance that included Free France and Russia.

The military intellectuals made relatively little attempt to deal with grand strategy, largely because none of them had firsthand experience making it. Some contribution in a historical fashion was made in *The World Crisis* † by Winston Churchill in which he described his role in the First World War and in the work that he

* Our knowledge of this period will remain incomplete until after the first volume of the *Grand Strategy* series of the official histories is published. Sir Winston Churchill was not in the Government during the decade 1929-39, and for this period his works consist of histories of other periods and books of speeches.

† New York, 1923-31.

and Lord Haldane did in attempting to establish a Ministry of Defence in 1919 and he alone in 1936. But until Churchill as Prime Minister assumed the post of Minister of Defence in 1940, politics prevented anything stronger than the weak Minister for the Co-ordination of Defence of 1936 being established. The Ministry of Defence came in 1947, but it was not until 1964 that the various duplicate Service Secretaries were replaced by a single Minister and a single Chief of Staff. Churchill himself was a magnificent war-time Prime Minister, but his interwar record in various peacetime offices, especially as Chancellor of the Exchequer, 1925-29, did little for the Services and nothing for grand strategy.

Beneath grand strategy lies strategy, the movement of forces in peace or war so as to achieve the advantage. For non-belligerent democracies this means primarily the distribution of their strength so as to maintain the status quo in a world changed by new align-ments amongst or within states, by technology, and by new weapons. In Britain for centuries the unwritten emphasis had been upon the maintenance of a two-power standard by the Royal Navy. But the First World War showed that more than a mere numerical superi-ority in ships was needed. Quality, technical excellence, staff work, and highly trained leadership were also vital.* In the interwar years the growing deficiency in quality and quantity left the Royal Navy hard-pressed to deal with the excellent German navy of 1939. The basic strategy of the Royal Navy remained that sketched by the American Admiral A. T. Mahan and so well described by Captain S. W. Roskill in the official *The War at Sea*.† But British strategy went wrong before the First World War and in violation of a sound tradition became involved in the immediate support of a Continen-tal power, France, for centuries the normal foe. This fatal link was not destroyed until the German *panzers* fortunately thrust the Brit-ish out at Dunkirk in 1940. Thereafter, Britain reverted to her traditional maritime strategy of protecting the vital sea lanes, re-building her military strength, and striking offensive blows at the time and place of her own choosing.

* See the definitive work by Arthur Marder, *The Anatomy of British Sea Power* (New York, 1940, reissued at Hamden, Conn., 1963) and the sequel *From the Dreadnought to Scapa Flow* (New York, 1961- ). Corelli Barnett's *The Swordbearers* (London, 1963) and S. W. Roskill's *The Art of Leadership* (1963) are provocative.

† See especially Chapter I of Volume I and Chapter XXIX of Volume III, Part II.

Traditionally after 1661 Britain had maintained a small royal bodyguard at home, expanded upon necessity as a shield against invasion, while garrisons were kept overseas to protect rich colonial possessions and vital naval bases. Continentals were paid to fight British wars in Europe. Only occasionally, as in the War of Spanish Succession, as in the defence of Hanover, or as in the Napoleonic Wars, was a British Army landed on the Continent to undertake a major campaign. From 1815 until the beginning of the staff talks with France in 1906, the British Army was a colonial force, and its thinking until well after the First World War was that of the leadership of the Army in India. The 1914-18 war did place in the War Office a great many men whose experience of war was mainly gained in France. But while they laboured to return their Service to the 1914 budgetary level, they were given no guidance as to the role of the interwar Army until 1936, when it was decided that it would revert once again to a colonial force. Then suddenly in 1939 conscription was reintroduced, and the War Office was informed that it was to raise fifty-five divisions for service in France. Norway and Dunkirk ended this misuse of British forces. Thereafter, as Roskill notes, except for the abortive expeditions to Dakar and Greece, the Army settled down to a traditional British role, the defence of Egypt falling under the heading of colonial protection. Ultimately, of course, the strength was created with which to clear North Africa and invade Italy, France, and Burma.

British strategy in the interwar years can only be described as inadequate. But a good deal of the blame for this must be placed upon the political leadership that failed to provide grand strategy and the means even to maintain the traditional British posture where the surface forces were concerned. The position was even more grievous for the new third Service, the Air Force.

Here the claim was made, as in the Mitchellian American counterpart, that the aeroplane was an utterly new weapon of war and that, therefore, none of the older rules applied to it. Yet what did airmen do but adopt Clausewitz's concept of paralysing the will to war of the enemy? A deterrent striking force is a feasible conception if the foe is convinced that it has the power to do the job. The British aerial deterrent was bad strategy because it was neither credible nor capable. As Sir Charles Webster and Noble Frankland have pointed out, it had neither the equipment nor the training to deliver the blow, and war soon proved it a blunted sword.* More-over, the basic strategy adopted was false in that the emphasis was put first upon a blow against an enemy and only secondarily and with extreme reluctance upon defence of the island air base and industrial arsenal. If it had not been for the change of direction instituted in 1936, radar and fighters might never have been devel-oped and the Battle of Britain lost in 1940. Shamefully little was done about either Army Co-operation (the tactical air force) or the protection of seaborne commerce (Coastal Command and the Fleet Air Arm).

At the bottom of the scale lie tactics, action taken when in contact with the enemy. All that need be said of them here is that they must obey, within the limitations of each action, the principles of war. These are variously given, but generally include selection of the objective, protection of communications, concentration of effort, economy of force, and the use of surprise.†

The tactical level is that at which strategic equipment becomes operational. Until about 1850 there was relatively little change in communications and weapons. Then came steamships, railways, tele-graphs, rifled guns, and a little later in the century torpedoes and submarines, with, just after 1900, telephones and wireless, internal combustion engines, aeroplanes, tanks, and the machine guns. It has been claimed that all of these inventions were in their day revolu-tionary, especially the aeroplane and more recently the atomic bomb. The longer view is that they were not. The simple upward curve of human development and of the increase in knowledge shows by com-parison that even the aeroplane has developed within the general structure of society. Aircraft were not the first nor the last weapons to be considered by their adherents so radical as to change the fundamentals of war. The blame for this misconception must lie upon the fact that their proponents were young and ill-educated and that they either came from a society that had failed to understand the significant changes taking place in the industrial world or from that particularly sheltered, intellectually isolated group, the mili-

---

* *The Strategic Air Offensive against Germany,* I (1961), 1-135. See also David Divine, *The Blunted Sword* (1964).

† See E. J. Kingston-McCloughry, *Global Strategy* (1957), p. 33, and Fuller's and Liddell Hart's versions given below. The principles of war were often mentioned, but never enumerated, in British military manuals until after the 1914 War. For an excellent survey of tactics in the 1939-45 war, see Fuller's *The Second World War* (1948).

tary caste. For instance, official specifications for military aircraft in Britain have all too often lagged behind what designers could produce five years before the type was due to be operational.*

Rapid technological change has usually had to be used by leaders whose acquaintanceship with its products has been at best superficial. The generals of the First World War had little practical knowledge of the machine gun, barbed wire, or siege warfare. Their experience of war was limited either to minor engagements or to maneuvers. They simply could not comprehend the vast problems of moving massed forces over ground churned to mud by massed artillery. Industrial power and bad generalship simply slaughtered the infantry. Late in the war armies began to find new ways to cross no-man's land using combat teams or tanks. But these methods had to be forced upon them. In the meantime they had tended to neglect one of the most important of all the principles of war—surprise.

But it was not simply the vast agglomeration of men produced by conscription and of material provided by an industrialized society that they did not understand. Too often both military and civilian leaders have regarded remarkable new weapons of war as requiring whole new laws of operation, or at least being able to discard the old principles of war. The most recent examples are airpower and the atomic bomb. The latter in particular has developed into something of an impossible weapon. No statesman with a thorough understanding of war dares use it now because it will return to spoil the peace.† Furthermore, the atomic bomb cannot be used against a primarily agrarian society without defying the principle of economy of force and without the danger of bringing the user to national bankruptcy. To put it over-simply, in order to understand new weapons, it has been necessary to obtain new maps on which the increase in range and power can be seen in perspective. If the weapon is too unwieldy for the job at hand, then either the emphasis has to be upon something more conventional or upon diplomacy and peace-keeping.

What appears to have exercised a far more important effect upon

* This statement will be documented in my forthcoming work on the British aircraft industry, *Production and Politics*. Early examples of it can be found in *The British Rigid Airship* (Hamden, Conn., 1961).

† The satire on this in the movie *Dr. Strangelove* (1964) could be viewed with extreme alarm for some of the characters were only too close to life. See also the 1962 Lees-Knowles lectures by Sir John Winthrop Hackett, "The Profession of Arms," *The Times* (London), 4-6 December 1962, p. 13.

organizations in the twentieth century than the actual nature of particular weapons, is the generally alarming increase in the cost of defence. War has become too large a part of the national budget to be left to the soldiers. This has caused some remarkable changes in the actions that the civilian Higher Direction has been prepared to take, as witness the installation of Mr. McNamara as Secretary of Defense and of his whiz kids in the American Pentagon.* Certainly political and economic reasons have played a most important part in the evolution of the defence organization in Britain. The creation of the Ministry of Defence in 1919 and in 1936 was defeated largely because Winston Churchill was the logical candidate for the Secretaryship. The Royal Air Force and the Air Ministry came into being because of production problems. The Ministry of Supply was created in 1939 because the War Office could not handle procurement and the Ministry of Aircraft Production in 1940 because the Air Ministry was incapable in this vital activity. All of which raises once more the important point in regard to an understanding of the position of the military intellectuals in Britain in the interwar years: why were the armed forces neglected? †

First, there was a failure of leadership caused both by the neglect of defence and lack of interest in it on the parts of Bonar Law, Stanley Baldwin, and Ramsay MacDonald. When the Prime Ministers did not consider the subject important, why should others? Second, there was a great insistence upon orthodox finance and upon disarmament,‡ which helped create a mammoth unemployment that the politicians were unable to solve but that absorbed their attention. Third, the leadership of the day, largely ignored by the "lost generation" that went into business instead of politics in reaction to the conduct of the 1914 war, was not interested in things foreign or intellectual and wished to forget the bad dream of the Last War, which had done so much to destroy the comfortable Victorian world in which it had matured. Fourth, there was the Englishman's traditional dislike of unpleasant facts and basic theories as well as of dirty, noisy machinery, to which must be added a certain snobbishness. Fifth, there was a great belief in unpremeditated, *ad hoc* gov-

* See William W. Kaufman, *The McNamara Strategy* (New York, 1964).

† This is a question that I discussed in *Armed Forces in Peacetime* in the chapter on politicians and defence.

‡ Fuller in his *The Second World War*, p. 25, lays the blame on a financial war with the United States.

ernment, which seems to have degenerated since the Second World War into playing the political game for that game's sake. Sixth, there was the nature of English "public school" education, which still stubbornly places the emphasis upon the classics and gentlemanly pursuits, to the neglect of applied science and government. Until the Fisher-Selbourne reforms in the Royal Navy early in the century, engineers were hardly considered officers.* In the British Army of the interwar years gunners, for instance, were a lesser breed of officers and "did not hunt." All of these things were subtle and indefinable. They amounted to an unwillingness to discuss that most unpleasant of all subjects, the possibility of another major European war, an affair quite different from a colonial skirmish, which might be regarded as a form of hunting. And last, it might be added that the inefficient practice of "muddling through" has been made into a virtue that has possibly calamitous underpinnings.

Simple as the rules of war are, their application is complex and requires study and understanding by the Higher Direction and not merely by a host of subcommittees of the Committee of Imperial Defence as happened in the years 1918-39.† War affects the whole of society, and so the responsible officials owe it to their constituents to discuss it and never to allow any one school of thought to hold undisputed sway.

* In addition to Marder's works, see Geoffrey Penn, *"Up Funnel, Down Screw!"* (London, 1955).
† See Franklyn Arthur Johnson, *Defence by Committee* (1960).

*Book One*

# Operational Research: The Exponents of Sea- and Landpower

# *Chapter III* — The Military Intellectuals

The military intellectuals in interwar Britain can be divided into two groups: the official thinkers on the staffs and in the military graduate colleges, and the independent pundits.

The work of the Service staffs in the interwar years is only just beginning to be revealed in the official series, *United Kingdom History of the Second World War*. Naval staffs concentrated on routine chores, military * on returning to the status quo of 1914, and the Air Staff on a war the Air Force had not the equipment to fight. Neither the Naval nor the Imperial General Staff made any clear usable war plans until after the Munich crisis in 1938. This was not entirely their fault because of the lack of Higher Direction.† This lack of focus must have been felt in the staff colleges, where officers were trained to run major commands and the Admiralty, the War Office, and the Air Ministry. The emphasis was on the study of selected campaigns.

### The Official Intellectuals: The Staff Colleges ‡

Relatively little is known about what took place in the staff colleges. It does appear that these schools in training officers for higher

* The term "military" (in typically ambiguous fashion) means both pertaining to the Army and matters dealing with armed forces. We need some new word such as "armial" to cover the former meaning with greater clarity.

† The best book on the Higher Direction in the interwar years is Franklyn Arthur Johnson, *Defence by Committee* (1960).

‡ The main work is A. R. Godwin-Austen, *The Staff and the Staff College* (1927). More recently there is *The Eighth Report from the Estimates Committee* of the House of Commons, *Service Colleges (H.C. 296), 1963-64; (H.C. 229), 1963-64* and *Session 1964-65, Special Report 3. Service Colleges (Departmental Observations upon the Eighth Report . . . ) (H.C. 88)* (1965); A. C. T. White, *The Story of Army Education, 1643-1963* (1963). Harold Florian Clark and

commands took little interest in grand strategy, the overall conduct of a war. Nor did they pay too much attention to the logistical side of strategy, the art of the general, other than to discuss its relationship to the Quartermaster-General's Department. Grand strategy was left to the Committee of Imperial Defence and its subcommittees, while instruction in it was the business of the Imperial Defence College, which opened its doors in 1927. Though this new organization was not a fountain of theories and ideas, it did serve as a stimulating training ground. Before we examine it, however, a few comments on the senior service schools are in order.

It is difficult to ascertain what went on at the R.A.F. Staff College at Andover during the interwar years. But the early failure of Army Co-operation in the Second World War and its subsequent development along the German model, the paucity of maritime air equipment, and the late switch-over to a Home Defence Force composed of fighters all indicate that insufficient attention was paid to these matters. Or it may well be that the recurrent economy drives forced policy makers to take the safe course so that new ideas were never tested in the field. This despite the fact that an emphasis on research had been one of the original aims of the R.A.F. The few memoirs that discuss this blame economizing, claiming that those who went to Andover and later to the Imperial Defence College were dynamic. But even though they often held staff appointments afterwards, the very youth of the Air Force made it difficult for them to provide proof that their ideas were sound. Some air-inspired concepts appeared, such as dive-bombing at the annual interwar Hendon Display, but they were indulged in as much because they were spectacular stunts as because they were practical tactical propositions. The Second World War in France and the Western Desert revealed that the new equipment was modifiable to new tactical doctrines, but that these

H. S. Sloan, *Classrooms in the Military* (New York, 1964), John W. Masland and Laurence I. Radway, *Soldiers and Scholars; Military Education and National Policy* (Princeton, 1957); Gene M. Lyons and John W. Masland, *Education and Military Leadership: A Study of the R.O.T.C.* (Princeton, 1959), and Gene M. Lyons and Louis Morton, *Schools for Strategy: Education and Research in National Security Affairs* (New York, 1965) cover the widening American interest in these subjects. (The account in Lyons and Morton of the Duke-University of North Carolina Seminar is inaccurate and slights my role in organizing that group.) The only two works touching this for Britain: William Snyder's *Politics of British Defence Policy* (Columbus, Ohio, 1965) and Lawrence W. Martin's article, "The Market for Strategic Ideas in Britain," *The American Political Science Review*, LVI, No. 1 (March 1962), 23-41.

were at first lacking. As proof of this one has only to look at a picture of a Hurricane in spring 1939 and another towards the end of its operational life in 1942. Designed to a specification calling for two fixed guns in the fuselage, by 1939 it had eight machine guns in the wings and a fixed-pitch, two-bladed wooden propeller. By 1942 it had switched to four 20 mm. cannon, a constant-speed airscrew, long-range tanks, and on occasion two 40 mm. anti-tank guns.

The other staff colleges, at Camberley for the Army and Greenwich for the Senior Naval Officers' War Course, depended to much the same extent as the Air Force staff college on the nature and desires of the Commandant and of the instructors. Fuller was at Camberley for a while, but Archibald Wavell did not join the faculty because he was offered a post not commensurate with his rank. K. G. B. Dewar might have served at Greenwich, but politics in the Admiralty debarred him. The most appropriate of these appointments was that of Richmond to be the first Commandant of the Imperial Defence College, but his tenure of that post was limited, because of inter-Service rivalries, by prior arrangement. To a certain extent the failure to send the most provocative officers to the staff colleges was counterbalanced by the practice of inviting Liddell Hart and others to be visiting lecturers. But it must also be taken into account that by the thirties many students at the colleges were gentlemen who had little experience of war, at least at the command level.*

THE OFFICIAL INTELLECTUALS: THE IMPERIAL DEFENCE COLLEGE

The Imperial Defence College (the I.D.C.) was proposed immediately after the Great War of 1914-18 by Sir Maurice Hankey, the ubiquitous Secretary of the Committee of Imperial Defence and of the Cabinet, and also by Sir George Aston. It was opposed "in one quarter." † But in 1925 Hankey got the idea accepted in prin-

* John Masters in the second part of his autobiography, *The Road to Mandalay* (1960), gives a good description of the work of junior officers at the staff college at Quetta, India, just prior to the Second World War.

† Air Chief Marshal Sir Arthur Longmore, *From Sea to Sky* (1947), p. 175. From what Longmore says it is not clear as to whether the opposition came from a Service ministry or from the Prime Minister. But as Lloyd George and Bonar Law were both for defence economies, no doubt they supplied the veto. For Aston's side, see *The Fortnightly Review*, CXV (April 1921), 622-639. See also Franklyn Arthur Johnson, *Defence by Committee* (1960), pp. 179, 210-211.

ciple by the newly created Chiefs of Staff Committee, and in January 1927 the I.D.C. opened its doors. It was administered by the Admiralty to which the War Office and the Air Ministry paid grants-in-aid. The Commandant was appointed in succession by each of the three Services for a two-year period. Six officers from each of the armed forces and fourteen appointees from the Civil Service, the Dominions, and the Indian Army composed the annual class, which met at 9 Buckingham Gate, London. Their syllabus for training in Imperial strategy included the higher strategic and administrative direction of war, the nature of the armed forces, civil defence, politics and the conduct of war, the economic, social, industrial, and financial resources of Britain and the Commonwealth, foreign policy and international relations, and visits to various military and industrial establishments.

The usual procedure was for the small staff, consisting in the normal military fashion of officers who had just taken the course, to be supplemented by outside lecturers from the various government departments in London.* In addition, games of the sort that Sir Henry Wilson had introduced at the Supreme Allied Headquarters at Versailles in 1917 were played. In these every possible war in which Britain was likely to be involved was fought out by two syndicates.

Each syndicate consisted of a Prime Minister, Service Secretaries, Chiefs of Staff, and the like. The results of each game were analysed and a paper prepared upon them, but these were regarded as strictly unofficial documents and had apparently limited, if any, circulation in official circles. (This seems a pity since at least one of the solutions reached by a syndicate—that Singapore would be taken from the landward side—proved correct in 1942.) Apart from the general lack of interest in war in higher policy-making circles, several other explanations may be offered for this neglect of I.D.C. studies. Many important people were still trying to make the transition from the day of informal personal talks and hand-written notes to the impersonal multilithic paper-weighted system of twentieth-century government. Moreover, the "lost generation" were either dead or shunned politics in antipathetic memory of the hated politicians, as the soldiers imagined them to be, of the First World War. Lastly,

---

* This would, of course, have made even wider the influence of the Civil Service mandarins described by Thomas Balogh in Hugh Thomas' *The Establishment* (1959).

most of the I.D.C. studies were made by bright junior personnel, few of whom actually went from the I.D.C. to positions of influence. For the sake of their careers, they had to seek commands rather than staff work. If a man became too good a staff officer, he was likely to be kept tied to an ambitious commander to the detriment of his own career.

The I.D.C attempted to overcome the parochial training with which the Service colleges and staff colleges indoctrinated their students, but it was too small and too few senior officers had passed through it by the time they reached high command for the I.D.C. to be influential. With the limited number who had passed through its portals in the dozen-odd years of its pre-1939 existence something of an old-school-tie atmosphere grew up because of a common shared experience.* By 1935, when Arthur Longmore (later Air Officer Commanding-in-Chief, R.A.F., Middle East, in the Second World War) was Commandant and Giffard Martel, one of the pioneers of armoured warfare, was there, each course ended with the students being asked how the expansion of British forces should proceed. Officers present then raised the question of the wisdom or effectiveness of the Prime Minister as Minister of Defence and of a War Cabinet without ministerial administrative responsibilites. In general, they concluded that much would depend upon the personality and desires of the Prime Minister of the day.

In 1937 and 1938 the classes toured the battlefields in France and Flanders, noting the apparent slump in French morale and industry, while in 1937 the Commandant went to the German maneuvers, where he was impressed by the 88 mm. guns later so deadly in the desert, the Fiesler Storch Army observation aircraft, Heinkel 111's, Dornier 17's, a mass attack by 800 tanks, and the new U-boats. But he was not allowed to see the anti-aircraft weapons or parachutist demonstrations. The last student paper in which Commandant Longmore had a hand, that of 1937, dealt with a hypothetical war against Germany and Italy, and the students gave, as it turned out a year later, much too much credit to Poland and Czechoslovakia. At the same time they came to realize that the British government was

* The Royal Military College of Canada is at present the only establishment where the inter-Service attitude is encouraged from the start by having a tri-Service undergraduate body in which it is hoped an institutional loyalty will gradually provide cohesion in the higher commands. It was re-opened on this basis in 1948, in part to supply future United Nations commanders and their staffs.

sadly lacking in information about Japan, the official enemy since 1922, and her likely actions. Martel accused the I.D.C. of being devoid of an overall concept of defence and of being afraid to generate criticism and controversy.*

The staff colleges laboured under the difficulty that their instructors and students generally came from the same closed society. Except for a few officers sent from the other Services, the main group at each staff college was composed of officers from that Service. This was, as has already been noted, less true of the I.D.C., whose student body was more carefully balanced. On the other hand, in the interwar years there was a group of younger officers in the British services, particularly in the Army, who were determined that in any future war the politicians should not be able so easily to meddle in military affairs as they had in the First World War. This newer elite, Field Marshals of which Earl Wavell † and Lord Alanbrooke were the most prominent 1939-45 war examples, concerned itself with developing an ability to communicate with the political leadership upon equal terms. They were realists. They did not want to exclude politics from war, but to re-strike what they considered a desirable balance between the makers and the executors of military as well as national policy. This resurgence of military interest in the direction of war and the conduct of peace occurred at a time when British politicians showed less interest in and understanding of foreign affairs in peace and war than for many decades past. The result was that the politicians failed to meet the challenge of this new type of professional advisers. Except for Churchill and a few sometime-officers and technical specialists, they have yet to meet the Services on a common ground. In a sense the politicians are suffering from having won two world wars, and their present position is not unlike the smugly complacent high brass after the First World War. Per-

* Longmore, pp. 175-185; Sir Frederick Dreyer, *Sea Heritage* (London, 1956), p. 280; Sir Giffard Martel, *Outspoken Soldier* (London, 1949), pp. 362-366, contains a memorandum on the I.D.C. which appears to be misdated December 1931, instead of 1935, when Martel actually attended the college.

† Field Marshal Earl Wavell died before he could write his memoirs, and his son was killed in Kenya before he finished collecting material for his father's biography. The task has since been carried through the first part of the Second World War by John Connell's *Wavell, Soldier and Scholar* (New York, 1965). Wavell himself contributed to a number of official manuals, wrote the standard life of Allenby, by whom he was much influenced, and delivered an illuminating series of the Lees-Knowles Lectures at Cambridge in 1939, *Generals and Generalship* (Harmondsworth, Mddx., 1940).

haps they need to be sent to the Institute for Strategic Studies. Yet today, more than in the years 1918-40, many thoughtful writers are discussing national defence. In the interwar years the group was more limited, and there was virtually no American contribution.

## The Unofficial Intellectuals: The Seapower Advocates

Captain H. G. Thursfield, R.N., the editor of *Brassey's,* Sir Archibald Hurd, from 1899 to 1928 on the editorial staff of *The Daily Telegraph,* and Hector C. Bywater, a maritime journalist, produced solid professional writings based upon recent history and current events, but, though Bywater possessed imagination tempered by an acute sense of what was possible, none of them wrote on the great principles of warfare, nor did they really attempt to make a fundamental change in any aspect of naval administration or in the conduct of strategy.\* This breach was filled by the one great scholar in the Navy of the day: Admiral Sir Herbert Richmond.

## The Unofficial Intellectuals: Admiral Sir Herbert Richmond

Admiral Sir Herbert Richmond achieved flag rank in 1920.† Born in 1871, he entered the Royal Navy at the usual early age of

* Besides Hurd and Bywater, there was also Lt. W. (now Sir) Stephen King-Hall, who won the 1918 Naval Gold Medal Prize Essay contest of the *Journal of the Royal United Service Institution (JRUSI)* with his work, "The Influence of the Submarine in Naval Warfare in the Future," *JRUSI,* LXIV (August 1919), 359-381. See also his "Speculations," *JRUSI,* LXV, 1920, 155-163, on tanks, and LXVI, 1921, 47-57, on the battle fleet; Maj. R. B. Pargiter and Maj. H. G. Eady, *The Army and Sea Power* (1927), a historical survey from the Renaissance to 1918; Lt/Cmdr. J. M. Kenworthy, *Freedom of the Seas* (1928) and *The Real Navy* (1932), written in defence of the Fleet after the mutiny at Invergordon in 1931.

It is possible that Bywater deserves more space than he has received in this volume and that he has been unfairly relegated to a lesser place because he was first of all a journalist.

The background for British naval writing is to be found in the works of Admiral Alfred Thayer Mahan; in Earle, *Makers of Modern Strategy,* pp. 446-456 (the article by Theodore Ropp on "Continental Doctrines of Sea Power"); in Peter M. Stanford, "The Work of Sir Julian Corbett in the Dreadnought Era," United States Naval Institute *Proceedings,* LXXVII (January 1951), 64-71; in Sir Henry Newbolt, *Submarine and Anti-Submarine* (1918); in S. W. Roskill, *The Strategy of Sea Power; Its Development* (1962) (the Lees-Knowles Lectures for 1961); and D. M. Schurman, *The Education of a Navy* (1965).

† On Richmond, see Arthur Marder, *Portrait of an Admiral: The Life and*

fourteen and rose steadily to be Assistant Director of the Operations Department at the Admiralty, 1913-15, and then captain in succession of the battleships *Commonwealth, Conqueror,* and *Erin.* Thus he was a rival of Jellicoe's Captain Charles Madden and of Beatty's Chatfield. After Beatty arrived at the Admiralty as First Sea Lord late in 1919, he called in Richmond to write a tactical manual as the Royal Navy did not possess one. Part of this work was delegated to Lt. Stephen King-Hall, late intelligence officer with the Harwich submarines, who proceeded to produce "the first official textbook on the art of [cruiser] war or any other aspect of it ever issued by their Lordships for the guidance of naval officers." *

In February 1920 Richmond, the ablest naval officer of the day (said Marder) and the most irresponsible (said Chatfield †) was posted to command the Senior Officers' War Course at Greenwich, when it was re-started. The students consisted of about twenty captains awaiting appointments who were allowed to attend for a year. Unlike the War Office, which required two years, the Admiralty felt that twelve months were sufficient for teaching the intellectual principles of war and higher command. Richmond was suspect as he was something of an intellectual, a type always feared and distrusted by the ordinary officer until he proved himself a seaman and a gentleman. Proof of the attitude of the Admiralty may be found in two incidents connected with the course. Richmond was reprimanded for having Admiral Albert P. Niblack, President of the United States Naval War College, the home of Mahanism, speak without permission, which would have been refused. And when the 1922 economy drive's "Geddes axe" fell, nineteen out of the twenty-four present as students on the course or on the staff were retired from

*Papers of Sir Herbert Richmond* (Cambridge, Mass., 1952), which is basic; a short sketch is that by G. M. Trevelyan, "Admiral Sir Herbert Richmond, 1871-1946," *The Proceedings of the British Academy,* XXXII (reprint, 1946), with a naval insight by Rear-Admiral Henry Thursfield; also see the account in the D.N.B., 1940-50 (1960). Prof. Donald Schurman of the Royal Military College of Canada has recently completed a study, as yet unpublished, "The Pens behind the Fleet," which places Richmond in the Colomb-Mahan-Corbett school of nineteenth century naval writers. (See p. viii.)

* King-Hall, *My Naval Life, 1906-1929* (1951), p. 170. This is not strictly true, as the old naval signal books contained a lot of information upon maneuvers and had become standardized in Queen Anne's reign.

† Lord Chatfield, *The Navy and Defence,* II, *It Might Happen Again* (London, 1947), p. 60. He was also attacked by P. R. C. Groves in *Behind the Smoke Screen* (London, 1934), pp. 162-170.

the Service. Richmond was always incensed that the Admiralty did not regard courses in naval history and strategy as a fundamental part of the naval officers' education and that what training in this there was was given late in their careers.

After he left the Naval College at Greenwich, Richmond published an article on "Co-operation" in which he showed that in the periods of Britain's greatness her statesmen had always held a clear-cut and definable view of the national interest that guided them in the making of strategy. Co-operation, he said, could be effective only when the purpose was known and the supremacy of one Service decided upon so that money could be properly allocated. It was necessary to study defence as a whole in order to ascertain which arm would play the dominant role, as no country could afford to be supreme on land and at sea. He called for the study of war as a whole in its long historical context and not of just the narrow ideas of the other Service prior to 1914. His conclusions showed that he had a far better grasp of the all-embracing nature of war and its preparations than had most of the responsible persons of his day. What he urged was the establishment of a British Imperial doctrine of war, the teaching of this to all officers early in their careers, and its use as the basis for staff college studies, for future planning, and for practical preparation for war.*

In 1923 Richmond was posted to command the East Indies Squadron. In April 1925 he was promoted to Vice-Admiral and shortly thereafter became unemployed. In September 1926 as representative of the Senior Service he was appointed the first commandant of the Imperial Defence College, which opened in January 1927. His two-year term ended in 1929. He was then promoted to Admiral. The new Labour Government wanted him as First Sea Lord, but the Admiralty successfully resisted. He had been a founder of *The Naval Review* in 1913,† which their Lordships viewed with suspicion rather than as a source of Service opinion, for it sought to educate junior officers in high matters of war and command. He became *persona non grata* not only for his letter to *The Times* of 21 November 1921

---

* "Co-operation," *JRUSI*, LXVIII, 1923, 391-404.

† Started in 1913, *The Naval Review* provides an outlet for naval officers who want to get something off their chests. The issues are restricted for twelve years, but may after that time be seen at the Imperial War Museum. Its contents are much like those of the U.S.N.I. *Proceedings* and suffer on occasion from not only editorial selection, but also, as during the First World War, from outright censorship by the Admiralty.

advocating the 10,000-ton battleship, but also for his expression of certain ideas at the Royal Institute of International Affairs (Chatham House), for which he received a reprimand.* His letters to *The Times* of 21 and 22 November 1929, arguing once more against the materialistic Admiralty policy of big battleships and the numerical limitation of fleets, finished his career as a naval officer. On retiring from the Navy in 1931, he became a professional historian, the career upon which his reputation now rests. As a thinker he was outside the mainstream of naval thought and direction.

But that does not mean to say that he did not have something to contribute. He did, for dissent is essential to survival. It may well be argued that Richmond was one of the few rational high ranking naval officers. Certainly his sound historical evaluations were based upon scholarly study, naval experience, and patient analysis.† In 1921 when the Admiralty idealists wanted 59,000-ton monster battleships, a line pursued by the Japanese in their *Musashi* and *Yamato* of 83,000 tons—the 59,000-tonners were regarded as the best compromise of the conflicting demands of fuel for speed, guns for destructive power and defence, and of armour and internal watertight protection—Richmond, the anti-materialist overly concerned with surface raiders, argued that Britain needed as an ideal warship one of less than 10,000 tons, capable of 24 to 28 knots or at 15 of cruising

---

* This cannot be documented as meetings at Chatham House are private and only material published in *International Affairs* may be attributed to the group. Since this was a private meeting, the Admiralty's action seems all the more invidious.

† Richmond's works fall into three categories: First come the papers he edited for the Naval Records Society: *Papers Relating to the Loss of Minorca in 1756* (1913), and *The Spencer Papers*, III and IV (1924). Then there are his own historical works: *The Navy in the War of 1739-48* (1920), *The Navy in India, 1763-1783* (1931), and the unfinished *The Navy as an Instrument of Policy, 1558-1727* (1953, edited by E. A. Hughes). The third group may be divided between popular wisdom and more serious works of broad scope. In the former category are *Naval Warfare* (1930), *Naval History and the Citizen* (1934), *The Navy* (1937), *The Naval Role in Modern Warfare* (1940), *British Strategy, Military and Economic* (1941), *The Invasion of Britain* (1941), *Amphibious Warfare in British History* (1941), *War at Sea Today* (1942); in the second, *Command and Discipline* (1927), *National Policy and Naval Strength* (1928), *Economy and National Security* (1931), *Imperial Defence and Capture at Sea in War* (1932), *Naval Training* (1933), *Sea Power in the Modern World* (1934), *The Naval Officer in Fiction* in *Essays and Studies by Members of the English Association*, XXX (Oxford, 1945), and the greatest of all his works, *Statesmen and Sea Power* (1946). *The Navy in the War of 1739-48* was begun in 1907 and completed in 1914, but publication was delayed by the war.

8,000 miles, and armed with 6-inch guns. This line was ultimately developed by his disciple Captain Bernard Acworth, who went rather too far back when he insisted that the ships burn coal. (Such an attitude was compatible with operations in the North Sea or the Channel, but, as the next war showed, would seriously have handicapped Britain in dealing with long-range U-boats in the Atlantic and diesel-powered raiders on the broad oceans.

### THE UNOFFICIAL INTELLECTUALS: THE OLDER MILITARY WRITERS *

Apart from Richmond, there were relatively few writers on broad strategy. Some dallied with it in the influential *Journal of the Royal United Service Institution (JRUSI)*, the major general Service magazine. Occasional articles appeared in the Navy's confidential *The Naval Review,* while the airmen had their own *Journal of the Royal Air Force College.*

The major periodical that carried the most frequent writing on military affairs was *The Nineteenth Century and After* (called *The Twentieth Century* from December 1950), followed by *The Fortnightly Review, Blackwood's,* and *The Saturday Review.* The most persistent names were those of Sir George Aston, since 1904 Professor of Empire Defence at the Army Staff College at Camberley, and Sir Frederick Maurice, who officially retired from the Army in 1929, having already gone into education, being in 1927 appointed Professor of Military Studies at the University of London.† Part of his fame rests on his attack on Lloyd George in "the Maurice Debate" in the Commons of May 1918.

* The best source for the earlier thought of the British Army is Jay Luvaas' *Education of an Army* (Chicago, 1964). There is still much to be done in the examination of the works of the many minor military writers, a few of whom I have mentioned merely incidentally. Many useful bibliographical lists are available from the former War Office Library, now the Ministry of Defence Central Library, whose Librarian, Mr. D. W. King, is most helpful to scholars. For an interesting survey of British military literature, see The Prince Consort's Library (Aldershot), *Centenary Exhibition, the Book Display* (1960). For a guide to the general nature of British naval, military, and aeronautical thought as seen largely by serving officers, see *The Consolidated Author and Subject Index to the Journal of the Royal United Service Institution* (Ann Arbor, Mich., 1965).

† Sir Frederick is sometimes confused with his father, also a major-general, Sir John Frederick Maurice (pronounced Morris), who died in 1912 after writing the official history of the Boer War. His son was Director of Military Operations at the War Office, 1915-18, in succession to Major-General Sir Charles Callwell, the author of *Minor Wars* and editor of the diaries of Sir Henry Wilson.

Taken chronologically, it was Sir Charles Callwell who first raised in the interwar years the question of the making of broad strategy. He had been concerned with the Dardanelles inquiry, and in reviewing "Wully" Robertson's *From Private to Field Marshal* he commented that the former C.I.G.S. (Chief of the Imperial General Staff) raised for Englishmen certain questions. What was the position and what were the responsibilities of the professional advisers of the Government when taking part in Cabinet discussions? Callwell felt that it was the duty both of the Prime Minister as chairman to elicit and of the dissenting officer to put forward his views as they might affect several departments. But at the same time he recognized that the expert was present to advise his superior and not to oppose him. Yet, if a senior officer did not express his opinion, was he to be taken as concurring in such a decision? If as a servant of the Crown a military man expressed a contrary opinion that was accepted, could he then be held accountable for the subsequent executive decision? What if the Minister had formed his opinion without consulting his expert advisers, should the advisers then remain silent? Callwell felt that at least in wartime they had to speak up, for if they did not points might be overlooked that the Prime Minister should have known, as they affected several departments. Moreover, should a Minister fail to reveal these divergent opinions of his advisers, was he breaking faith with his colleagues? As an officer was constitutionally a stranger at a Cabinet meeting, he was at a disadvantage as to his right to speak, while at the same time the fact (much truer in the twenties than in the forties) that he had difficulty in expressing himself, let alone in putting his thoughts in politician's language, tended to make his advice of much less weight than that of more fluent persons.*

At the same time, in 1921, Sir George Aston made a public plea for the revival of the C.I.D. (Committee of Imperial Defense) and the creation of what came to be the I.D.C.† But on the whole publishers were not inclined to take chances on more than a few works in this field, and of those most were by reputable authors. After several years of apathy, a succession of volumes, coinciding with a new batch of literary memoirs of World War I, began to flow off the presses following Liddell Hart's *Paris, or the Future of War*.

---

* *The Nineteenth Century and After*, XC, December 1921, 1062-1071.
† On the postwar history of the C.I.D., see Franklyn Johnson, *Defence by Committee*, pp. 165-275. On the I.D.C., *supra*, p. 27.

Lieutenant-General Sir Gerald Ellison, Deputy Quartermaster-General at Gallipoli and at the War Office, 1917-23, produced in 1926 *The Perils of Amateur Strategy as Exemplified by the Attack on the Dardanelles Fortress 1915,* which lambasted Churchill and appraised Lord Fisher's Baltic Plan, but at the same time was a plea for the creation of a rational system for Imperial conduct of war that would take into account the peculiar needs of a democratic system.

This was followed in 1927 by J. Holland Rose's *The Indecisiveness of Modern War and Other Essays.* Rose, Vere Harmsworth Professor of Naval History at Cambridge, discoursed upon the problems of war and national policy in the light of the indecisiveness of the First World War. Like Aston and Callwell before him, Rose felt that the complex progress of mankind had brought committees in which the modern politician shone because he was an able debater, but that this had the danger that he usurped the functions of both the administrator and of the military adviser and thus placed himself, in Rose's view, in an impossible position simply because he could steer Parliament, leaving the Services to bureaucratic management. At the same time Aston brought out an edited collection of lectures delivered at the University of London in 1925 and 1926 by such distinguished men as Sir Charles Oman, Admiral Richmond, General William Ironside, Air Vice-Marshal Sir Robert Brooke-Popham, Sir Harold Hartley and Admiral Sir Cyprian Bridge and covering both Service and civilian views as well as calling for more study of military history. But on the whole *The Study of War for Statesmen and Citizens* is a disappointing book, valuable today only for what it reveals of the thought of the twenties.*

Meanwhile, others had been exploring the American Civil War in a wider vein, and one of the fruits of this was the appearance in 1926 of Sir Frederick Maurice the younger's *Governments and War,* his Lees-Knowles Lectures of 1925.† Basically he studied the functioning of the Union high command to see how Lincoln had managed and to compare his work with Maurice's own experience close to the top of the British military and political Higher Direction in the First World War. In 1929 Sir Frederick published *British Strategy:*

* To see how dangerous it is to guess as to the future, read Prof. A. M. Low, "How We Shall Fight in A.D. 2023," *The Nineteenth Century and After,* XCIV, September 1923, 354. These predictions were surpassed within ten years.

† The American title, *Statesmen and Soldiers of the Civil War: A Study of the Conduct of War,* is more accurate.

*A Study of the Application of the Principles of War* in which he presented the Clausewitzian *offensive à outrance* viewpoint as it was left dangling by the First World War. He did not see war as a social phenomenon, and he made the mistake of saying that the object of war was achieved by the *destruction* of the enemy's armed forces rather than by their *defeat*. For Sir Frederick war was a political act whose object was to create a change of policy that could only be attained when the will of the people to fight was overcome. He believed along with many others that the advent of airpower had changed the principles of war rather than merely affecting them as other material developments had done. At the same time he noted that since 1919 there had been a revulsion against using war as an instrument of national policy—the Briand-Kellogg Pact having been signed while he was writing *British Strategy*. Maurice may be classed as a middle-of-the-road writer who found himself unable to break away from his background and training. He was at his best as a historian as in his later *Lessons of Allied Co-operation: Naval, Military, and Air* published in 1942 and based upon the official histories, memoirs, biographies, and Command Papers, and upon his own experiences in the Higher Direction of the First World War. But in all his works he was more a historian than an original thinker.

On the periphery of the thinkers, but much in the center of the publishable writers was Lt/Cmdr. J. M. Kenworthy, 10th Baron Strabolgi. Often provocative and exasperating, his books and speeches were too close to daily events to have more than a momentary impact.*

Again there was a publishing lull during the Disarmament Conference (1932-34) and the economic depression (1931-35), always excepting Richmond, Fuller, Liddell Hart, and one or two disciples. Then as rearmament quickened the public's interest, military articles began to pour from the pens of journalists as well as military writers. (But on the larger subject of Imperial strategy there still remained relatively few informed debaters.) Notable amongst the new contributions was an article in defence of the Chiefs of Staff system and against a Ministry of Defence by the late

* See *Peace or War* (New York, 1927); *New Wars: New Weapons* (London, 1930), a plea for more money for the Air Force and none for battleships, which is a fair insight into thoughts on the subject at that date.

C.I.G.S. Field-Marshal Lord Milne, assisted by Lieutenant-General Sir Ronald Charles, the late Master-General of Ordnance.*

As Milne pointed out, the C.I.D. had become surrounded by committees so that at every meeting some one of the fifty-odd committees had to report. The annual report of the Chiefs of Staff on what the country needed in the way of defence was based upon a Foreign Office appraisal and the whole was censored by the Treasury. (The Chiefs of Staff, though, were still servants and not Ministers, so they lacked access to the Prime Minister to impress their views firmly upon him.) Milne was against a Ministry of Defence because it had already been examined after the war and found useless owing to the complexity of weapons, duplicate and rival staffs, etc. What Milne favoured was the system as it was in which the Cabinet made broad strategy and each Service Ministry then worked out its plans to make it reality. But he admitted that the system really lacked co-ordination and that its main difficulty came from financial control under a government that annually ignored the warnings of its top military advisers. Moreover, as the Prime Minister never presided at the C.I.D. meetings, each Service tended to present its own ideas as to the defence of places upon which the Cabinet asked for advice. There was no overall concept of Imperial defence. So Milne favoured what was created in March 1936, a Minister for the Co-ordination of Defence. One wonders whether or not his was a planted article.

In opposition to Milne was the long-time Financial Controller at the War Office, Sir Charles Harris, who decried the whole Ministry-of-Defence conception. He argued that what was needed was a Minister of Supply.† In 1939 such an appointment was made, and in 1940 the office of Minister for the Co-ordination of Defence died a natural death when bellicose Winston Churchill, "the amateur strategist," succeeded pacifist Neville Chamberlain, the defence-conscious appeaser.

Both Victor Germains and Major-General H. Rowan-Robinson contributed general books and specific attacks upon certain of the military intellectuals just before the war broke out again in 1939, but as they were critics of Liddell Hart and Fuller, they will be treated later.

* "The Higher Organization of National Defence," *The Nineteenth Century and After,* CXIX (March 1936), 303-317.

† "Our Defence Organization," *The Nineteenth Century and After,* CXXL (April 1937), 500-511.

### THE UNOFFICIAL INTELLECTUALS: MINOR MILITARY WRITERS

One of the common postwar games is to try to determine what were the lessons of the last war. Since the Crimean War the practice has been to write official histories in which raw materials are placed in accessible form and from which officers can draw the appropriate lessons. But two difficulties arise: such works are not unbiased; and after modern mondial struggles, it takes a tremendous amount of time for the finished works to appear.* Before their publication, others will try to elucidate the general conclusions. It is often easy enough to say what were the textbook mistakes and to point to the unusual but successful ideas adopted. But it is much harder to focus upon the new weapons and to say which of them will be the most vital in the ensuing years, for they are the ones that will need the most study, analysis, and development before the next war, by which time they may be obsolete.

Among the writers in this vein, Lt. King-Hall's analysis of the means of getting behind the German lines in 1918 stands out for his prescience in pointing to the future of airborne jumping over and tank thrusts through the opponent.† Colonel H. Rowan Robinson (later Rowan-Robinson) noted that position warfare of the First World War was hard on the lower ranks, but could be directed by fools in the upper who dreamt in terms of heroic actions and failed to study the dull conflicts such as the Russo-Japanese War. He advocated that emphasis in the peacetime Army be placed upon a fast mobile British Expeditionary Force that could break through the enemy and then use its unlimited mobility to roll him up. If a stalemate should occur, the solution was not more guns but different tactics. He also urged the study of enemy equipment in peacetime

---

* Of the British official histories of the First World War, the naval was not completed until 1931, the air until 1937, and the military until 1949. In the case of some other participants, such as the Germans and the Italians, the process of publishing the 1914 war volumes is still continuing in 1965. On the British histories of the Second World War, see my "A Government at War," *Stand-To* (Canberra, Australia), March-April 1963, pp. 11-15, 32, and July-August, pp. 19-27, reprinted in *The Library Quarterly* (Chicago) in abbreviated form, XXXIV, No. 3 (July 1964), 240-248. More information on both official histories and on military historical departments will be found in the forthcoming volume *Official Histories,* to which the official historians of various nations are contributing. This is to be published by the Eisenhower military history program at Kansas State University.

† "Speculations, I," *JRUSI,* LXV, 1920, 156.

so that what was captured could be used in war to increase mobility.*

Other Service writers called attention to the need to consider scientific and mechanical advances and their relation to war. Lt/Col. W. D. Croft in "The Application of Recent Developments in Mechanics and Other Scientific Knowledge to the Preparation and Training for Future War on Land" strongly attacked the horse as useless in modern war, advocated the lightening of infantry, and pointed to the menace of air attack on lines of supply.† He also wrote "The Influence of Tanks upon Tactics." ‡ Croft was an infantry commander (Scottish Rifles) who had been on the first postwar staff college course and in 1922 was in command of the Tank Battalion at Aldershot. He said that the answer to the tank was not the anti-tank gun but, in Mahanic terms, another tank. Moreover, he asked why make the infantryman do what he does not do in civil life, walk everywhere, and thus exhaust him before a battle? In commenting upon the lecture, Major-General W. H. Anderson pointed to the seven steps to the future: (1) scientific investigations of weapons, (2) experimental designs, (3) the thought of experts and enthusiasts, which was usually ahead of that of the Army and the nation, (4) foreward thought in the Army to back up the experts, (5) acceptance by the unthinking higher military authorities, (6) the views of the financial authorities, and (7) the opinions of the fighting soldier who sees only what is issued and how it works.

Lt/Col. J. C. Dundas of the Royal Artillery put the case for anti-tank guns,§ but concluded that the best defence was a tank, never

---

* "The Relations of Mobility and Firepower," *JRUSI*, LXV, 1920, 572-579. In the Second World War the British made the Sten gun ("the Woolworth" as it was popularly known) to use up captured German 9 mm. ammunition, then had to manufacture 9 mm. to use up the Stens. One difficulty in fast-moving wars with adopting most enemy equipment is that it may lead to misidentifications and casualties to one's own side. See especially accounts of war in the Western Desert, 1940-43, in Major-General I. S. O. Playfair, *The Mediterranean and Middle East* (H.M.S.O., 6 vols., 1954 ff.); Gordon Landsborough, *Tobruk Commando* (London, 1956); Virginia Cowles, *The Phantom Major* (1958); and in Donald Crisp, *The Brazen Chariots* (1958). Misidentification in and from the air was a frequent problem and led to the adoption on D-Day of the black-and-white striping of aircraft in addition to the standard national markings on planes, tanks, and trucks, and to the garbing of the R.A.F. Regiment in khaki instead of the traditional R.A.F. smoke-grey-blue, which had a Germanic hue in 1944 in the eyes of many infantrymen.
† Second Prize Essay, 1919, *JRUSI*, LXV, 1920, 443-476.
‡ *JRUSI*, LXVII, 1922, 39-53.
§ *JRUSI*, LXVII, 1922, 106-111.

theless. Colonel Commandant L. C. L. Oldfield of the Royal Artillery in "Artillery, and Lessons We Have Learnt with Regard to It in the Late War," and Brevet-Major O. W. White in "Battle Supply" analysed other needs.* More controversial and provocative was Major-General Sir Louis Jackson's "Possibilities of the Next War." † Various other writers already mentioned also contributed to these Service debates, but none of them rose to eminence of any lasting sort comparable to that achieved by Fuller and Liddell Hart.

## THE UNOFFICIAL INTELLECTUALS: MAJOR-GENERAL J. F. C. FULLER

The most original of the British tactical military thinkers was Colonel (later Major-General) J. F. C. Fuller, the operational brain of the Tank Corps.‡ John Frederick Charles Fuller, born in 1878,

---

* *JRUSI*, LXVII, 1922, 579-599, 93-105.

† *JRUSI*, LXV, 1920, 71-89. Jackson had before the war delivered an equally startling talk, on the impact of airpower, that was a springboard for other speakers in the pre-1914 years.

‡ Though Fuller has written extensively, the only evaluation of his work in all its ramifications from tanks to yoga to politics has been, until the end of 1964, David H. Zook, Jr., "John Frederick Charles Fuller, Military Historian," *Military Affairs*, XXIII, No. 4 (Winter 1959-60), 185-193, and now the chapter in Jay Luvaas, *The Education of an Army* (Chicago, 1964), where Fuller is aptly called "The Discordant Trumpet."

In the back of Fuller's *The Reformation of War* will be found a bibliography of his writings from 1914 to 1923, though what was for official use and what was public is often unclear.

His books are: *Tanks in the Great War* (1920); *The Reformation of War* (1923); *Pegasus' Problems of Transportation* (1925); *Yoga: A Study of the Mystical Philosophy of the Brahmins and Buddhists* (1925); *Atlantis: America and the Future* (1925); *Sir John Moore's System of Training* (1925) and *British Light Infantry in the Eighteenth Century* (1925) (originally produced in 1914 as *Notes on the Training of the New Armies, 1797-1805*); *Foundations of the Science of War* (1926); *Imperial Defence, 1588-1914* (1926); *On Future Warfare* (1928); *The Generalship of Ulysses S. Grant* (1929); *The Natural History of War* (1930); *India in Revolt* (1931); *Lectures on F.S.R. II* (1931); *Lectures on F.S.R. III (Operations between Mechanized Forces)* (1932) (now called *Armoured Warfare*); *India: the dragon's teeth* (1932); *War and Western Civilization, 1832-1932* (1932); *Generalship: Its Diseases and Their Cure: A Study of the Personal Factor in Command* (1933); *Grant and Lee: A Study in Personality and Generalship* (1933); *Empire Unity and Defence* (1934); *The Army in My Time* (1935); *Memoirs of an Unconventional Soldier* (1936); *The First of the League Wars* (1936); *The Last of the Gentlemen's Wars: A Subaltern's Journal of the War in South Africa, 1899-1902* (1937); *The Secret Wisdom of the Qabalah* (1937); *Towards Armageddon: The Defence Problem* (1937); *The Conquest of Red Spain* (1937); *Decisive Battles* (begun in 1923, issued in 1929, and revised 1939-40); *Machine Warfare* (1941) (a entered the Army in 1898 at the age of twenty after one year at the Royal Military College. He was soon posted to India where he became an agnostic and read widely in anti-religious literature. During this period he learned to think systematically and to reduce things to fundamentals. He found that seven eighths of what he was taught was useless, but that "obsolescence is a good whetstone." While in India he developed the idea that all depended upon weaponpower and acquired the nickname of "Bonaparte" or "Boney" not only for his looks but also for his habit of saying, "Give me the power and limitations of any weapon you like, and in half an hour I will give you a reasonable tactical answer." * As David Zook puts it, basically Fuller felt that weapons rather than dogmas were and are the key to victory. After the First World War Fuller saw the need for mechanization as the real lesson to be learned from that immortal machine-gunned stalemate.† It was an idea that had begun to disturb him after the Russo-Japanese War. He was already, before the First World War, coming to be an intellectual in the Army, at a time when officers were not noted for their brains. In the war he rose rapidly to Chief General Staff Officer of the Tank Corps. Before he became involved with tanks, Fuller had been Chief Staff Officer

version of *Lectures on F.S.R. III); Decisive Battles of the U.S.* (1942); *Armoured Warfare* (1943) (another version of *Machine Warfare); Armament and History* (1945); *Watchwords* (1945); *Thunderbolts* (1946); *The Second World War, 1939-1945: A Strategical and Tactical History* (1948, revised 1954); *A Military History of the Western World* (3 vols., 1954, 1955, 1956); *The Generalship of Alexander the Great* (1958); *The Conduct of War, 1789-1961: A Study of the Impact of the French, Industrial and Russian Revolutions on War and its Conduct* (1961); *Julius Caesar: Man, Soldier, and Tyrant* (1965).

Fuller contributed the following pieces to *The Journal of the Royal United Service Institution:* "The Revival and Training of Light Infantry in the British Army, 1757-1806" (1913, p. 1187); "The Procedure of the Infantry Attack" (1914, p. 63); "The Tactics of Penetration: A Counterblast to German Numerical Superiority" (1914, p. 378); "The Training of the New Army, 1803-1805" (1916, p. 779); "Moral, Instruction and Leadership" (November 1920, p. 656); "The Application of Recent Developments in Mechanics and other Scientific Knowledge to Preparation and Training for Future War on Land" (Gold Medal Military Prize Essay for 1919), (May 1920, p. 239); "The Development of Sea Warfare on Land and its Influence on Future Naval Operations," Lecture (May 1920, p. 281); "Mechanization of Modern Armies (February 1925, p. 73); "The Berlin Problem" (May 1962, p. 149). The gap from 1925 to 1962 is partially explained by the rift between Liddell Hart and himself on the one hand and Captain Altham, R.N., the editor, on the other. In addition Fuller contributed to a number of Service and other journals.

* Letter to Robin Higham, 11 May 1962. See also his *Memoirs* (1936).
† Captain David H. Zook, Jr., *Military Affairs,* XXIII, 186 (Reprint).

of the Machine Gun Corps (Heavy Section). As, in 1916, it was a cardinal rule that these weapons should never go into action with less than 5,000 rounds belted up and available, it became obvious to him that one of the greatest needs of the day was some way in which his men and their equipment could be kept going during an advance. An armoured fighting vehicle that could move over no-man's land was the answer. His long battle against the War Office and Douglas Haig caused him to refer most irreverently to the Field Marshal as a "stone-age general" whom he blamed for almost ruining England by his stubborn offensive at Ypres and his equally rock-headed defence on the Somme.* Fuller claims for himself, with considerable justice, that it was his tactics that created the breakthrough on 8 August 1918 and let Haig obtain victory. While Ernest Swinton and Hugh Elles fought the Battle of the Tank in London, Fuller fought it at G.H.Q. in France and produced the plan that might well have revolutionized warfare in 1919 if the fighting had continued. In 1918 Fuller went to the War Office, which he contemptuously called a "glutinous mass," for the next four years. In 1922 he became Chief Instructor at the staff college at Camberley, having by then already made a name for himself as not only an astute tactical thinker but also as a writer. In 1920 he had embarrassed the Admiralty by winning the Naval Prize Essay contest at the Royal United Service Institution with a piece that he, with malicious mischief, claimed had been submitted as a joke. Their Lordships were so incensed that it was not accorded the usual publication but had to appear two years later in *The Naval Review*. After his term at the staff college, and subsequently as Military Assistant to the C.I.G.S., he was given command of the new experimental brigade at Aldershot. But as he felt that he was to be too hemmed about by restrictions to make a success of it, he threatened to resign from command of the 7th Infantry Brigade and from the Army. He then was appointed G.S.O. 1 (General Staff Officer) to Ironside, who commanded the 2d Division. There Fuller had fun making the usual training exercises something more akin to war, with chance playing its part. In 1929 he had a brief spell in command of a brigade on the Rhine, which was evacuated, and then of one at Catterick until promoted to Major-General on 14 September 1930 and placed

* The most recent appraisal of Haig is John Terraine's controversial *Ordeal of Victory* (New York, 1963). Almost every recent work on the Western Front has something to say about British generalship.

upon half pay. He refused an appointment to command at Bombay as he considered it a waste of his talents. In 1932 his acid little book, *Generalship: Its Diseases and Their Cure*, appeared and on 14 December 1933, at the age of fifty-four, he was placed on the retired list.

His works became the textbooks for the French, Russian, and American armies and were absorbed by the Germans often through the writings of Liddell Hart who expanded them. But his impact in England was far less. The explanation is simple and regrettable. He attacked the system and those who operated it, and this made him *persona non grata* to too many people. At the staff college, for instance, he would say to an officer, "You are a seventeen-and-six-penny man—what I mean is that you couldn't get seventeen-and-sixpence a week in civil life!" [*] His memoirs are full of astringent remarks about the War Office and senior military personnel, none of which was likely to endear him to that archly conservative class, the normal Army officer, particularly the cavalry types.[†] Moreover, he could make embarrassing discoveries such as that the *Field Service Regulations* talked of the principles of war, but, since they never stated them, few officers knew them. Like many practical intellectuals, he was decisive, clear-thinking, alert, and had a wide-ranging mind, while at the same time he cared nothing for the Army's favorite—the horse. Yet, again ironically, it was he who fundamentally saved the cavalry from the entrenched role that they had played in the First World War and revived their mobility using modern mechanical horsepower in the Second. Also ironically, though he discarded historical analogy in favour of new weapons, he was forced to seek historical evidence to defeat the Haig-mindedness of his superiors and of the general public, which refused to recognize the relationship of war to civilization. He still believes war is an outgrowth of the moral poisoning of society.[‡]

Until he produced *Tanks in the Great War*, little of Fuller's writings had appeared outside of the Service. With that lucid and authoritative work, based on enemy and Allied sources as well as upon his

[*] King-Hall, *My Naval Life*, pp. 207-208.

[†] For a fictional study of a World War commander, see C. S. Forester, *The General* (London, 1936), as well as Liddell Hart's biographical sketches, *Reputations Ten Years After* (1928); also Fuller's *The Army in My Time*.

[‡] On this point see Michael Howard's review of Cyril Falls, *A Hundred Years of War*, in *The New Statesman*, 2 January 1954. See Zook, *Military Affairs*, XXIII, 189.

own unbeatable personal knowledge, he rose to national and international prominence. What made him such a powerful writer was that he saw the interdependence of industry and war in the modern world. His 1919 *JRUSI* Military Prize Essay pointed out that pure science, physical science, applied science, and moral science formed the base of a pyramid of which war was the apex. In almost epigrammic form he summed up his basic ideas with "To understand the past and to judge the present is to foresee the future" and "Warfare is both a science and an art" and can be conducted only by persons who have studied the evolution of civilization and the four sciences. An army is a combination of men, movements, weapons, and protection whose actions must be based upon the principles of war and upon psychology.*

Like Liddell Hart, Fuller wanted the continued use of gas, which he viewed as a civilizing influence upon war.†

## The Unofficial Intellectuals: Captain B. H. Liddell Hart

The doyen of the military critics was B[asil] H[enry] Liddell Hart. Born in Paris on 31 October 1895, educated at St. Paul's School and Corpus Christi College, Cambridge, where he read history, he was an officer who served much of the First World War in the front-line trenches with the King's Own Yorkshire Light Infantry. Severely wounded, at the end of the war he was engaged in training troops. In 1920 at the age of twenty-five he was asked by the War Office to write the official postwar manual on infantry training, which he did under the strong influence of that master of the subject, General Sir Ivor Maxse, to whose notice as Inspector-General of Train-

* *JRUSI*, LXV, May 1920, 239-274. The Fullerite principles of war:
        (1) the principle of the objective,
        (2) the principle of the offensive,
        (3) the principle of the security,
        (4) the principle of the concentration,
        (5) the principle of the economy of force,
        (6) the principle of the movement,
        (7) the principle of the surprise,
        (8) the principle of the co-operation.
These are affected in war by time, space, ground, weather, numbers, morale, communications and information, supply, armament, obstacles, formations and observation. They are still the commonly accepted ones.

† See J. B. S. Haldane, *Callinicus: A Defence of Chemical Warfare* (London, 1925), and Charles H. Foulkes, *"Gas!": The Story of the Special Brigade* (London, 1934).

ing of the British Armies in France he had come. (But it was typical of the War Office mind of the day that his brief chapter on outposts was removed and replaced instead with the old 1914 one, which Liddell Hart felt was entirely inapplicable.) * He was then appointed to edit the official *Small Arms Training Manual*. Much of what went into these two works was based upon his own ideas evolved and experimented with in 1917 and known then as his Battle Drill system and explained and elaborated in his first articles in the *JRUSI*.†

* *The Tanks*, I, 200. On 24 November 1960 Capt. Liddell Hart prepared some notes on his personal experiences and reflections for a talk to the Rotary Club. These contain much useful material, but have not apparently been published. It was originally expected that my book would be published somewhat ahead of Liddell Hart's own memoirs, which he was forced by the publishers to reduce from their original 300,000 words to 228,000, at which he balked at cutting them further. The compromise agreed to was to issue them in two volumes, the first of which appeared in May 1965 and was very well received; the second followed in November. Unlike Fuller, Liddell Hart timed his so that the great bulk of his writing and his influence was past before they appeared. It is hoped that Fuller's autobiography will be re-issued with a postscript to carry his life and thoughts from 1935 to 1965.

† "The 'Ten Commandments' of the Combat Unit: Suggestions on Its Theory and Training," *JRUSI*, LXIV (May 1919), 288-293; "Suggestions on the Future Development of the Combat Unit: the Tank as a Weapon of Infantry," *JRUSI*, November 1919, pp. 666-669; "The 'Man-in-the-Dark' Theory of Infantry Tactics and the 'Expanding Torrent' System of Attack," *JRUSI*, LXVI, 1921, 1-22; and "The Soldiers' Pillar of Fire by Night: The Need for a Framework of Tactics," *JRUSI*, LXVI, November 1921, 618-626. Some of these ideas were also expressed in the *Royal Engineers' Journal* and reprinted with illustrations in *The Military Engineer* (U.S.A), XIII, 1921, 315-320, 409-414, as "The Science of Infantry Tactics." It is interesting that very little has been written about Liddell Hart and his work.

There are a few short pieces: in *Kunitz's Twentieth Century Authors* (1942 and a supplement in 1955); a bad article by "Irving M. Gibson" (pseudonym of Professor A. Kovacs of St. Johns University in Brooklyn in 1947) in E. M. Earle, *The Makers of Modern Strategy* (Princeton, 1943, reprinted without corrections in 1952). (Liddell Hart wrote a strong objection to this piece, which was written in the shadow of the fall of France; it is undated, but Kovacs' Francophile reply to Earle is marked 8 April 1947. I am grateful to Dr. Jay Luvaas for providing me with copies of both these documents.) Considering the vast output of the man, it is surprising that until recently there were practically no appraisals of Liddell Hart's work available, even in the military journals. Book reviewers have had their irresponsible say, but only in Luvaas' *The Military Legacy of the Civil War: the European Inheritance* (Chicago, 1959), pp. 216-225, and in the whole chapter in his new *The Education of an Army* (Chicago, 1964), in Colonel Robert J. Icks, "Liddell Hart: One View," *Armor*, LXI (November-December 1952), 25-27, in Lt. (j.g.) John W. Walden, "Liddell Hart," *Military Review*, Vol. XXXIV, No. 6 (September 1954) (re-

After a spell in the new Army Education Corps,* in 1924 he was, for "medical reasons," placed upon half pay by order of the anti-intellectual C.I.G.S., The Earl of Cavan, and wrote his first important popular work, *Paris: or the Future of War*, which appeared the next year. In the meantime, Maxse had obtained for him a position with *The Morning Post*, of which the former was a director, and upon the death of Colonel Charles Repington † he succeeded to his job at *The Daily Telegraph* as the only full-time military correspondent

print), and in General of the Air Force Chassin, "Un grand penseur militaire britannique: B. H. Liddell Hart," *Revue de Defense Nationale,* October 1950, pp. 334-346, have there been real attempts at evaluations.

The most recent material on the background of Liddell Hart's own work, besides his memoirs, is the book of essays edited by Michael Howard, *The Theory and Practice of War: Fifteen Essays Presented to Captain B. H. Liddell Hart on His Seventieth Birthday* (1965). As this was not to be published until the end of 1965, I have not been able to see more than the Table of Contents kindly sent me by Captain Liddell Hart.

Liddell Hart (and he used to be known as Capt. B. H. L. Hart) has an extensive bibliography of his own, just in books: *New Methods of Infantry Training* (1918); *The Science of Infantry Tactics* (1921); *Paris: or the Future of War* (1925); *Great Captains Unveiled* (1926); *The Re-Making of Modern Armies* (1927); *Reputations: Ten Years After* (1928); *The Decisive Wars of History: A Study in Strategy* (in 1941 as *The Strategy of Indirect Approach*, in 1942 as *The Way to Win Wars*, in 1945 a second edition was entitled the same and in 1954 the title was changed to *Strategy: the Indirect Approach*) (1929); *Sherman: Soldier, Realist, American* (1929); *The Real War* (later *History of the World War, 1914-1918* (1935)), (1930); *Foch: the Man of Orleans* (1931); *The British Way in Warfare (When Britain Goes to War* (1935)) (1932); *The Future of Infantry* (1933); *Col. Lawrence: The Man behind the Legend* (1934); *T. E. Lawrence: in Arabia and After* (1934); *The War in Outline, 1914-1918* (1936); *Europe in Arms* (1937); *Through the Fog of War* (1938); with Robert Graves, *T. E. Lawrence to His Biographers* (1939); *The Defence of Britain* (1939); *Dynamic Defence* (1940); *The Current of War* (1941); *This Expanding War* (1942); *Thoughts on War* (1944); *Why Don't We Learn from History* (1944); *The Revolution in Warfare* (1947); *The German Generals Talk (The Other Side of the Hill* in the U.S.A.) (1948); *The Defence of the West* (1950); *Strategy: the Indirect Approach* (1954); *The Red Army* (1956); *Deterrent or Defence* (1960); and *The Tanks: the History of the Royal Tank Regiment, 1914-1945* (1959); *A History of the Second World War* and his *Memoirs* (I [1965], II [1965]). Several of these volumes are revisions of his earlier works and others contain reprints of his military journalistic articles for *The Daily Telegraph, The Times,* and other publications. See also Brian Bond, "Second Thoughts on War: a conversation with B. H. Liddell Hart," *Military Review* (September 1965), 23-32.

Liddell Hart was the Military Editor of the *Encyclopaedia Britannica* and contributed many articles to it over the years.

* See A. C. T. White, *The Story of Army Education, 1943-1963* (1963).

† On Repington, see Luvaas, *The Education of an Army.*

in Great Britain. He retained this post for a decade, then in 1935 he joined *The Times* in a similar post and as defence adviser. During some eighteen months of the next four years he became very influential at the War Office, where the new Secretary of State, Leslie Hore-Belisha, put in sixty-two of his reforms including the retirement of the senior officers left over from the First World War. In May 1937 the Minister for the Co-ordination of Defence, Sir Thomas Inskip, had asked him to write a memorandum on Army reorganization. In this paper Liddell Hart recommended doubling the number of guns in the four anti-aircraft division, but not till the Germans invaded Austria in early 1938 did this find favour with the General Staff at the War Office. It was for Inskip that he also wrote the paper on the need for home defence air forces as opposed to Trenchard's deterrent force. In 1939 he had a nervous breakdown and left *The Times*. And after the fall of France in 1940 for some years his military reputation was in decline, but it has risen again slowly in the nineteen-fifties and sixties. Liddell Hart has always been didactic and though he has been labelled a prophet, he bridged the gap between the tank vanguard led by Fuller and the main body of infantry, cavalry, and artillery under the War Office. More than any other writer of the period, he attempted to create a defence philosophy for Britain that would blend modern military ideas with traditional British disinterest in armed forces in peacetime. At the same time, he was a prescient military correspondent. Perhaps the most fascinating part of a review of Liddell Hart's work is the evolutional portrait of a human mind that emerges.*

## CONCLUSION

Both the official and the unofficial military intellectuals were in part captives of the system in which they matured. This was true whether or not they went to the staff colleges or to the Imperial Defence College or merely grew up in the Service. Thus we find that the sort of careers that Richmond in the Royal Navy and Fuller in the Army enjoyed were typical. The same can be said later on for

* As Jay Luvaas has noted in *The Civil War; the European Legacy* (Chicago, 1959), p. 219, n. 44, Liddell Hart's *Thoughts on War* provides a most useful source for the intellectual historian in the way in which his original ideas are classified by subject and dated. It must be noted, of course, that these raw materials are most useful when combined with a study of the research and other activities upon which he was engaged at the time that the inspiration occurred.

Sykes and Trenchard, both of whom were approximately contemporaries of the other two. Though Richmond was somewhat anti-materialist, nevertheless he was, like Fuller and the airmen, very interested in weapons and their effects. As a group they had lived in a period of transition that had left far more of a mark upon them than would be the case a generation or two later. In contrast, Liddell Hart was so young and his military service so short that his vision was far wider, making him more of a Jomini than a Clausewitz, more a strategic thinker than a tactician. These differences must be borne in mind in considering what they wrote.

The impact of the First World War on their thinking is also important. In their various ways, the pundits were concerned that Britain should not be bled white in another futile, un-British, Continental conflict. Their approaches varied with their background. Richmond, imprisoned by his battleship background, paid less heed to the submarine than might have been expected. Fuller, Sykes, and Trenchard sought to fight a mobile war, and a short one, if war there had to be. Liddell Hart took a wider view and showed the greatest growth in intellectual awareness of the problems of war.

# *Chapter IV*—The Pundits of Seapower

Traditionally the Royal Navy has been the silent Service. Its writers have been few and its greatest exponent, apart from the recent writers Prof. Arthur Marder and Captain S. W. Roskill, has been the American Admiral Alfred Thayer Mahan in his series on *The Influence of Sea Power upon History, 1660-1815*. The Navy was not well served in the interwar years when career-consciousness and the Admiralty's limited view of *The Naval Review* and of the courses at Greenwich were no encouragement to officers to put their pens to paper. Moreover, two of the leading critics, Fred T. Jane of *All the World's Warships* fame and Sir Julian Corbett, the official naval historian, were dead by 1925. This left only the less-effective Sir Archibald Hurd, Hector C. Bywater, and Captain H. G. Thursfield, whose need not to antagonize their sources curbed their tongues. Add to this a long period in which there was no publicly acknowledged enemy, and one has gone a long way to explain the lack of naval writings of stature without mentioning the normal difficulties of a naval career often at sea in far away places.

## Admiral Sir Herbert Richmond

Sir Herbert Richmond wrote a good deal in the interwar years, though not with real freedom till after 1930. Despite his years as Assistant Director of Operations at the Admiralty just before and during the early part of the First World War, his work suffered from the fact that he was forty-seven in 1918 and seventy-two in 1943, when he delivered the lectures (later entitled *Statesmen and Sea Power*) upon which his reputation principally stands. Correct on the larger issue of strategy, he was much less attuned when talking of weapons. His mind grew but slowly in the interwar years and never really broke with the century in which he was raised.

On 21 February 1923 Richmond had the honour to deliver the Raleigh Lecture on History to the British Academy. He chose as his subject "National Policy and Naval Strength, the seventeenth to the twentieth Century." He gave a stimulating survey of the relationship of these two forces, a subject that remained close to his heart and later became one of the keystones in the gateway to knowledge that he bequeathed to the English people.* In *National Policy and Naval Strength* (1928), he enlarged upon these ideas and sought to show, as he had in 1923, that size of vessel was not so important as a sufficient quantity of ships to meet the needs of an individual state. He elaborated upon this theme in 1931 with *Economy and Naval Security,* written at the time of the Depression crisis, in which he pressed the case for the limitation of warships to 6,500 tons (the size of light cruisers generally capable of dealing with armed merchant raiders, though not with the 10,000-ton German pocket battleships then just being placed in service), saying that this was perfectly adequate for trade protection provided that they did not have to meet vessels with a superior armament (which the German ships possessed!). After all, the first purpose of a navy at any time was to protect commerce by controlling sea communications. The limitation of numbers he felt was absolutely useless as that was a matter dictated strictly by the actual needs of individual national security. In this he had some effect upon Prime Minister MacDonald, who stopped battleship construction till 1937, but not sufficient to prevent Mac-Donald from agreeing to a limitation of cruisers in the London Naval Conference of 1930.

Already known as a naval theorist and historian, in 1931 Richmond delivered both the Lees Knowles Lectures at Cambridge and a series at the University of London. In editing these for publication, he added a most useful table of the functions of Imperial defence. These showed the extent of his thought and the ability he had to present the most complex patterns in simple form in conformity with his view that the basic concepts had to be driven home early in an officer's career.

*Imperial Defence and Capture at Sea in War* contained a great deal of sound advice. Unlike many other writers, Richmond was vitally concerned with the functions of armed forces in peacetime as well as in war. Fighting might have more appeal to the public imag-

* *Proceedings of the British Academy,* X, 1923, 339-354.

ination, yet survival depended upon what preparations were made not only for such occasions, but also on the means to avoid fighting at all. Thus the duties of the Services in the normal periods between conflicts were the preservation of order, maintenance for war, and training. Richmond called for the concentration of units so that suitable detachments could reach threatened points *in time* instead of the current policy of individual ships wandering all over the world. Though underrating them, he saw aircraft in their place, but argued that they were not capable of supplying that constant impression of authority by which peace was kept. As for an army, Britain needed, he thought, 90,000 men abroad and the same number as reliefs at home, for bases abroad were too vital to be lost at the start of a conflict. At the same time, he felt—and this was disliked by Sir Charles Madden, the First Sea Lord in 1929—Britain was keeping too many ships in commission while destroying her reserves, so that when war came she would have to wait while those still in reserve were modernized and new ships built.

Richmond was right in these respects. One of the Navy's immediate problems on the outbreak of war was a shortage of all classes except battleships and a very definite lack of anti-submarine equipment and doctrine. Throughout most of the war the Fleet Air Arm was badly equipped, due as much to the Admiralty's peacetime refusal to spend funds on developing the proper aircraft as to the Air Ministry's reluctance to supply them. This meant that, during the important years before Allied victory in the Mediterranean in 1943, with the exception of the attack on Taranto, the Navy was never able to operate either an offensive or a defensive carrier task force. Thus in many ways, for perhaps the wrong reasons, Richmond was correct in underestimating the effect of aircraft. But during the Second World War the Royal Navy suffered considerably from enemy air attacks, nearly all by landbased aircraft, as did the invaluable merchantmen that it was escorting.

In much the same way, his estimates of the importance of blockade and capture at sea in wartime proved farther afield. He felt the Admiralty was too U-boat-minded. It may have been so immediately after the First World War, but after 1929 the Admiralty obviously came once again under the spell of the "gunnery crowd." Since the submarine was immune to gunfire in most actions, gunnery officers were much happier concentrating on the pleasant thought of bringing the pocket battleships and other surface units to action. Richmond helped the Admiralty concentrate on the surface raider by his emphasis on the part cruisers and destroyers would play in raiding British commerce. With lessons of the First World War in mind, the Germans were, of course, hedging their bets. Under Grand-Admiral Raeder both very large surface raiders and U-boats were developed. The British Admiralty had to prepare the Royal Navy to meet both. It must be said to Richmond's credit that he did see that an enemy might, as the Germans nearly succeeded in doing by bombing in 1940-41, undertake the possible subjugation of Britain by attacks on her coastal trade and more particularly upon her ports. He was by no means convinced, however, that the submarine was a really dangerous threat though he credited it with considerable diversionary effect. While reading his words today, it must be borne in mind that they were written in the wake of the London Naval Treaty of 1930, which was popularly regarded by the Service as a victory for the Americans and the materialists, the advocates of the numbers game, to the neglect of strategic purpose and tactical need.

In 1933 Richmond tackled his favourite subject with *Naval Training*, in which he urged that a number of changes be made in the system set up in 1902. One of the chief suggestions was that the age of entry into the Service for officers be raised from thirteen to eighteen with applicants being chosen from the good "public" schools as in the case of the Army. This mode of entry had been available since 1913, but only to a limited few. He also wanted better training in military history and the abolition of the system of trying to educate midshipmen in academic subjects while they were also serving afloat as officers.

The year 1934 saw Richmond return once again to the well-worn theme of naval security as yet another naval conference loomed upon the horizon. He continued to condemn the doctrines dominating the world's navies as false dogmas adhered to for no rational reason. A case in point was the 35,000-ton battleship, which the United States Navy finally justified on the ground of a lack of bases overseas when Britain under Richmond's pressure called for the reduction of this type to a maximum of 25,000 tons, without fuel or water.* *Sea Power in the Modern World* recognized that blockade could be applied

---

* In general the idea of using battleships as monitors in support of amphibious operations found little favour, for the latter were after Gallipoli generally distrusted, until after Pearl Harbor. In the U.S. Navy their use as task-force command posts came really with the Japanese kamikaze attacks on carriers in 1944.

effectively only if the maritime power was allied to a land power and that it would be effective only against a nation seeking world domination. At the same time he pointed out that airpower was not a substitute for seapower for airpower could not transport an army overseas nor maintain it there. For this reason, he argued, seapower remained a better weapon for collective security than airpower. But as far as the size of the naval instrument was concerned, it needed to be big enough to do the job assigned and no larger. In other words, he was calling for economy of force and for making use of the mobility and power of surprise that seapower afforded. As far as ratios were concerned, if the world desired them, then the thing to do was, he said, to start with what the smallest power felt it needed for the security of its merchant fleet and sea routes, and then to work up from there, rather than down from the top with the result that powers such as Italy were left feeling insecure. Finally, he observed that whatever ratios were agreed upon, these would be the ones that would have to be imposed upon Germany, then already secretly building U-boats and openly developing pocket battleships.

He also began to write more for popular periodicals such as *The Nineteenth Century,* in which, in support of Liddell Hart,* he published a blast at the military mind. He noted, as others before and after have also, that peacetime routine corroded the military mind, which became saturated with paper work and lacked stimulation to think of war, while the twin gods became orthodoxy and conformity. Richmond wanted not the abolition of traditions, but of suppositions. His was the approach of the loyal but inquiring scientific critic. He loved the Navy and wanted to see it do its job well. He felt, rightly, that it could not do this if it were ruled by ideas that were untested and based upon statements and presumptions not founded upon careful investigation. Like many such vital minds, he was disturbed that well-intentioned questions and suggestions were met with unthinking hostility on the part of the Admiralty, and by administrators in general, who not only felt that such ideas held personal reflections upon themselves, but also that, if adopted, they would make more work and upset the pleasant and well-ordered routine. His next sally, therefore, was no more politely received in Whitehall.

* "The Service Mind," CXIII, January 1933, 90-97.

"The Case Against Big Battleships" in August 1934 pointed out that the Admiralty had completely muddled itself as to what was a capital ship. He noted that every ship of war was a compromise between fighting power, speed, and endurance and that its function, therefore, governed its design. Size did not make for invulnerability, while the function of a battleship could, if other powers were limited, be as well satisfied at 22,000 tons as at 35,000, while the 10,000-ton Washington Treaty cruiser was still a large but useless size. Moreover, if ships became too large and vulnerable—and he noted that the bigger ships at Jutland were sunk with fewer hits than those at Tsushima a dozen years before—the Higher Direction became afraid to use them for fear of loss. (This happened at the Admiralty in 1939 with regard to aircraft carriers, which Fuller had already predicted would be the new capital ships.) Moreover, as Britain could not afford to have many large ships, she would be better off building the small ones she needed for the defence both of big ships and of convoys. It was ironic that the British experts had started the trend to bigness in the eighteen-nineties and that other powers wanted capital ships because the British said they were necessary! Late in 1934 Richmond wrote that he felt that Germany should probably be allowed to re-arm, but just over a year later he hoped that none of the powers, then meeting at London, would decide to go further with rearmament.* At the time he suggested that allies in the classical balance of power role were far better than the greatest fleet, while parity, unless it took account of the Shotwellian points,† was meaningless.

Richmond praised the appointment in 1936 of a Minister for the Co-ordination of Defence but proved to be overly optimistic as to what that gentleman would accomplish. Nevertheless, he gave good advice in saying that British naval strength had never before 1921 been based upon fixed criteria, but always upon political prob-

* *The Nineteenth Century and After,* CXVI (August 1934), 186-193; "Naval Disarmament," *The Nineteenth Century and After,* CXVI (December 1934), 640-650; "Naval Rearmament," *The Nineteenth Century and After,* CXIX (January 1936), 38-46.

† On 12 March 1919, Prof. J. T. Shotwell had written in *The New York Times* that parity made no sense unless the following were taken into account: location of naval bases, the extent of the merchant marine to be protected, the proximity of trade routes to hostile coasts, and dependence upon overseas supply in terms of the amount per head of population, upon which basis Britain rated 196 and the United States only 77.

abilities. At the same time that fixed ratios had been determined, naval strength was becoming far more difficult to measure owing to the complexity of modern warhsips.* At the time that this was written, all but the Anglo-German Naval Agreement had lapsed, and Britain was feverishly rebuilding her neglected navy.

By the time he came to review Bernard Acworth's *Britain in Danger* in 1938, Richmond had changed his mind about U-boats and was prepared to call the Admiralty at fault in not being prepared at once to institute convoys and at the same time to guard against surface raiders.†

On the whole the broad pattern of the war proved Richmond correct. But he sadly misled the Admiralty as to the importance of surface raiders while neglecting the close-support role of the carrier against U-boats and aircraft. Not that the Admiralty either cared much for his views or would have done otherwise given the Board and officers it then had. Apart from the limited number of battleships, the war was really fought by small ships and aircraft carriers. In both these categories Britain was woefully short. Moreover, despite the 1917 scare, trade protection had been regarded much too optimistically, and the Admiralty was forced from the opening day of war to convoy. As so often had proved the case, tactics disallowed on maneuvers as improper were exactly those used by the Germans.‡ But it was on the much broader field of the making of policy and strategy that Richmond was so signally vindicated. The 1939-45 war called for unified strategy, allies, and the co-operation of both the three armed forces and of the entire nation for victory. Britain lost Singapore because it was not properly protected and manned as a result of the country's having persisted in a policy that was bound to place it in jeopardy. Due to the shortage of fighters and other anti-aircraft defences, Malta was only with difficulty kept as an operational base. The historical practice of shepherding convoys with battleships again had to be adopted due to the failure to knock out or bottle up the big German ships that were designed to be used as raiders or as potential menaces until a battle unit was completed. In Grand Admiral Raeder's view, a trade war against England was

---

* "The Minister of Defence," *The Nineteenth Century and After,* CXXI (April 1937), 512-521.

† "Some Naval Problems: Britain in Danger and Captain Bernard Acworth," *The Nineteenth Century and After,* CXXIII (February 1938), 193-203.

‡ Rear-Admiral Ben Bryant, *Submarine Commander* (New York, 1961), p. 36.

the proper German naval role, and events proved him correct as the First World War had already indicated it might.

Richmond's best work came after 1940 when he produced his classic *Statesmen and Sea Power,* in which in a broad sweep he sought to educate both politicians and naval officers to the strong interrelationship of political and military strategy. In it he summed up his two main lines of thought: what had been and what should have been the naval policy of the civil government and of the Admiralty, and how it was carried out by the officers in command with the forces that the country placed at their disposal.

In *Statesmen and Sea Power,* his Ford Lectures at Oxford in 1943, Richmond laid out with perfect clarity the theme that he also later developed in the unfinished *Navy as an Instrument of Policy* volumes.*

He began by quoting Sir John Fortescue, the eminent historian of the British army who had made the pertinent point that it was statesmen who decided when to strike, where to strike, and how to strike, which meant that the armed forces were mere weapons of grand strategy. The essence of the book is to be found in the idea that it is the duty of statesmen in peacetime to make sure that the armed forces have the materials, the men, the bases, and the logistical backing as well as the reserves with which to act quickly and decisively at the politician's command. And the corollary to this is, of course, that public leaders must not blame the armed forces for failure when leaders force them into war for which they are improperly manned, equipped, and provided. In a long and careful as well as extensive survey of British naval and diplomatic history from the days of Elizabeth to the surrender of Japan in 1945,† he graphically exposed the mis-statesmanship of the interwar years through which he had lived.

He was careful in the Introduction to define seapower as

> that form of national strength which enables its possessor to send his armies and commerce across those stretches of sea and ocean which lie between his country or the countries of his allies, and those territories to which he needs access in war; and to prevent his enemy from doing the same. And who is the Statesman? He is that civil authority responsible for the maintenance of this power in peace and its effective use in war as a national weapon.

---

* See also the newer work by Captain S. W. Roskill, *The Strategy of Sea Power* (London, 1962).

† The lectures were not published until 1946.

Thus, he said, the statesman must see that the country has a sufficient standard of naval strength in relation to other powers, the requisite fighting instruments, bases, shipping, and seamen, and a dynamic shipbuilding industry. Moreover, the statesman must not allow the weapon of economic pressure to be blunted by neutrals who have traditionally desired to make profits out of every conflict.

In Richmond's appraisal of the handling of national maritime policy, famed Queen Elizabeth I came off poorly for she lacked singleness of purpose, the ability to concentrate the efforts of the fleet upon one object at a time, and she neglected the use of surprise. Sir Francis Drake was blamed for what should have been laid upon the sovereign's shoulders because *she* had failed to make adequate preparation and had misdirected the plan of attack. As he noted throughout the book, the cheapest way to make war is not always in the long run the most inexpensive, for dissipation of effort is generally far more costly than striking an expensive blow at the very beginning. The cheapest way, of course, was to have a credible deterrent that prevented war from breaking out in the first place. Time and again in *Statesmen and Sea Power* he also pointed up the lessons of Elizabeth's campaigns as the need for an offensive strategy, saying of the 1590's that "the objects of war are never attainable by defence alone, as all experience of war by land and sea had abundantly shown, the functions of a fighting force cannot be restricted to the necessary, but negative, processes of defence, even if it were possible to attain security merely by beating off an attack." He also vigorously attacked the economizers, who were inclined to agree with vociferous neutrals and hazy-headed humanitarians that belligerents would respect in war rules laid down on paper in peace. He knew only too well that in a showdown human beings only recognize force.

After the passing of good Queen Bess and the early Stuarts, the Navy ceased to be a purely royal possession and became a national service that in the Dutch Wars proved that, used offensively, the Navy could defeat Continental powers by depriving them of the maritime commerce upon which they depended. The statesmen of the Commonwealth and Restoration period successfully aimed their weapon precisely at the enemy fleets that guarded trade; this was sound military policy. Once again, this policy, as always, led the enemy to resort to neutral shipping, an action that, Richmond asserted, was rightly met by a harsher application of the blockade and of definitions of contraband. The wars with France made England's position more vulnerable and so called for a higher standard of strength than in the conflict with the Dutch. The Royal Navy had now to be prepared to counter invasion, meet several French fleets or contain them, convoy British trade, and at the same time keep a large enough reserve to balance the losses in battles and storms that might occur. Moreover, as Britain was by the latter part of the seventeenth century a colonial power, her statesmen had the additional responsibility of protecting these naval and commercial outposts. The story of the wars against France was one of alternate glorious periods, when English men and materiel were in top condition, and of depressing periods, when peacetime neglect saw the Navy embarrassed in war, often after failing to be a deterrent.

Starting with William of Orange, English statesmen found themselves split between the *continental* and the *maritime* schools of thought. The former wanted to send troops to fight in Europe, the latter to make use of the true mobility and surprise power of the fleet to weaken the enemy at sea and overseas, which was more in their true interest. Once absolute command of the sea had been obtained, then, in Richmond's opinion, and only then, was it safe for Britain to employ her forces continentally to bring down an aggressor. In attaining ascendancy at sea, she had always to bear in mind that the main fleet of the enemy had first to be destroyed, for then all other expeditions could be conducted with maritime impunity. When there was a failure to do this, as in 1781 off the American coast, then disaster would follow. The wars of the eighteenth century showed the folly of underestimating the need for cruisers, the most versatile and important of all naval vessels. (It will be remembered that Richmond had pointed with horror in the late twenties to the steady reduction in cruisers and small craft. The actual number of cruisers fell below the fifty that the Admiralty of the day called the minimum in 1930, though in 1888 this figure had been 186 at a time when Britain had fewer possessions than after the First World War.) Richmond continued with a fine pen to draw the picture on down to his own day, showing how neglect of the basic principles of seapower, a well-prepared, adequate navy ready to seize control of the seas, always left a maritime Britain in jeopardy.

Sir Herbert Richmond is one of the Royal Navy's tragedies. Though he rose to high rank, for he was an efficient officer and a loyal seaman, he was not really allowed to exercise his talents in policy-making. His rebellion against the materialists jeopardized his success because the Admiralty was controlled by the battleship-minded after the First World War. Due to inter-Service jealousies, he was denied more than a two-year stint as Commandant of the Imperial Defence College, and, when his words began to reach high political personages, he was let out to pasture in scholarly fields. The Navy's loss became History's gain, for he turned his competent scholarship into intellectual influence of a wide order.

## CAPTAIN BERNARD ACWORTH

Much less important than Sir Herbert was Captain Bernard Acworth, a submariner who had been a turret officer on the battle-cruiser *Indefatigable* at the Dardanelles and after the war the captain of an anti-submarine-warfare destroyer. His works were written for popular consumption with the artistic aid of Dr. Oscar Parkes, the learned and well-informed editor of *Jane's Fighting Ships*. Acworth's first work, *This Bondage: A Study of the "Migration" of Birds, Insects, and Aircraft, with Some Reflections on "Evolution" and Relativity* (1929), was a wide-ranging nature study that ended in favour of airships and against the R.A.F. This appeared just at the time when the large experimental British airships *R100* and *R101* were to fly; by the end of 1930 the latter had crashed and the former was waiting the fall of the sword of Damocles. He lacked Richmond's more rational approach to air matters, though both of them wanted a Fleet Air Arm under naval control. In 1930 appeared his *Navies of Today and Tomorrow*, which argued against the materialist followers of Admiral Lord Fisher, the famous "Jackie," responsible for the numerical limitation of warships and in favour of the "blue-water school" led by Admiral Sir Reginald Custance (1847-1935). Custance had long fought for the study of naval history and had argued for the building of many ships of moderate tonnage, powerful of armament, though slow of speed in preference to armoured cruisers. Custance had been retired from the Navy in 1912 because his views were not popular. Acworth argued strongly in *Navies of Today and Tomorrow* that fleets must not patrol trade routes, but must, as Clausewitz and Mahan had argued, seek to knock out the enemy fleet in order to seize the strategic initiative in the land campaign, to obtain an easy defence of trade, and to blockade effectively the enemy's ports. There was no short cut, he said, to effective seapower by foregoing fast battleships for cruisers, submarines, and aircraft. But at the same time he called for the careful study of the torpedo as a weapon and the re-evaluation of the gun as the only one.

The difficulty was that Acworth never really came to grips with the problem of an assault upon British maritime strength by a power that refused to create a battle fleet, engaging instead in a guerrilla three-dimensional rather than a conventional surface attack. The Second World War was to show that though some big ships were needed to counter the small enemy battle "fleets in being," the basic shield and sword against enemy commerce raiders were small escort vessels, baby flattops, and long-range aircraft. Even the mighty *Tirpitz* was sunk late in the Second World War by a combination of midget submarines and heavy bomber attacks, rather than by surface forces. In the Pacific, United States Navy submarine forces found the Japanese, who tended to base their naval ideas upon those of the Royal Navy, unprepared and unable to deal with underwater attacks. The war in the Pacific was almost exclusively a matter of actions between carrier task forces or of amphibious assaults and with corollary surface battles, generally at night when air support was least effective. Heavy guns alone won few if any battles throughout the war except for Oldendorff's victory at Surigao Strait in the vast Battle of Leyte Gulf.

In all his thoughts in *Navies of Today and Tomorrow* Acworth reflected the current differences of opinion amongst British and other naval officers. There had been a strong trend away from the battleship after the war and one extreme of this was the motor-torpedo-boat school developed especially by the Italians, another the air-over-all; and yet the gunnery group still exercised dominant control at the Admiralty because most of the senior admirals had been captains at Jutland and had grown up in a Navy dominated by guns. An example is Lord Chatfield, Lord Beatty's captain at Jutland, who was First Sea Lord from 1933 to 1938, succeeding Sir Charles Madden, Jellicoe's captain. Moreover, in this 1930 work Acworth was still so dominated by his hatred of the R.A.F. that he failed to take into account the coming impact of airpower upon the war at sea. Increasingly after 1930 one side gained the strategic advantage as a result of delivering a knockout blow by air such as at Taranto or at Pearl Harbor. It was the inability of the Royal Navy to close German bases that compelled the Admiralty in the Second World War to demand so much of Bomber Command's time to fight the Battle of the Atlantic over France and Germany. In fact, the more of Acworth one reads, the more reactionary he sounds, as he was against 16-inch guns for their inaccuracy and long range, against torpedoes as large and chancy, against mines because the paravane had defeated them, against fire-control because it was too complicated and centralized. Given his own way, he would have returned to the simplified, coal-burning warship firing at point-blank ranges. Yet he had a point here, too. Coal was an easy, self-contained natural resource in Britain, but it required more men to handle it per ton than did oil and, as it could not be replenished at sea, limited the radius of a warship's action.

On the mechanical side, he also had just grounds for complaining that the materielists had complicated weapons by their search for perfection to such an extent that their efficient use was above the capabilities of young ratings and officers who would have to operate them, especially in small ships like destroyers and submarines. Certainly his expert opinions on submarines were easily documentable. The unimproved *L*'s were fine boats, which were preceded by the freak *K*'s and followed by the *M*'s, *R*'s and *X-1*, while the *O*'s and *P*'s were mechanically cluttered up, especially with wireless, and suffered heavy casualties in the Second World War. Though Acworth did not put it this way, what he implied was that in peacetime a constant evolution takes place that is never battle-tested and results in many improvements of doubtful value simply because people in all departments have to be kept busy. (How like commercial life, too!) One of the first results in war is a general cry for more officers and men to handle all these materials under active service conditions.

His next work was *The Navy and the Next War* (1933), which was reissued in 1935 with an eighteenth-century-style title, *The Restoration of England's Sea Power being a Second Edition of The Navy and the Next War with Four New Chapters, Including "Collective Security," "Air Power and Sea Power," and "The Anglo-German Naval Treaty."* A trenchant attempt to counter the air mania, as he saw it, of the day, it called for a return to balance of power or strategical independence. The first edition had been well reviewed, and Acworth was gaining stature as a right-wing navalist. His attitude in 1935 was, in his own words:

Afraid of everything we are unprepared to defend ourselves against anything. Instead, we have saddled ourselves with the cost of an Air Force that cannot defend us from the air, an Army that cannot undertake Continental warfare on the scale apparently contemplated, and a Navy that cannot even guarantee the food supply of this teeming island. . . . No apology is needed, therefore, for endeavoring . . . to sort the sheep of legitimate apprehension from the goats of groundless terror.

In 1937 he returned to the attack originally delivered in *Navies of Today and Tomorrow* with fresh demands for small, efficient, coal-burning ships including 13-inch-gunned battleships priced at £1,000,000 apiece. He also supported Richmond's plea to be aware of surface raiders and revealed that the Admiralty's plan was to send a battlecruiser and an aircraft carrier (a vessel Acworth considered utterly useless) with flights of torpedo-bombers to patrol the trade routes, which actually was one of the first methods used in 1939. He claimed that the Sea Lords supported the idea of 2,000-ton, 6-inch-gunned sloops, but that First Lord Eyres-Monsell was against them, so the Sea Lords urged Acworth to write about them.* Acworth did not think much of the new, air-conscious navy, just granted control of the Fleet Air Arm in 1937.

The principal problem with Acworth was that he was correct in his broad conclusions on the non-existence of British naval policy and in his suggestions as to what it should be from a political stand, but he muddied the waters and his reputation is corroded by his attempts to be specific about types of vessels and tactics, especially since he based these upon a seaman's outlook that took no account of the general technological progress of society and of contemporary enemies. But perhaps this was inevitable since he had not Richmond's historical knowledge and breadth of view. The latter made this contrast evident in his comments on *Britain in Danger,* but Richmond agreed thoroughly that there was no British naval policy.†

One cannot pass from the naval writers without giving a brief nod to Russell Grenfell. He is perhaps best remembered today for his wartime book, *The Bismarck Episode* (1948), which had qualities of fiction in its mood of suspense. In addition, he wrote two strictly

---

* *Britain in Danger: An Examination of Our New Navy* (London, 1937), p. 49. See also Stephen King-Hall, *My Naval Life* (London, 1951), pp. 263-266, on his own secret study of warship design and naval policy in which he concluded that no co-ordination existed.

† *The Nineteenth Century and After,* CXXIII (February 1938), 193-203.

historical works, *The Men Who Defend Us* (1938), an attempt to rehabilitate the Navy after the Invergordon affair and in the face of rising need of the men's services, and *Main Fleet to Singapore* (1951), an early exposition of the failure of British strategy that led to the loss of *Prince of Wales, Repulse,* and Singapore in 1941 and 1942. In addition to these, just before the Second World War he produced a provocative little study of naval strategy based upon his lectures at the Royal Naval College at Greenwich called *The Art of the Admiral* (1937). This was followed in the next year by *Sea Power in the Next War,* one of the volumes in the series edited by Liddell Hart.

In the latter Grenfell sought, as did other writers in this series, to make a balanced judgement. He felt that as far as the evidence then available was concerned, war experience had not shown that aircraft would be very effective against warships, while at the same time more thought needed to be given to battleships and less to aircraft. However, the psychological influence of aircraft would be there, and their impact would be greater upon larger units. If there was a historical precedent, it was that of the mental impression made by submarines in the First World War. The striking weapon of both these third-dimensional machines was the torpedo, and Grenfell was in tune with the thought of the day when he emphasized its psychological effect at Jutland and its future tactical one.

Both the motor-torpedo-boat enthusiasts and the airmen led by Trenchard were advocates of the efficacy of this ship-killing weapon. Trenchard had proposed shortly after the 1914-18 war that the R.A.F. take over defence against invasion on the ground that torpedo-bombers were cheaper, more mobile, and as effective as a Fleet. Though the Air Force was denied this role at home, it was given a major place in the Singapore scheme. Yet little was done to develop either torpedoes or their delivery systems as the 1939-45 war showed only too well.

On the matter of invasion, Grenfell argued that it was only an academic problem as far as Britain was concerned, but that for Australia and New Zealand it was a reality in those days of Japanese aggression in the Far East.

In the period 1918 to 1939 the Navy seems to have suffered from a dearth of critics. The explanation for this would seem to lie in the facts of Service life in the interwar years, in the anonymity of

*The Naval Review,* which contained much ill-thought-out criticism, to which the Admiralty was indifferent, and to the nature of life at sea, which gave little time for reading and writing as compared with military life. Yet it is only being fair to point out that in Richmond, despite his nineteenth-century outlook, the senior Service had a competent critic and in Acworth a runner-up equal to the few produced by the other Services, with the exception of Fuller in originality and Liddell Hart in contemporary stature.

# Chapter V — The Advocates of Mechanized Landpower

While we talk of "seapower" and "airpower," the term "landpower" has far less meaning. Thus to categorize Fuller and Liddell Hart as the advocates of landpower may be delimiting their sphere of influence too narrowly. Yet they both did concentrate their energies primarily on matters affecting the Army. Furthermore, unlike the seapower and airpower pundits, their work was complementary. Though they were a generation apart in age and experience, nevertheless they both emerged at the end of the First World War with the idea that the infantryman could be given a better chance through the application of mechanization and of better generalship. Within a very few years they were brought face to face, found they had much in common, and have ever since supported each other. Thus it was quite fitting that in late 1963 they should have been awarded Chesney Medals in a joint ceremony.*

## J. F. C. Fuller

It was in the realm of tactics that Fuller made his greatest and most original contribution. He looked at operations in World War I and saw that they raised three questions for the offensive: how to keep men alive, how to keep weapons functioning, and how to retain movement. The solution was the tank, which made man master of his weapons and not a pack mule,† as Fuller put it. But it was no good providing the weapons if the commanders lacked brains. Thus Fuller became a crusader for intelligent commanders

* *The Times,* 1 November 1963; *JRUSI,* CIX (February 1964), 68-72.
† The infantryman of 1918 had to be able to carry as much as 70 pounds of weight in clothing and equipment.

and, above that, for intelligent statesmen who would realize that the role of the Army is to prevent war, not to stop it from spreading. Like most partisans, he occasionally overstepped the bounds of reality, such as in his predictions of one Service by 1950 because tanks would be both submersible and flyable. In his 1919 Essay he called for a reorganization of the structure of government to provide a Ministry of Defence with an Imperial General Staff under whom would be the Navy, Army, R.A.F., Science, and Industry, in which each department of the Staff would be organized into a thinking section (historical, statistical, and planning functions), a liaison section, and a routine section. Lord Haldane also made similar proposals in the official British documents series *Cd. 9230* (1918). Fuller also wanted manuals that would show each member of the forces the role he was required to play, and a tactical university. He demanded a New Model Army of reduced cost and increased efficiency because it was based on mechanization and not upon the horse.*

In 1923 there appeared *The Reformation of War* in which Fuller's theme was that the 1914 war was not the last war; therefore, Britain had to prepare for the next one. His language was as usual so blunt as not to win many converts. He admitted to being a heretic because "novelty is a mental laxative which is not tolerated by the military monk." War was not mysterious, but the most commonsense of all sciences, yet the fools (taxpayers) who paid for it knew nothing about it. In much that he said—as for instance, "the desire of man is peace; the law of life is war" with fear and love the two extremes—there was a straight reflection of the teachings of Darwin, Pavlov, and other nineteenth century scientists. He saw the causes of war as the valour of ignorance,† as the barbaric army out of touch with national progress and the national spirit, as the economic forces including the need for raw materials, manufacturing manpower, and free markets in which to sell, and as revenge. These rash wars of conquest know no ethical limitations. In any war—and Fuller regarded peace as a state of war—the morale of the enemy should be attacked first, his

* He also contributed to the *JRUSI* "The Development of Sea Warfare on Land and Its Influence on Future Naval Operations," LXV, 1920, 281-287, and "Moral Instruction and Leadership," LXV, 1920, 656-674; and "Tanks in Future Warfare," *The Nineteenth Century and After*, XC (July 1921), 93-108, in which he put the case for the tank very succinctly and upon a war and not a battle basis. His wider views are found in "The Purpose and Nature of a Fleet," *The Nineteenth Century and After*, XC (October 1921), 699-714.

† The title of a book on this theme by the American, Homer Lea (1907).

resources second, and his defences only at the end. Fuller based this upon the tactical plans of the tanks evolved in 1917 and intended for use in 1919 on a large scale. The idea was to punch through a weak part of the enemy line and then to exploit the gap with fast tanks that would hit the enemy rear, psychologically his most unstable area and source of reserves and supplies. And in the modern day when entire nations go to war, he said, then the population is at war and attacks upon civilians are justified, an idea that the airpower enthusiasts carried to an extreme. As to weapons, he noted that "a weapon is a means of imposing by force a policy upon an adversary" with the least loss to either side. As the "security of peaceful prosperity is the object of war, not slaughter," the ideal weapon should possess the following characteristics: production should not detrimentally affect prosperity, it should be simple to manufacture in peace and in war, its nature should be unknown to the enemy, it must economize time on the battlefield, it must incapacitate without killing, it should permit an antidote being known to the side using it, and it should effect no permanent damage to property. As all the weapons of traditional warfare were based upon the concept of destruction, the world must switch to gases. These could be made non-lethal, did not destroy property, were cheap, secret, and helped the chemical industry in peacetime, too. But this humanitarianization of warfare, he estimated, would only be possible if there were no major war until 1972, by which time the traditionalists could be converted or retired. The carrier for gas that would make its effects universal was, of course, the aeroplane.

But here Fuller was led astray when he began to predict too much into the future types rather than tactics. In 1923 he saw the airship having a great role as an aircraft carrier; it was in fact a flop. He thought that if he was correct and that aircraft alone could dominate the world, then a great squandering of money on armies and navies could be stopped by the abolition of surface forces, though he foresaw, correctly, a considerable future for the submarine. Trenchard was at the time arguing for a greater role for the R.A.F. Fuller was, however, quite right in saying that the vital question of the day was: could a hostile nation be forced to change its will by an independent air attack? He answered this in support of the massive first blow such as that envisaged by the Air Ministry. But he did not think that such a blow might, at least for some time, end the war if civilian morale held, for he talked of the tank as the gas-proof, bomb-proof fighting vehicle on land. In *The Reformation of War* he was speaking from a transitional period, and some of his ideas applied to the actual situation that he faced in trying to get the Tank Corps safely established within the British Army and others to what he visualized as the foreseeable development of war in the modern world.

Fuller devoted considerable space in both his 1919 Essay and in *The Reformation of War* to the actual composition of armoured divisions. At first his new divisions were to be heavily infantry and horsed, but in 1923 he was less specific, though discarding infantry in view of the rapid increase in the speed of the tank from 4 to 25 m.p.h. At the same time he suggested that the use of mobile artillery would see the development on land of the long-familiar duel at sea between guns and armour.

In *On Future Warfare* (1926) he set forth his conception of the ideal army of what he called "the Artillery Cycle" of warfare. This would have a heavy division comprised of 320 tanks, each with three crews that could act as infantry when needed, and a light division, not equipped with infantry or artillery, to play the cavalry role. The final division would be a "pursuit" group lacking artillery and infantry, whose job would be to clean up after a battle.

His ideas contrasted with those of Liddell Hart's "New Model" division of 1922, which was to be completely mechanized and composed of units that could be made into individual combat teams. Each theorist was working, of course, from his own vantage point and experience: Fuller creating what he regarded in 1919 as possible of acceptance, while Liddell Hart strove more for the maximum efficiency based upon his own thoughts evolved on a larger scale than that of an infantry platoon. The Fuller school men were able to place the majority of their ideas in the official manual, *Mechanized and Armoured Formations* (the 1929 "Purple Primer"), while Liddell Hart's ideas were accepted by the Germans and used most successfully in 1940 when the combination of tanks and motorized infantry proved so deadly.

In "The Progress of War," a 1926 article,* Fuller reiterated his plea for the use of gas while at the same time pointing to fundamental truths about the military situation regarding Germany and France. As Germany mechanized, he foresaw armies becoming

* *The Nineteenth Century and After,* C (October 1926), 481-496.

increasingly linked to their air components both for action and for supply. (But it was not until *The Second World War* (1948) that he called air transport revolutionary.) He felt that as long as Europe remained unfederated, war was inevitable, and that in these circumstances Britain had either to maintain a strong friendship with the United States or to resuscitate Germany militarily. To guarantee the frontiers of a strong France made no sense at all. (But it was, we know now, just that action on the part of Britain that allowed France to dominate the Continent in the first dozen important years after the 1918 Armistice.) He then launched an appeal for a return to the professional armies of old in modernized, scientifically armed, mobile form commanded by able men who could act independently. He followed this up in May 1927 with another article that was a plea that principles be connected with policy that in its turn must be based on conditions.* In "Science and War" † he appealed for thinkers on, and students of, war. The whole essay was a brilliant little history of the influence of science upon tactics, making the point that until soldiers studied war and not just campaigns, they would be no better than butchers.

The 1928 Briand-Kellogg Pact struck him as absurd, and he said so. The constant was the search for peace: "War is not an enigma, but a fact, yet it is treated as an enchantment which can be destroyed by a spell, a formula written in ink and repeated by a circle of politicians." War, he said, in 1934, is neither good nor evil in itself, for its nature is determined by its goal, nor can it be ignored or exorcised. The only way to be rid of it is through reason.‡ War will disappear only when it has lost its utility, but industrial wars of destruction are absurd for the object of modern war is economic not political control. He ended with the prediction that war would become ridiculous only about the year 2050, when all danger would be removed by having it fought by robots.§ He followed up these ideas with *The Natural History of War* in 1930.

In 1931 he produced a work upon Indian problems that exposed

* "The Changing Conditions of War," *The Nineteenth Century and After,* CI (May 1927), 685-693. *On Future Warfare* (1928) was a collection of his articles from the years 1919-27.

† *The Nineteenth Century and After,* CIII (January 1928), 88-96.

‡ "War and Western Civilization," *The Nineteenth Century and After,* CXV (April 1934), 394-403.

§ "The Elimination of War," *The Nineteenth Century and After,* CIV (November 1928), 650-658. See also pp. 766-776, a reply by A. G. Baird Smith.

the chaotic nature of Indian politics, but in which he also accused the British of doing no more than to ferment trouble that the Army was called upon to put down. In it he tended to be Fascist in outlook, which, when coupled with his interest in oriental religions, gave the impression that he was unstable and detracted from the real genius of his military works.

In 1932 came his *Lectures on F.S.R. III (Operations between Mechanized Forces)*, which was carefully read by his fan, General Heinz Guderian of the German Army. The Russians at once issued 30,000 copies to their forces, later increasing distribution to 100,000, and the Czechs and Spanish followed in principle, while, moaned Fuller, sales in England to 1935 totalled less than 500 copies.* Yet in this work, now known as *Armoured Warfare,* he provided a carefully annotated handbook upon the conduct of mechanized warfare that should have been acquired and read by all British officers, whether or not they belonged to the Tank Corps, to the cavalry, infantry, or artillery, not to mention the other branches. Doubtless part of the poor sales was the result of a feeling by the general public that this was simply a military handbook and one that not even armchair generals would read. But the latest annoted edition is readable by all. In *Armoured Warfare* Fuller was most anxious to make the point that defence was just as vital as offence and that it was a gross mistake, particularly liable to arise in peacetime, to believe that there was something cowardly and undignified in defence. War, he correctly noted, was not simply defence or offense, but rather for it to be waged successfully, there had to be a judicious use of the two. The *offensive à outrance* of the French left him cold and horrified as did the idea that new weapons change the old fundamental principles of war.

The year 1932 also saw the publication of a number of manuscripts to which he must have put the finishing touches after he ceased active service, including *War and Western Civilization, 1832-1932: A Study of War as a Political Instrument and the Expression of Mass Democracy.* In this he challenged the concept of democracy that he felt was mere demagogy, for not the will but the emotions of the people provided the driving force, "the drug," that gave them a war hallucination. He claimed that since 1832, when the great Reform Bill was passed in England, the world had marched steadily

---

* *Memoirs,* 455; letter to Robin Higham, 17 April 1962.

forward materially, but had made no attempt to look at man's soul, to understand human beings, and through that knowledge to avoid war. Although an agnostic, his talk of the abyss into which mankind with its magic and lack of godliness was falling sounded like the words of a Christian minister. He saw not only the failure of the military, the General-Staff mind, to grasp the fact that inventions had changed the time span in which world events took place, but also that civilian populations had become craven mobs. Moreover—and remember that he did ultimately lend his name to the Fascist cause— Fuller felt that public opinion on any important issue was bound to be wrong because it generalized the views of the most ignorant. Unfortunately it was the expression of sentiments such as these that tended to obscure in many minds the brilliance of his purely military views. It is not wise to mix political and military ideas. What he had to say about the German use of gas was sound and so were most of his other observations upon the conduct of war, which included the demand for a scientifically trained, modern army for the League of Nations based in Britain.

Late in 1932 there also appeared *Generalship; Its Diseases and Their Cure: A Study of the Personal Factor in Command*. The thesis was that modern war had become as impersonal as modern business, and this made for the futility of a conflict such as that of 1914-18 because the generals were unknown to their troops and knew not the ground over which they fought. Fuller pointed out that the average age of the world's one hundred top generals was 40.36 years, whereas the British generals of 1932 averaged 59.9 years,* and that Army officers were groping about for a solution that would permit the re-establishment of the old relationships in a force constantly suffering from social and industrial pressures. Command, like management, had become dehumanized, said Fuller, whereas the rule should be *"The more mechanical the weapons, the less mechanical must be the controlling spirit."* The solution, then, was to deputize more and to let the general possess the physical courage to be seen far forward. In the Second World War, be it noted, generals not only did this but also made sure it was known they did by good public relations. Wavell, the New Zealander Bernard Freyberg, George Patton, Rommel, and Montgomery (who went so far as to use a double) †

* This was a point that Liddell Hart expanded upon later. See *The Defence of Britain,* Chapter XIX, "The System of Promotion."

† [M. E.] Clifton James, *I Was Monty's Double* (London, 1954).

became legends even to the opposing troops. Compare these with the chateau-bound commanders of the First World War.* The trouble, said Fuller, was that in peacetime the petty mind that is expert on small details makes a reputation and smothers initiative in others, but when the time comes it cannot cope with war at all. The rifle increasingly, and then the new artillery, drove the general back off the battlefield, while his increasing age when on active command made such a position more tolerable. The telephone chained the whole Army together and kept subordinate commanders on a wire when they should have been out leading their men. In order to control this electrified force, the staff at headquarters had become, said Fuller in 1932, a collection of spruce flunkeys and not of colonels prepared to sally onto the field to see that plans were carried out. (Radio did much to break the field-telephone wire in the Second World War.) The modern staff had tended to become the brains and the general a rubber stamp.† The solution Fuller proposed was to hand-pick a list of officers aged thirty-five to forty-five and to give them active command on the outbreak of war for they would have had battalion commands and anything higher was, in peacetime, administrative and not leadership training. The job of the G.S.O.1 (Chief of Staff) should be executive so that the general could get out of headquarters as much as possible. This general theme was pursued in his *Grant and Lee* of 1933 (reprinted in 1959), in which he also argued that the 1864-65 campaign in Virginia was the first of the modern ones in which a new tactical approach was used to counter the rifle bullet, which had come to dominate the battlefield. Nevertheless, he maintained, "Seven-eighths of the history of war is psychological." In the course of writing *Grant and Lee* he reread the great nineteenth century classic, G. F. R. Henderson's *Stonewall Jackson,* and came to the conclusion that it was highly romanticized and that Jackson was Henderson's "ideal soldier."

Like many military thinkers and politicians of the day, he was

* Leon Wolff, *In Flanders Fields* (New York, 1958), p. 228, tells of Haig's Chief of Staff crying when he saw the battlefield for the first time at Paschendaele and saying, "Good God, did we really send men to fight in that [mud]?"

† Fuller did not comment on the Navy, but others bear him out that "staff-ococus" was its curse, too. Yet the very fact that admirals had to sail with the Fleet and share all its dangers gave them a more heroic stature than that achieved by the generals. Beatty and Keyes kept their popular reputations in peacetime, even if Jellicoe's became somewhat tarnished.

involved in the revival in the mid-thirties of the debate over a Ministry of Defence following the creation of the Commonwealth in 1931. In *Empire Unity and Defence* (1934) he strongly supported the idea, but unlike most other debaters, he wanted the new organization limited strictly to planning and direction, leaving administration to the three already established Service departments. His own idea was a return to the directional unity that had given William Pitt the Elder his successes in the Seven Years' War. Fuller's Ministry would, then, be composed of three branches. The Political Department was to concern itself solely with the making of home, Imperial, and foreign policy. The General Staff, headed by the Chiefs of Staff Committee, was to think out and make plans for the operations in peace and war that the Political Department called for in their policy memoranda. The General Staff would control grand strategy, supply and manpower, while the third branch, the Finance Department, would calculate what each action would cost. In order to provide for Imperial unity, not only was each of the Dominions to have a similar organization to control operations of the forces in its area, but also the Committee of Imperial Defence and the Imperial Conference system were to be replaced with a permanent Imperial Council composed of the Deputy Prime Ministers of the whole Empire. Fuller argued that such a Council would provide a sure means of averting war by the very unity of its collective action. It was an idea that Joseph Chamberlain had raised in 1897 and that the 1922 Chanak crisis over the Turkish Straits had shown was badly needed. Nor was this approach new to Fuller; he had expressed it in his 1919 prize essay and in *Imperial Defence* in 1926. But at the same time, while recommending unification, he also urged a strategic realignment. Either Britain had to adhere to the League of Nations or to the Empire. Personally Fuller was for an alliance with Italy to isolate the Franco-Prussian problem. Earlier he had been for the Japanese alliance, but by 1935 he called for friendship with the United States to control Japan in the Pacific, as the Atlantic was more important to Britain than the Far East. Russia, for the next ten years, was, he thought, out of the picture, but could after that be defeated. As for Imperial defence, the need was first to protect London from air attack and then to provide a string of bases for mobile air support of any outer area that might be attacked, for Commonwealth States could not afford their own air forces. For the co-ordination and direction of such a strategy a Ministry of Defence was needed.*

The attack on the Higher Direction, both military and political, was continued and his general ideas further elucidated in *The Army in My Time* (1935) and in his *Memoirs of an Unconventional Soldier* (1936). In the former he pointed out for future guidance that the lessons of the Great War of 1914-18 were that grand strategy depends on policy and that it in turn must be based upon a political knowledge of the war. Policy is carried out through the strategic plans of the Commander-in-Chief (C-in-C), who must be replaced if he fails culpably. In the latter work he mischievously described his own life in the Army from his days as a subaltern (given in detail in *The Last of the Gentlemen's Wars*) to his retirement in the early thirties after fighting the Battle of the Tank in France and Whitehall. Once again a major theme was the stupidity of officialdom, especially in high Army and War Office circles. It was as much the literate man's revenge as the work of Robert Graves in *Goodbye to All That* or of Siegfried Sassoon in *The Memoirs of a Fox-Hunting Man* and his other tales. But where they were humanitarians, intelligent persons rebelling against war itself, Fuller showed that war, while always likely, did not have to be inhuman if the Higher Direction took advantage of inventions and productive capacity as well as relearning the basic rules of the game.

In addition to the works already mentioned, he wrote a number of books upon contemporary issues such as *India in Revolt* (1931), in which he attacked democracy and the handling of the nationalist movement by use of the Army, *The Dragon's Teeth* (1932), *The First of the League Wars* (Ethiopia) (1936), in which he predicted that mechanized forces would overrun Poland and France in a fortnight, and *Towards Armageddon* (1937) covering British defence problems in the days of rearmament. Two of these must be commented upon.

Written on the eve of the Geneva Disarmament Conference of 1932-34, *The Dragon's Teeth* was a study of war and peace in which he emphasized the close interrelation of the problems of war and peace and their common causes. He exposed the Versailles settlement, examined the economic consequences, and predicted that Russia

---

* "Imperial Defence," *The Nineteenth Century and After,* CXVII (February 1935), 129-140.

would become the new supra-European power. His conclusion was that of an eighteenth century *philosophe:* that the influence of civilization could end war when a spirit of peace and a system of universal laws existed, an end that could only be brought about by the education of Man. His own spirit comes through well in the Preface:

[Politicians] are moral cowards; they distrust the people because they are afraid of them; consequently they are afraid of telling them the truth.

Since the close of the War people have been living in an atmosphere of political lies. There is no policy, because without courage there can be no principles. Each party when out of power has simply anathematized the party in power, not to improve government, but to oust government. . . .

We have had enough of these people with their quack medicines and infallible cure-alls, and I think it is about time we ceased to delude ourselves into believing that any world settlement can be arrived at until the public takes an intelligent interest in world problems; and such interest demands knowledge. . . .

. . . I have attempted to show [in this book] where the present causes of war lie, that war and peace are closely related—for it is peace which creates war—and how eventually war may be eliminated; but only by recreating peace—that is, by drastically changing our social order. I have not attempted to be pleasant or unpleasant, but instead to be truthful. My quarrel with France is not with her people, but with her politicians, whose fearfulness, vindictiveness and selfishness are precipitating another war. My admiration for Russia is not engendered by her Oriental despotism, but by the energy she is showing, which puts most other nations to the blush. If I decry professional soldiers, it is not for personal dislike of an honest and modest body of men, but because their work is fatuous; they are not preparing for the next war but for the last war but one, and are consequently a danger rather than a security.* If my dislikes are pronounced, it nevertheless will be found that one and all are based on principle: I cannot tolerate cowardice, untruthfulness and sentimentality. I do not believe that life is the most precious thing in this world, and when it is considered so, I do believe that a civilization is definitely in its decline. I believe that personal convictions, faith, courage and heroism are far nobler than mere living, and that without

---

* What can one think when one reads of such tactical training as the following: "A spectacular cavalry charge was one of the incidents of the Army manoeuvres on Salisbury Plain yesterday. The charge took place in the bright sunshine of a perfect autumn morning and in the face of 'devastating' machine-gun fire. It was witnessed by military attachés of fourteen countries. . . ." (*The Sunday Times,* 20 September 1931) It may be remembered that such tactics failed against bows and arrows at the Battle of Crecy in 1346.

them life is no more than a rudderless ship. Every animal seeks to live, yet even a wolf-bitch will sacrifice her life for her young. When a nation or a civilization falls below the level of self-sacrifice for an ideal or a principle, then it is finished, and it will inevitably be replaced by a more heroic one.

War faces us today just as grimly as ever, and it is not going to be abolished by peace pacts and disarmament conferences. . . .

These truths have not diminished with time.

In *Towards Armageddon* Fuller first pointed out that the real question for Britain to face was what was *the* defence problem? He began his answer by declaring that the 1914 war had shown the need in twentieth century civilization for political authority, for national discipline, economic self-sufficiency, and for scientific weapons in both war and peace. The war had shown that the decisive factors were seapower, starvation, propaganda, and air attack. But what had occurred since the conflict was "an armament regression." Unfortunately, at this juncture his old polemical spirit appeared, and he went beyond the then limits of public credulity by calling communism an Asiatic upheaval that could be faced only by a consolidation of Europe such as Mussolini had given Italy. While there is no doubt that he did then and still does feel this strongly, by injecting unpalatable political reasons into his appeal for national discipline he laid himself open to hostile criticism. Yet he was correct when he called British rearmament in the mid-nineteen-thirties a "planless muddle" suffering from past financial stringency and lack of strategical direction. It was his hope in this book to carry to the forthcoming Imperial Conference the message that the Empire needed a central direction of strategy. The Minister for the Co-ordination of Defence he viewed as ridiculous, for how could a man charged with developing supply do so without a strategy to guide him? Convinced as he was that Hitler did not want war, he asked for what kind of war was Britain preparing? He saw the greatest danger as an air blow, for the aeroplane had become the master weapon, though he admits now that in this he vastly overrated the concept that civilian morale would collapse.*

Obsessed as were many others with the probability of the national will collapsing, he saw conscription primarily as a means of raising a disciplined force of internal police to stiffen the public during the aerial onslaught. Looking at the totalitarian states and their ability

* Letter to Robin Higham, 17 May 1962.

to concentrate power and considering that the advantage among equals lay primarily in surprise, he foresaw, as did the airpower enthusiasts and their Parliamentary supporters, that the first blow of a new war would be the last. Thus with the national will as the target, the nation's surest shield would be discipline. Though he wanted to impose a Fascistlike efficiency upon the British constitutional base, he appeared to many to be much farther to the Right. At the same time he urged that material, human psychological, and tactical requirements be carefully studied and plans made. Thus he called for greater agricultural self-sufficiency, protection of the ports so that imports could be unloaded, a problem that the Navy was overlooking in its concentration upon defence at sea, and an alliance with Russia as a counter to Germany after the latter had been allowed to recreate the Holy Roman Empire. In addition, he advocated not only a Minister of Supply but also the establishment of an armaments industry in India, and equal pay and conditions of service for workers at home and men in the Services. He concluded with a study of air-, sea-, and landpower in which he plumped for the Navy putting the Army ashore to hold bases from which the Air Force could operate and thus establish an aerial *pax Britannica* in Europe. (This was, in fact, a Government plan.) He predicted that the next war would start with a "little blue lie" put out in ignorance by some money-oriented Englishman who failed to understand that new life-making rather than money-making forces were abroad. Britain's problem, then, in the last analysis lay in how to avoid death by internal decay. Much of what he said was correct, but unpopular.

Fuller joined Sir Oswald Moseley's Fascist movement not from naivete but for two sound reasons. First because he believed a vocational electorate along the lines of the corporate state system then in vogue in Italy was more suited to modern industrial democracy than the geographical franchise arrangements then pertaining. He based this reason upon the fact that the only thing the voter really knew anything about was his job. Second because Moseley was for a fully modernized and mechanized army. Fuller believes that the great mistake of the Moseley movement was to imitate the Black Shirts in Italy since this enabled enemies of that group of super-loyal patriots to be attacked effectively by their opponents. That Britain may well have needed discipline is attested to in the revelations of the official histories of the Second World War. There the Government's concern with the collapse of national morale under bombing is made strikingly evident in plans to mobilize the Army as an internal police force.

Like other military writers he capitalized upon the Second World War market for military books with *Decisive Battles* (1939-40), later expanded and re-issued as *The Military History of the Western World* (1954-56); and *Machine Warfare*, a new version of *Lectures on F.S.R. III; Armament and History: A Study of the Influence of Armament on History from the Dawn of Classical Warfare to the Second World War*. In this last title, a short, provocative, and readable book he hammered away again at his favourite themes of weapon power and the relation of war to society. He wrapped the whole up with his *The Second World War: A Strategical and Tactical History*. More recently his studies, notably of Grant and of Lee, have been augmented with *The Generalship of Alexander the Great*, with *The Conduct of War, 1789-1961*, and with *Julius Caesar*.

Fuller was the most original British military writer. He had the fortune to be born with an enquiring mind and the good luck to be thrown into close contact with the machine-gun and the tank, the most revolutionary devices to be thrust upon the Army in a century. But he still might not have prospered as a theorist if he had not been gifted with a barbed pen. It was, of course, too sharp to make him a popular prophet like Liddell Hart, but this was, perhaps, to his advantage for he later enjoyed the leisure in which to create his more famous books. But above all else, he had the higher military experience that allowed him to write with authority and humour of people and events still remembered.*

Fuller has, as anyone in his position generally has, some weaknesses. He was so eager to convince the Army of the need to study economic and political forces, that being an agnostic himself, he overlooked the hold that religious or political beliefs could have on the ordinary man whom the Government of any modern country has to convince. He also went somewhat astray in some of his predictions of the directions and limitations of mechanical progress. He was criticized by Sir Frederick Maurice and Victor Germains for postulating a

* For more recent comments upon Fuller, see the reviews by Michael Howard in *The New Statesman and Nation*, 16 April 1955, p. 550, and 28 July 1956, pp. 109-110.

Science of War,* but for this he should be forgiven, for not only did he believe war was an art but he also had to pound home the idea that it was much more than waving one's baton on the field of battle, that modern war was a vast logistical enterprise. His reputation has suffered from the many personal enemies whom he made, but like Liddell Hart's it has increased in stature as the years have passed, especially since the Second World War in Europe was such a tank war and since so much that he wanted in *Towards Armageddon* came to pass.

Fuller had a much wider geographical experience than Liddell Hart. He served in India and visited Ethiopia during the Italian campaign there in 1935. Yet his *The Second World War, 1939-1945: A Strategical and Tactical History* shows that despite his talk of the traditional British strategy, he has the typical soldier's lack of interest in the war at sea, especially the Battle of the Atlantic. On the other hand, his view of the strategic air offensive against Germany, while extreme, has proven to be well founded, though he was overly anti-Churchill, perhaps not fully appreciating that statesman's problems in 1942.

Fuller's contribution is two-fold. He stimulated thinking, especially in tactics, while pointing out that the tank, like many new weapons, had been abused in the First World War. Second, he accented the fact that war is a scientific art that has to be studied, especially since it has become mechanized. He helped push the British Army into the modern world by trying to make it reflect that actual society from which it drew its manpower, rather than the limited dying élite from which it obtained its officers. In other words, he made it aware of the Industrial Revolution. His general theme may be summed up in a few words from his *The Second World War* (p. 153):

> In the end, as we shall see, it was superiority of weapon power, and, therefore, of industrial power, which was to become the final arbiter. Nevertheless, weapons themselves are but a frail reed to lean upon unless they are used with intelligence. That is, in accordance with the principles of war applied according to strategic conditions and tactical circumstances.

* Victor Germains, *The "Mechanization" of War* (London, 1927, Foreword by Maurice).

## B. H. Liddell Hart

Having played at military games as a youth, Liddell Hart already had some ideas of tactics when the First World War broke out. As an infantry officer he saw the appalling conditions under which men had to act in the face of bad generalship, if any leadership there was. By the end of 1916 and the Somme battles of that year, his concept of the combat unit had begun to emerge and it was published in the 1917 British Army pamphlet *S.S. 143*. In that piece the platoon emerged as the basic unit that contained all the infantry weapons but was still capable of subdivision to increase mobility and tactical strength. Conditions in France were thought not to allow troops to be withdrawn from the lines for training. But after the Germans successfully infiltrated in March 1918 in their near-successful offensive, the British were forced to change their views and the new counteroffensive and more open warfare gave the combat unit status. The chief difficulty was the indoctrination of junior officers and N.C.O.'s with principles that were neither too rigid nor too hedged about with exceptions to make the system work. Thus he called for "the pillar of fire by night," a beacon of doctrine.* In describing and attempting to lay down the doctrine for combat units, Liddell Hart began to feel his way towards the strategic indirect approach. He urged that the attacking group should make the best use of the ground to achieve surprise while a support group covered them. Once they were forced into a fire-fight, then the resupplied covering group should leapfrog through. At the same time he avoided the unifocal view of most military writers by analysing also the defensive problem. While he adopted the expanding torrent tactics for the offensive used by the Germans in 1918, he called for combat units to make up the defence with a willingness *à la* Haig to die on the spot. The defence, he said, should be composed of mutually supporting strong points that contain the offense in enfiladed funnels. Later in *The British Way in Warfare* he applied these same principles to war as opposed to battles. In his early infantry work he had used the analogy of two men groping for each other in the dark as the basis of infantry tac-

---

* As he complained in *The Current of War* (p. 50), it was not until his protest in 1922 over the reworking of his infantry text that the War Office awoke to the fact that these manuals were written for junior officers and N.C.O.'s and not for generals so that, therefore, it was essential that they be readable at *all* levels. Wavell made the same complaint in the 1930's.

tics; in later works he enunciated the same principles for national wars. Each side needed to be able to guard as well as to attack, to concentrate quickly, and to have alternative objectives. As early as the end of the war he was thinking in psychological (the word was then new) terms and noting that it was the morale side of war that needed the greater study.

It must be remembered that at this date Fuller was only just succeeding in getting the actual principles of war * spelled out in the British *Field Service Regulations* and that his plan, adopted in 1918 by the General Staff for the unfought 1919 campaign had aimed at breaking the German will to fight by armoured smashes through the lines followed by swift attacks upon the German headquarters and supply areas. It was from this base that both the British military and air strategists in the interwar years worked. In *Paris* Liddell Hart saw bombing of industrial capacity as one way to get past the shielding Army to the heart of a nation.

Where Fuller used the principles of infantry tactics for the principles of war, Liddell Hart used them in human terms. He called the elements Mind, Movement, Weapons, and Protection; the elementary principles Objective Mobility, Hitting, and Security; and the accentuating principles Surprise, Co-operation, Concentration, and Economy of Force.† Liddell Hart early recognized that one of the major

---

* The principles of war vary with individual writers. Cyril Falls in *The Art of War* (London, 1961) (p. 10) gives them as ideals: concentration or economy of force, surprise, aggressive reconnaissance or readiness to fight for information, and maintenance of the aim. Falls was one of the official military historians of the First World War and later Chichele Professor of War at Oxford. In 1941 he produced *The Nature of Modern War*, which he amplified as a result of criticism into *Ordeal by Battle* (1943). Liddell Hart gave the principles as:
  (1) Adjusting your ends to your means,
  (2) Keeping your object always in mind,
  (3) Choosing a line (or course) of least expectation,
  (4) Exploiting the line of least resistance,
  (5) Taking a line of operation that offers alternative objectives,
  (6) Ensuring that both plan and disposition are flexible and adaptable to circumstances,
and two negative ones:
  (7) Not throwing your weight into a stroke when your opponent is on guard, and
  (8) Never renewing an attack along the same line (or in the same form) after it has once failed.
(*Strategy* (1954), pp. 348-349).
  † Quoted in Liddell Hart's *The Current of War*, p. 7; see also *The British Way in Warfare*, pp. 106, 301-304.

problems of war was training and of that necessity, the indoctrination of the lowest fighting leaders with basic rules that would not be knocked out of their heads by the noise and confusion of combat. "Simplicity," he said, "is the key to victory."

By 1922 his vision was increasing. He pointed out that the horse would have to go out of the Army because it was disappearing in civilian life, though in 1925 Haig still called it indispensable. On the other hand, he failed to appreciate that low-level tactical aircraft might, as their speed increased, achieve surprise.

Liddell Hart was converted to the Fullerite armoured warfare school some time between 1921 and 1923.* He accepted the inevitability of mechanization when, after he had written the postwar infantry manual, he was asked to draft the footslogger's case against mechanization. The resulting document satisfied his superiors, but disturbed him. From then on he felt himself forced to make the case for mechanization. He found that in 1918 the War Office had discovered that this gift from the Industrial Revolution reduced the food needed by a division by two thirds, that only a fifth as much "fuel" was needed to move a ton of supplies 100 miles by lorry as by horse, that a ton of petrol needed only 48 cubic feet of shipping space while a ton of compressed hay consumed 270 feet, oats 70 feet, and straw 416 feet, that more forage than ammunition was supplied during the First World War and that four times as much food for horses was sent to Egypt during the conflict as was sent for men. Moreover, he became convinced that masses of artillery not only made it difficult for anyone to move across the battlefield and thus exploit a breakthrough, but also that massed artillery was highly vulnerable to the new air weapon. By 1923 the new Vickers tanks capable of 20 m.p.h. were outrunning the infantry.

Though he says his conversion dated from 1921 to 1923, he had weakened earlier than that when in 1919 he wrote "Suggestions on the Future Development of the Combat Unit: The Tank as a Weapon of Infantry." † While he then said that the infantry would remain the decisive arm only as long as it was modernized and its mobility restored by the adoption of the tank, he saw armoured forces only as infantry weapons for breaking trenches and not in the

* Writing in 1929, he said 1923 (*The Current of War*, 97), but in 1934 he gave the date as 1921 (*When Britain Goes to War*, p. 297). He now says 1919. (Letter to Robin Higham.)

† *JRUSI*, LXIV (November 1919), 666-669.

Fullerite sense of the dominant and decisive striking force. And in the early years after the war the general use of tanks was limited on maneuvers to useless attacks upon prepared infantry positions because the umpires and the conditions governing operations in England, even with the use of the Maneuvering Act, forbade reality by excluding supply bases from the field.

In 1922 he produced a paper on a "New Model Army" that was rejected by the *Journal of the Royal United Services Institution* as too radical, the new C.I.G.S., the Earl of Cavan, being anxious to quash controversy and nonconformity. This article eventually appeared, however, in *The Army Quarterly* in October 1924. The future German *panzer* general, Guderian, read it and immediately had it translated and issued to the German Army.* This was the beginning of Liddell Hart's conception of blitzkrieg. The "expanding torrent" method of attack, which he had perfected as an infantry tactic, was coupled to the long-range independence of the Mongol forces of Ghengis Khan through the adaptation of mechanization. The fundamentals of the idea were the exploitation of the breakthrough by a rapid and sustained deep strategic penetration undertaken by mobile forces operating independently towards variable objectives so that both tactical and strategic surprise were maintained. As he read more in the next few years, the basic idea was strengthened by examples culled from Sherman's operations to the sea and by analysis of the raids by Nathan Bedford Forrest in the American Civil War. In the 1922 article he did not attempt a long-range forecast, but, while accepting that land tactics might well emulate those of the sea, he did conclude that mammoth tanks, such as the French later developed to no useful purpose, would not be likely to find practical use. He differed from Fuller in calling for both the use of mechanized infantry (his "tank-marines") in an offensive role and for heavily gunned tanks, though while in 1919 Fuller had accepted infantry in the attack, he had dropped them by 1923 for all but guard duties. Fuller's ideas tended to dominate at the War Office and the importance of tank-borne infantry and of gun-armed tanks

---

* Heinz Guderian, *Panzer Leader* (New York, n.d. [c. 1956]), p. 10. Guderian himself says that as early as 1922 he began to read Liddell Hart, Fuller, and Martel because the Germans lacked knowledge of tank and other operations conducted by the Allies. To Liddell Hart he gives the credit for developing the idea of long-range armoured strokes with a combined division as well as for many other useful suggestions.

came to be recognized only in the Second World War.* Liddell Hart's conversion resulted in what he considers to have been his most influential work, *Paris: or the Future of War,* published in 1925.

*Paris* is not the 1919 Peace Conference, but rather the classical archer who slew Achilles by shooting him in the heel. The book had great impact because a copy was given by Trenchard to the incoming C.I.G.S., Sir George Milne, and after he had read it, he called in Liddell Hart and discussed the ideas presented. The result was that the Fullerites were given a break and an experimental armoured force created for maneuvers. Liddell Hart also used the occasion to call for an operational research organization,† but this continued for many years unrealized except in the writings of the pundits. Liddell Hart and Milne came, however, to a parting of the ways when Milne failed to live up to his promise in the face of the well-entrenched War Office and Army as well as the orthodox financial inertia of peacetime.‡

In *Paris* Liddell Hart branched away from the infantry view to a national one. He noted that civilization could not stand many more callous and careless wars like the 1914 one, while any nation that neglected its defences or attempted neutrality was, as history showed, bound to fall. He attacked the "military Bourbons" then in power, who, despite the lessons of the war, persisted in the idea that the true objective of armed forces was the enemy army. He blamed this upon the myopic vision of hero-worshippers of Napoleon, who studied only his campaigns and not all wars. This had led to the senseless multiplication of numbers rather than to the adoption of the increased firepower made possible by new industrial techniques. For the distortion of Napoleon he blamed Clausewitz, a theme that he developed at length in *The Ghost of Napoleon* (1934).§

---

* As the defender of the infantry, Liddell Hart has written a number of mimeographed notes on these problems for those who ask him for details.

† Liddell Hart claims to have been the originator of the concept of operational research. This must be taken with a grain of historical salt. Certainly in Britain in the First World War there existed a small statistical section at the Admiralty that supplied Prime Minister Lloyd George with the necessary facts to enable him to insist upon the introduction of convoy. Today, of course, the subject is a considerable one. In 1963 the Air Ministry published A.P. 3368, *Operational Research in the Royal Air Force,* and there are now several American studies on the subject.

‡ Liddell Hart, "Seven Years: The Regime of Field-Marshal Lord Milne," *English Review,* LVI (April 1933), 576-586.

§ See also Henry Ridgely Evans, *The Napoleon Myth* (Chicago, 1905).

The "Napoleonic fallacy" stemmed from the fact that Clausewitz never finished *On War* and that in many places his meaning is unclear. Those who studied Napoleon through Clausewitz tended to develop the cult of the unlimited war, whose only objective is the complete subjugation of the opponent. But Clausewitz had also pointed out that there were limited wars designed merely to gain some advantage along the frontier. More than this, military interpreters of his works confused victory with success; that is, they enlarged upon the idea of a tactical victory in battle and made it the same thing as the utter destruction of the enemy will. Life is rarely so simple, as Bismarck clearly demonstrated in 1866 after Königgrätz, when he refused to allow von Moltke to destroy Austria. Despite this obvious example, militarists developed the theme in the remainder of the nineteenth century that the offensive *à la* Bonaparte, ending in a rapid, smashing victory, was the only way in which to conduct a war, forgetting both that the world has seen few men of Napoleon's military stature and that it was the Corsican's offensiveness that finally caused his own downfall, as Clausewitz noted.

Already Liddell Hart was giving signs of increasingly broad reading that led to a series of books on the great captains of history and what made them successful. In particular he took a liking to Marshal Saxe (1696-1750), who knew that "a prosperous and secure peace is a better monument than a pyramid of skulls." * All of this preaching was, of course, a reaction to the senseless, un-British policy of engaging in a Continental war of attrition. The correct policy was to strike at the Achilles heel of an enemy; that was the proper aim of grand strategy, but unfortunately in peacetime, he noted, the British do not care and the dissenters are thrown out of the Service. The Achilles heel of the modern nation was its industrial complex, and so Liddell Hart supported strategic bombing as the golden arrow of Paris. Both Liddell Hart and Fuller acclaimed the use of gas as humanitarian and cheaper, a means to defeat the will of the enemy while leaving him to recover and once more be a customer.† Both pointed to the traditional orthodox militarist and the sentimental

* For the latest life of Saxe, see Jon Manchip White, *Marshal of France: The Life and Times of Maurice de Saxe* (New York, 1965).

† Gas was used by American forces in Vietnam in late March 1965. Essentially these were of the anti-riot type, but nevertheless, partly because of rather clumsy handling of the public relations side of the affair, there was a public outcry; see, for instance, the lead editorial in *The New Statesman*, 26 March 1965, "Vietnam: the Horrors Multiply." See also Clifford F. Rossweiler, "What's so

pacifist as being opposed to gas, and both quoted irrefutable statistics* to show how much more humane gas was. Yet in 1925 an interternational anti-chemical and anti-bacteriological convention was signed.† But gas was not used in later aerial assaults because it was discovered that not only was it difficult to transport but also that its effect in populated areas was vastly reduced by the ease with which even residences could be gas-proofed.

In *Paris* Liddell Hart devoted a few remarks to the Navy. He said that the destruction of the enemy fleet was only the means to an end that was either close blockade or invasion. He felt that the postwar battle of types overlooked this dominant fact and was thus based upon false assumptions. He fully realized the menace of the submarine, though he was overpessimistic as to its dominance if the enemy held the coasts of France and Ireland. Seaborne commerce was the British Achilles heel, so Britain had better watch what she was about, he said, or be prepared to face the consequences. She did not and had to fight the grim Battle of the Atlantic, 1939-45.

His concept of strategy being based on the analogy of hand-to-hand combat, he called for the ability to parry a blow and then to deliver a one-two punch. In such a strategic conception, the Army would have to provide one blow (until the day when airpower dominated everything). The way to achieve mobility, the only way to make the soldier useful, was to adopt the caterpillar or multi-wheeled cross-country vehicle, which would free the soldier from his dependence upon roads and railways,‡ made vulnerable by omniranging air-

Terrible about Germ Warfare?" *The Saturday Evening Post,* 30 January 1965, p. 12; and Hanson W. Baldwin, "After Fifty Years the Cry of Ypres Still Echoes— 'Gas!' " *The New York Times Magazine,* 18 April 1965, p. 28; Major Joseph Burns Kelly, "Gas Warfare in International Law," master's thesis, Georgetown University, 1960; and Subcommittee on Disarmament, Committee on Foreign Relations, U.S. Senate, "Chemical-Biological-Radiological (CBR) Warfare and its Disarmament Aspects," 29 August 1960 (Committee print).

* *The Reformation of War,* p. 82. Only one out of every thirty British gas casualties died, versus one out of every three hit by shells, bullets, or bayonets, 1914-18.

† *Cmd. 3604* (1930) and *Cmd. 3747* (1930).

‡ Another development after 1931 was the lightening of the Army and the abandonment of much of the material that was issued to cover every continguency. The result of the reintroduction of mobility may be roughly envisaged by contrasting the 900 yards of advances in the First World War with the nearly 900 miles in the North African campaigns in 1941-43, before logistics called a temporary halt.

craft. The true solution was the armoured vehicle, which in fighting terms meant the tank. Thus "New Model Armies," like Cromwell's Ironsides, would have to be developed to keep pace with both strategy and civil progress. He predicted that naval tactics would be adopted for both tank and air battles as cycles of defence and offence, armour, or gun, achieved temporary supremacy. In this respect he accused the generals of hypocrisy in their talk of mobility in the face of machine guns when their armies had no tanks.* The British Army of 1926 had 136 infantry battalions, but only 4 tank battalions (usually able to field about 8 tanks apiece), 2,176 infantry platoons to 136 machine gun platoons. Already by 1926 he was advocating motorized infantry of the sort that the Germans were to use so devastatingly in France in 1940 in such poetic justice against British pacifism.

In *Great Captains Unveiled* (1927), inspired by T. E. Lawrence of Arabia, he swept across history from Ghengis Khan to Wolfe of Quebec. Surprisingly, only four of the fifteen captains were professionals, and of these only Robert E. Lee was actually a product of the military academy. All the others were amateurs who had the priceless gift of independence and freedom, said the author, whose book was one of twelve assigned to officers of the newly formed Experimental Armoured Force.† His main theme was that audacity and perspicacity were winning qualities when combined with a sound knowledge of military history. It was the ability to undertake rapid movements, maneuver easily, and have an efficient supply service that made some generals so deadly. Moreover, Liddell Hart pointed out that the lesson of history was that a small professional army was better than a massive conscript one. This was a view he came increasingly to develop up to 1939 and again in later years, and some of his ideas have since been adopted in the British White Paper (*Cmnd. 124*) of 1957. Already by 1927 he was warning that the Germans under von Seeckt understood these things and were creating a different kind of army,‡ while the War Office continued to bumble along with a 1914 outfit augmented in theory by conscription. Again, from his infantry days, there begins to creep in Saxe's lesson that a wise general refuses battle when such action is unlikely to result in

---

* The last statement is from a 1926 article in *The Current of War,* p. 72.
† The complete list, which also included his *A Greater than Napoleon* (Scipio), will be found in *The Tanks,* I, 252n.
‡ See his *The Other Side of the Hill* (1948).

an advantage. Liddell Hart was later to develop this into the concept of dynamic defence.

Contemporaneously with *Great Captains* came *The Remaking of Modern Armies,* in which the theme of mobility, action, organization, and thought as expressed in various articles were marshalled to provide amplification of *Paris.* It was long his technique to give his columns permanence and wider readability by issuing them as collections. Primarily aimed at the British Army of the day, *Remaking of Modern Armies* contained, neverthelesss, much of enduring truth. Armies merely capable of defence were a useless expenditure. That might be an unpleasant thought for the pacifist. (But it is true that part of the will to fight is lost when the role is purely passive. Trenchard more than recognized this in his attitude that the best defence is a good offensive. Yet Trenchard and others failed to take into account that an offensive defence cannot be continuous any more than can a pure offensive, for the psychology of war demands successes that both lift the spirit and provide breathing spells, hopefully of permanent duration. Moreover, for certain nations, their situation, either geographical as in the case of Germany or political as with Britain and the United States, requires at least part of the standing professional military forces to undertake a holding action, even if necessary withdrawing in order to suck the offensive enemy into defeat by a counterstroke. It is thus important that troops—and these days politicians and the press also—be indoctrinated in these requirements in order to maintain morale.) What, then, Liddell Hart meant was that in order to be an effective defence force, the military guardians must be able to deliver a counterstroke, if their mere existence is not a sufficient deterrent. Further, that unless the troops themselves believe they can do this, their moral fiber will rot, as happened to the French in 1940.

Another theme that he continued to propound was that the Army could be mechanized for the same current expenditure if the infantry were drastically cut down and the savings on their pay allotted to the purchase of equipment. When economy was rampant in the early thirties, he reiterated the idea and noted that it was cheaper to pay the dole than to maintain a useless army. To regain mobility the reformed modern army had to resort to armour, petrol engines, new means of concealment, such as smoke or night or surprise, and the reversion to highly trained professional forces in order to restore mobility. To be used properly, the tank should not be frittered away

with the infantry, but should be used as a shock weapon, as Fuller
advocated. The other side of the coin was that it was essential for
officers to know and understand the tactics and character of a potential enemy, something again that reading and history could teach,
but staff colleges did not.

The professional generals of the First World War created little
feeling of respect in Liddell Hart, who, in 1928 severely criticized
their abilities in *Reputations Ten Years After,* a debunking of the
sort that might well have been called a Stracheyan *Eminent Generals.*
Haig, his former C-in-C who died that year, came off rather better in
criticism than he was later to do, though he was called the essence of
the English spirit, while his generalship was quietly damned. Once
again the general theme was the need for mobility and surprise while
at the same time recognizing the conditions of modern warfare without losing sight of the undying principles of war. Liddell Hart
stressed the importance of the morale of the fighting man, the ability
of the staff, and that high casualties in the early days of war were the
price of lack of preparedness.*

In 1920 Liddell Hart was tentatively offered a position with
Lt/Col. J. E. Edmonds, who was the official historian for the British
Army after the First World War. Edmonds, Deputy Engineer-
in-Chief of the B.E.F., 1918, was joint auther with Maj. W. Bir-
beck Wood of *A History of the Civil War in the United States*
(1905), and of the prewar English military writers was the only
one to break away from the hypnotic fascination of the Virginia
campaign and to look instead at the military picture as a whole.
Liddell Hart's position with him did not materialize, but friendship
with Edmonds ripened and continued for some years until Liddell
Hart revolted against what he regarded as the increasing dishonesty
of official history and of Edmond's falsification of casualties in particular. The connection, however, bore fruit in directing Liddell
Hart's gaze towards the western campaigns of 1864-65 in America.

His product in 1929 was *Sherman: Soldier, Realist, American.*
Here the independent historian set out to explore the mind of one
of the world's notable captains. Soldiers had become most interested
in the new fad of psychology after the 1914-18 war and the analysis

* In recent years there have been a number of books on the British in the
First World War ranging from Leon Wolff's devastating *In Flanders Fields*
(1957) through Correlli Barnett's *The Swordbearers* (1963) to John Terraine's
apologia for Haig (1964).

of the leader of the march through Georgia fits into the stream of both military and intellectual development. *Sherman* is both a classical military text and an important milestone on the road to modern military analysis. But it is also in the pattern of modern biographical art, though intellectual historians have yet to notice it. What fascinated Liddell Hart was that Sherman was considered by all who met him to be both the most original genius of the American Civil War and at the same time "the typical American." Moreover, Liddell Hart was interested in "project[ing] the film of Sherman onto the screen of contemporary history. For there are vital lessons to be learnt from this man, his character and his career, his struggle with his environment and his ascendancy over it—keys to the modern world and to modern war." The conscious exploitation of economic and psychological factors made Sherman a modern general who realized that the war could not be won by costly battles in Virginia half so fast as by an indirect approach. Unfortunately, says Liddell Hart in his Preface, the General Staffs in Europe failed to see this and faithfully repeated the Battle of the Wilderness fifty years later (without its being a holding action). *Sherman* remains a book well worth reading, as attested to by the fact that not only was it reprinted in 1957-58, but also issued as a paperback in 1960 in the United States as the Civil War Centennial approached.

But with this book as with a number of others, the story behind it is of greater importance to intellectual historians. Asked in 1928 to write a book on Lee, Liddell Hart chose Sherman instead, for his studies after the First World War had made him wonder how the Americans had broken the deadlock of the Civil War; he hoped to learn how military stalemate in Europe might also be avoided.

It was from the study of the campaigns in the South that Liddell Hart drew the lessons of the baited gambit and the alternative objectives, offensive strategy and defensive tactics, mobility and flexibility. Many of these ideas became permanently enshrined in *Strategy*, to which we shall come in a moment. So impressed was the British army with *Sherman* that in 1931 maneuvers included what was called "a Sherman march," in which the object was to see what equipment and paraphernalia could be dispensed with in order to lighten both the divisions and the individual soldiers. The result was a 30 per cent reduction in the number of vehicles per division and a very considerable relief to the poor pack-heavy soldier. At the same time *Sherman* was translated into German by Werner von

Blomberg, who was shortly promoted to field-marshal of all three German services. Though he put other Liddell Hartian works into German, also, the most avid reader of *Sherman* was, of course, Heinz Guderian. In America, General George Patton of World War II tank fame once made a tour along the route of Sherman's famous strategic penetration with a copy of Liddell Hart's book in hand.

*The Decisive Wars of History: A Study in Strategy,* since reissued as *Strategy: The Indirect Approach,* also appeared in 1929. It was a condensed history designed to bring out the salient points about war for professional soldiers in order to enable them to learn from the experience of others, for by 1929 junior officers had little or no fighting background of their own. In it Liddell Hart pointed out that "in the physical sphere the one constant factor is that means and conditions are invariably inconstant." Therefore, it was no use studying one campaign; all had to be covered. The real constant was human nature, which varied only by degree. He stressed that in strategy the longest way round was the shortest route to the objective since it achieved the psychological disruption of the enemy's equilibrium that the disastrous frontal assault could never achieve. Liddell Hart did not, of course, mean that a frontal assault might not upon occasion have to be made, but that if it were, then surprise and deception would have to be used to divert the enemy's attention so that the decisive blow would fall upon weakened positions. Such a massive local deception was executed at Megiddo in 1918 and was achieved on D-Day 1944.*

*Strategy* has become a classic, and its author's reputation will rest upon it far more than upon the nearly forgotten *Paris* of 1925. In *Strategy* Liddell Hart originally surveyed the twelve decisive wars in ancient times and eighteen of modern history to 1914, to which he added the First World War. In later editions was also included an analysis of the Second, in which he showed how well at first Hitler,

---

* In 1923 Winston Churchill published the second volume of his memoirs of the First World War, *The World Crisis,* which contained on page 36 his 1915 proposals re strategy. In this he defined the vital theatre as one in which a decision could be obtained at any given time; this might or might not be the main theatre of war. Second, if the fronts or centers of armies could not be broken, then their flanks should be turned, by an amphibious maneuver if they rested upon the sea. Third, the least-guarded strategic points should be selected for attack, not the most heavily. Fourth, in any alliance the weakest power should be eliminated first so as to make the stronger, if dependent upon him, fall. Fifth, no offensive should be launched unless the effective means, including surprise, of carrying it out were available.

who also reacted violently to the senselessness of the Western Front, used the strategy of the indirect, especially the psychological, approach to disrupt and unbalance his enemy so that military forces had little more to do than to give the final push to tottering edifices with few casualties to themselves. The thirty major wars covered more than 280 campaigns, but in only six of these had the direct approach worked to the advantage of the aggressor. Yet analysis of these six campaigns provided little justification for adopting a frontal assault, despite the fact that this was the traditional method of getting at the enemy. Curiously, he noted, generals had been led to adopt the indirect approach only as a last resort and not as the opening gambit, so that it was a policy of weakness and not of strength and suffered from the lack of power to make the really decisive punch. From his study, Liddell Hart was able to show that the most decisive campaigns had nearly all involved the economical indirect approach. Those Great Captains who occasionally tried the direct assault usually found that it left a blot upon their record. It was more promising to make the most unpromising indirect geographical approach than to make a frontal assault, for natural hazards were far less dangerous than human resistance. On the tactical level, the victor in almost all the decisive battles had his opponent under a psychological disability before he launched his attack.

Continuing his analysis, a basic kind of operational research, Liddell Hart put together the results of the strategic and tactical and concluded that most of the 280 examples fell into two groups: victories produced by the strategy of elastic defence, in which the opponent was sucked into a trap in which the decisive blow was then given by offensive tactics, or by a strategy of offence aimed to place the victor in a position upsetting to the enemy and capped with a tactical defensive. Both used the psychological lure or trap, which he termed the baited gambit. It was from these studies that he then moved on to the conclusion that the defensive was the stronger form of strategy as well as the more economical. When used offensively, the indirect approach has usually had a logistical motive that necessitated endangering or conquering the enemy's sources of supply. In a campaign against more than one enemy, it was always wisest to destroy the weaker partner first. In some of these ideas he was not, of course, too far removed from Clausewitz.

In much of *Strategy* as in his other historical and didactic writings, Liddell Hart attempted to make the point that it was no good, as staff colleges tended to do, studying one campaign, for the principles of war and of the art of the indirect approach could be mastered only by the study of all wars. Though at times he has called himself a scientist, a title which he can certainly claim in the face of the unscientific approach of most military commanders and politicians to the conduct of war, he is, nevertheless, correct in using the term *"art"* for the indirect approach. For leadership in war must be based both upon sound knowledge and upon an intuitive sense of the forces involved. As Liddell Hart has often stressed, this must be a matter of understanding the general principles not only of war but also of human psychology and human nature. In addition to his historical survey of war, *Strategy* contains a most useful concluding section in which the theory of strategy, the national object and military aim, and grand strategy are all examined. In these he pares away all illustrations and concentrates upon the undiluted essence of these topics, with the exception that he recognizes that grand strategy is the subject for another work owing to the fact that many of its principles are in conflict with those he has enunciated for the commanding general. Grand strategy is the realm of statesmen, who must, however, know what are the limits both of their own means and of their authority.

Of all his works, *Strategy* will remain his most influential in the long run, out-distancing his more confined historical studies, several of which are also classics in their own fields.*

Further studies of the First World War followed, including a biting analysis of the military mind in his review of Sir Ernest Swinton's *Eyewitness.*† In this review Liddell Hart proposed that the bright young officers in the Army should be allowed to have university fellowships so that they might escape routine and have a chance to study, as training for command was education in theory and

---

* In a letter to me dated 13 April 1962, Capt. Liddell Hart gave the following figures on the sales of his books in English: *T. E. Lawrence—In Arabia and After,* 34,000; *History of World War, 1914-1918,* 23,000; *The War in Outline,* 22,000; *The Remaking of Modern Armies,* 1,500 (plus 100,000 pirated copies in Russia); *The Defence of Britain,* 14,000; *Foch,* 3,000 in the original edition, but 146,000 in paperback; *Strategy,* 2,000 originally, 27,000 during the Second World War, and in 1954 the enlarged edition sold 3,000 in Britain, and 25,000 in the United States, where it is also in paperback. But these figures do not include recent reprintings.

† "The Tale of the Tank," *The Nineteenth Century and After,* CXII (November 1932), 595-606.

its only source in peacetime was in history. A modern example of the truth of this suggestion is Wavell, who was not only widely read, but able to write as well, which was highly unusual in a serving officer.

Having educated himself by research and writing, in 1933 Liddell Hart proceeeded once again to attempt to open the eyes of Englishmen with *The British Way in Warfare*. He pointed out that the traditionally successful and distinctively British conduct of war had been by means of mobility and surprise. Its abandonment for a Continental policy in 1914-18 had been disastrous, but might have been due to the fact that though the standard policy had been in existence for three centuries, no one had written of the theory behind it. This had led to a slavish imitation of the Continentals as they had set up schools and studied certain campaigns and wars. The great British mistake in 1914 had been to enter a war of attrition in which British policy had been shackled to that of a Continental ally. French policy was based upon the three Clausewitzian principles: absolute warfare with civilian mass armies, the overthrow of the main enemy first, with armed forces the true objective and battle the true means. The great interpreter of Napoleon had himself been elaborated upon by the French generalissimo Foch, who mistook tactics for strategy, said Liddell Hart. The study of history, which Napoleon himself had urged, showed that Britain's "businesslike tradition in the conduct of war" was economic pressure exerted through seapower with subsidies to Continental Allies. The correct policy, therefore, for the First World War should have been the supply of munitions and expeditions, not bogging down the Army in France.

He then proceeded to analyse strategy, and what he said applied equally to peace and to war. Grand strategy co-ordinates and directs all the resources of a nation towards the attainment of the political objective. Pure strategy is the art of generalship, the calculation of, and co-ordination of, the end and the means and the weighing of the force needed to achieve each immediate objective. The uncertainty of war (and of peace, too) had been aggravated by the failure to study it scientifically and to realize that the aim of strategy is to achieve the desired end with the minimum of fighting. It is the responsibility of government to indicate whether the defeat of the enemy is to be military or otherwise. The nature of modern civilization made, Liddell Hart felt, the true aim of modern war paralysis rather than destruction. Where the generals and their preparation for war were concerned, always a vexing problem, he said that they always prepared for the last war, which would be all right if they took up the reins where war had ended, and not where it started, while at the same time taking cognizance of weapons and inventions recently made available. He called upon them to study the war before the last one, but also particularly in the interwar years the American Civil War, the first of the great industrial, amateur, mass forces' struggles.* The British army, after its first instinctive return to 1914 standards immediately after the war, had actually moved ahead a few years, but it continued to delay establishing itself as a fieldable fighting force on the excuse that it needed to experiment further. But, said Liddell Hart, this was unnecessary as sufficient proof was already available (as evidenced by the 1929 issue of the armoured warfare manual) and the Germans were already building upon it. He then launched into his favourite theme—that the light infantry tank was the coming weapon and that the first national army to become armoured would have a tremendous advantage.

As early as *Paris* Liddell Hart had seen the coming importance of airpower. In *The British Way in Warfare* he stated that he felt it might well soon be the decisive weapon and would in future wars be much as the cavalry had been to the infantry in the past—the Air Force and the Army being the two components of military power. He foresaw what was to happen in France in 1940 and even more so in Crete in 1941, namely, that mechanized forces (in the Aegean, paratroopers) would make enemy air bases untenable and thus hamper the air offensive, while Britain might well be forced into starvation by the bombing of her ports and munitions factories. Though the Navy would continue to play its part in the wide spaces, many of its actions would in future be governed by the Air Force. What helped the Air Force, he felt, was that it started with the immense psychological advantage of being mechanized from the beginning.

---

* A possible explanation for the fact that generals tend to start the next war at the beginning of the last one is that the war books and planning in general in peacetime lay the emphasis upon mobilization and appear to have, in 1918-39 Britain, resulted also in a neglect of the potential enemy, as for instance the reluctance to let de Guingand go to France and Germany in 1937 (*Operation Victory* [London, 1947], pp. 15-19). There was an organization chart for a British Expeditionary Force and divisions assigned to it, but little thought had been given to its role, which Liddell Hart would not have had repeat that of 1914.

But the most important point that Liddell Hart emphasized was the maxim that if a nation wished for peace, it must understand war, not necessarily prepare for it. And by *war* he meant the very widest concept of that term, not the narrow purely military meaning that pacifists in particular have been wont to ascribe to it. Modern war affects all citizens, but at the time, he wrote, not even the Government was prepared to recognize that elementary fact.

It was in the period from 1932 to 1935 that Liddell Hart was constantly talked of as the new Deputy Secretary of the Committee of Imperial Defence. The idea was that he would be appointed Hankey's successor when that veteran organizer retired, and that he would modernize British defences. Unfortunately in 1935 Lord Trenchard, the former Chief of the Air Staff and no great friend of Hankey's, tried to get the Secretary ousted. Liddell Hart, despite the implication by Andrew Boyle,* had nothing to do with this action, but was discredited for he was regarded as a friend of the Air Force in the days when the Admiralty was desperately trying to defend the battleship in opposition to Liddell Hart's and other critics' ideas. Nor was the pundit entirely *persona grata* to the General Staff.

During the Second World War there was talk from time to time of placing Liddell Hart in charge of various operational research organizations, but either he was sent off to do specially urgent work or someone else was found who needed a post. The critic is rarely welcomed with open arms even in times of crisis.

In 1935 *The British Way in Warfare* was brought out in a largely revised form under the new title *When Britain Goes to War: Adaptability and Mobility*. Five of the old chapters were omitted,† and new ones added to give the book a more British point of view. The basic Chapter V was left intact as the lecture on strategy. The shift in emphasis was towards a war with Germany and an increasing cognizance of airpower. In 1933 Liddell Hart had predicted the likelihood of renewed trench warfare owing to the failure of staffs to study the problems of modern war and the lack of infantry mobility. By 1935 he was becoming convinced that motorization would favour the defence for it was essentially the means of bringing small arms, notably machine guns, into action. As he labelled himself "a prophet of mechanization," his word carried great weight. Yet he qualified his thoughts by noting that the attacker might be able to undertake

* *Trenchard* (1962), pp. 692-695.
† Chapters II, III, IV, IX, and XIV: XIII and XV were moved.

an assault, but that unless he could break right through, he could never act decisively. Here it seems, Liddell Hart's memories of those useless straggles across the Flanders mud came back to haunt him with the presumption that both the modern civilized armies of whom he was talking would be somewhat equally matched. The solution was also based upon the lessons of the last war—an armoured breakthrough or an end run in the indirect manner to strike at enemy airfields and knock his airpower off balance while the Air Force paralysed his industrial centers. In such lightning war, which the Germans so successfully developed into blitzkrieg, the unwieldy mass armies of Europe, with their vast disruptable communications, would prove to be greater liabilities than assets.

The war in Spain, beginning in July 1936, he regarded as the opening of the Second World War and said so at the time. Studying it, he produced *Europe in Arms* in 1937.* In this his analysis was more far-reaching and the work included chapters on air forces and capital ships (the Washington Treaty restrictions ended on 31 December 1936) and on the future of war. Writing in the pre-atomic decade he predicted that a "war to end civilization" (so often the fearful view of another great war) would in short order become a stalemate, made ridiculous and not decisive by the power of the defence on the ground that would of itself limit the air menace. Outwardly, at least, the trend of his thought was more and more towards a defensive position. It must be remembered that in 1937 he knew fairly accurately how poor British defence preparations were, how lacking the Government was in appreciation of the time lag between desire for design of weapons and their operational usability, and how the traditional British position was defensive up to and in the first few months after the declaration of war. He had long predicated that a successful offensive needed a ratio of strength of 3:1 over the defence, and lacking an armoured force any lesser combination looked like being stopped, at least as things then stood. He was moving steadily towards the two doctrines that were so castigated in the Second World War: limited warfare and dynamic defence, both of which Clausewitz had exposed.

It was in 1937 that Leslie Hore-Belisha became Secretary of State for War, and Liddell Hart his unofficial adviser. Hore-Belisha put into practice many of Liddell Hart's ideas, including the domina-

* The American edition had a special chapter on Spain tipped in.

tion of industrial considerations in supply that led to the purge of senior officers * and the concept of limited warfare that caused the British army to be prepared to fight non-Continental actions as an elite, mechanized force. Concretely he wanted three mechanized divisions overseas and three in the United Kingdom, the latter to aid France. The real problem, he wrote later,† was that the clamour for conscription and a doubling of the Territorial Army concealed the fact that Britain lacked the right weapons for the coming war. At the same time, in a paper prepared at Sir Thomas Inskip's request, Liddell Hart urged that the dangers of air attack be countered not only with fighters and proper anti-aircraft, but also in the field with armoured vehicles and by the creation of landing barges that could move cross-Channel and up the French rivers. His proposal to double the 600 guns allotted for the defence of Great Britain led to yet another Committee, whose scheme was dubbed "the Ideal Scheme" and was so disposed of in political fashion within the Service. He claims that this disregard of the national danger led at once to the purge of the Army staff.‡ By this time he was becoming more and more aware of the likelihood of a German attack on France, to whose defence Britain would have to go. Yet at the same time he was concerned to see Britain put into a traditional posture of defence while avoiding the mistakes made in the last war.

That struggle held a fatal, and literally profitable, attraction for him, which pessimistically caused him to emphasize the power of the defence and thus to discount the successful possibilities of a German blitzkrieg, though this was in fact being based upon the mechanical musclepower arguments that he and Fuller had been preaching and upon Liddell Hart's own studies, which showed that a deep penetration, a strategic rather than a tactical thrust, to the rear had the greater impact.§ It would, however, be less than fair not to say that he did not anticipate the German tactics so much as he failed to realize how appallingly bad the French Army would be in 1940. His own studies had caused him in 1928 to come to doubt

* Interestingly, similar cleansing action was taken in Germany and Russia in the latter thirties.

† This is recounted almost verbatim in *The Current of War*, pp. 121-123 and 171-173, and in *Dynamic Defence*, pp. 27-38.

‡ *The Current of War*, p. 123. Sir Frederick Pile, *Ack-Ack* (1949).

§ My interpretation here differs somewhat from that of Luvaas, *The Education of an Army*, p. 406.

Foch's plan of 1919, which had been based upon pinning the Germans back against what the French staff liked to call the impenetrable massif of the Ardennes. Apparently this concept was a delusion long perpetuated by a failure to view the ground. After contradicting in several books the idea that the Ardennes was impenetrable, in a memorandum of 10 November 1933 for Brigadier Patrick Hobart, the newly appointed commander of the tank brigade, Liddell Hart pointed out that in another war against Germany the role of a British Expeditionary Force would be to aid the French left wing by driving in on German rear communications where they passed through the Ardennes. This was used as the basic idea for the tank exercises of 1934. It may well be asked, then, why the British and the French were caught so badly in 1940 by the Germans led by Guderian, and again by von Rundstedt in 1944. Part of the answer must lie in the hostility of the General Staff in the late thirties to the pricking of their bubbles by Liddell Hart and to the aversion to any of the theorist's ideas after he became what the Secretary of State called "my partner," and to their concentration upon getting rid of such troublesome persons before these executors made their heads roll.* As Liddell Hart himself recognizes, the moment of influence brings a reaction that may well undo much of the good work accomplished in the period of accelerated decision and change. Moreover, as war approached, it became more and more difficult to write specifically about certain dangers, particularly as one was thought to have inside knowledge, especially of British weaknesses. Though the tie to Hore-Belisha was broken in 1938, the public and others continued until the war to think of the two as collaborators.

Liddell Hart also suffered from two dangers into which, in particular, a military theorist can fall. The power of the logical word took him rather beyond the realm of actuality because it involved prediction, and there has rarely been an accurate way of gauging how forces will fight, how their material, spirit, and generalship will stand the actual test of war. War is not unlike contract bridge. There are basic rules and codes, but every hand is different, and a lot depends on the psychology and the artfulness of the player holding it. The little elite who write bridge books tend, or so it appears to the reader, to lay down not only the general rules based upon

* See R. J. Minney, *The Private Papers of Hore-Belisha* (1960), a mutilated biography, and Colonel R. Macleod and Denis Kelly (editors), *The Ironside Diaries* (1962).

probabilities but also what the other players will hold and what they will do. The history of war and bridge is full of examples of commanders and players who know the rules and disobey them to reach success, while the ordinary player mistakenly regards the guiding rules as absolutes.

The fascination with the First World War resulted in yet another volume, *The Fog of War* (1938), in which Liddell Hart exhumed the behind-the-scenes materials to show how doctrines, dogmas, desires, loyalties, and personal outlooks confused the picture despite the blue-pencilled attempts of official histories to clarify it. The whole is most useful reading for historians interested in the human side of war and society, for, as Liddell Hart said, "History is a catalogue of mistakes. It is our duty to profit by them."

Just before war broke out in September 1939, he hastily published, in ten weeks from pen to print, *The Defence of Britain*, a very wide-ranging analysis of the situation as it stood early in 1939 with the sudden transition of the Continental situation by the elimination of the thirty-five-division Czechoslovak Army and—just after the book appeared—by the alienation of Russia. He was also at this time increasingly worried that Spain would be used as an Axis base. He felt that the Navy should continue to be strengthened in light craft while maintaining a limited number of battleships, as Britain's use of maritime economic pressure was declining in importance. The role of the Army either had to be expanded to help the French or to be left as it was, contracted, as the one Service upon which money could be saved. The crying need was for the air defence of Britain because it was now obvious that war would be fought at home and not abroad. Liddell Hart was strongly against Universal Service as the right remedy for the wrong war; what Britain needed, he said, was brains and machines: conscription of itself would do little to impress Germany. (And this is a view he has maintained in his postwar works.) But the heart of his doctrine was contained in Chapter V, "The Method of Defence—by Attack or Defence?" As opposed to totalitarianism, which called for the utter defeat of the opponent, he argued for the traditional war, which was restricted by the limited political objective for which it was fought. He feared a mass war would lead to national exhaustion and a bankrupt peace. On page 105 he stated fairly his position:

> The general deduction from experience that the defensive has a great and growing superiority does not, of course, imply that the

offensive can never succeed. It is likely to succeed, as already noted, in a campaign where the defender has no effective counter-weapons to nullify the offensive instruments such as aircraft and tanks. It may possibly succeed against an opponent of similar equipment if the attacker displays a great superiority of art, and thereby produces a great local superiority of fire and psychological threat.

. . . it is a common assumption that attack has usually paid in the past. This is contrary to the balance of evidence. Analysis shows that in the majority of the battles which are engraved in the pages of history, the loser was the army which was the first to commit itself to the attack, . . . History offers, to those who will inquire of it objectively, overwhelming evidence that the counter-offensive, after the enemy has overstrained himself in the offensive, has been the decisive form of action. . . .

. . . At the time Clausewitz wrote, as for all time past, even the largest forces were small in comparison with the area to be covered, and this limitation of their capacity for secure defensive extension made a purely defensive attitude unsafe. Whatever its local advantages, these were usually outweighed by its general risks. But since then there has been a great increase in the size of forces, accompanied by a still greater increase in the range of weapons, and the combination has produced change in the relationship of space to force. This emphasizes the need for a thorough re-examination of the basis of military ideas, and suggests that it would be wise to give due consideration to the new possibilities of national "defence" by defence in the true sense.

The bulk of the book was devoted, of course, to reforms in the Army and his part in them. The dominant theme was that the inefficiency of the War Office was costing the taxpayers money.

A contemporary, John F. Kennedy, later President of the United States, criticised Liddell Hart for underestimating the cost of putting Britain's defence into fighting condition and for deluding the voter by making him feel that limited war could be fought by small highly mechanized mobile units without disrupting the life of the country, at least during rearmament.* But as a recent principal adviser of the Government, could Liddell Hart in early 1939 go against its oft-declared policy?

One wonders how much consciously or unconsciously Liddell Hart's thinking on defence was influenced by the Germans. After all, ever since the days the Schlieffen Plan was created to counter the

* *Why England Slept* (New York, 1940), pp. 47-51. For an interesting note on the publication history of the book, see *The New York Times Book Review,* 27 August 1961, p. 8.

1894 Franco-Russian alliance, the Germans had had to think of fighting a defensive war on one front. In 1938 there appeared in Germany Field Marshal Ritter von Leeb's *Defence*, in which a strong analysis of the First World War was a prominent feature. Some of his ideas, according to his 1943 American translator, Dr. Stephen Possony, were incorporated straight from their original article form into the 1936 Red Army field service regulations and employed in 1941. Von Leeb, for instance, correctly pointed out that defence, while it pays bigger dividends for those who can wait while the enemy exhausts himself in attacks, is far harder psychologically on the soldier. Like Liddell Hart, von Leeb had read Clausewitz and had realized that the nature of war was determined by its causes and aims, as well as by the ways and means available for its conduct. He concluded that the First World War should have been fought defensively (as at Ypres) by a well-trained, offensively minded Army, using defence in depth and not linear tactics to avoid heavy casualties. On the whole, von Leeb's conclusions are very close to Liddell Hart's and may well have been as much influenced by him as vice-versa. They varied simply in reflecting the nation and the Army from which he came, while von Leeb himself went on to become an Army commander in the 1941 Russian campaign.

After the war started, on 9 September 1939, Liddell Hart sent the Government a memorandum calling for the renunciation of military attack as a means of meeting aggression on the ground that such a declaration would strengthen Britain's moral position and head off derision abroad and disillusionment at home. The first step in a new technique suited to Britain's circumstances, he envisioned it as setting Britain free to develop her traditional moral and economic pressures while leaving the forces free to counter any German attempt at aggression on the "British sanitary cordon." In grand strategy, Britain should seek Germany's weak flank while covering her own. At the same time he urged that no air offensive be undertaken for the present as the R.A.F. by no means had superiority, as the majority of Britons were only lukewarm for war and the temper of civilians was untested (and the war in Spain and China had shown that civilians, not military objectives, were the major recipients). An air offensive should be launched only when Britain was paramount in the air. We cannot know how much this advice affected the Government except by implication until the first volume of *Grand*

*Strategy* appears,* though much of the air evidence is corroborated by Volume I of *The Strategic Air Offensive Against Germany* (1961).

Liddell Hart's own apologia for his work in the thirties appeared in mid-1940. *Dynamic Defence*, written just after the German success in France in May, castigated the Chamberlain policy of appeasement as unhistorical and for its failure to contain aggression, noted that the air myth of a massive single strike breaking civilian morale had been eliminated, and laid the blame for the defeat in France upon a lack of understanding on the part of Allied generals of the nature of modern war. The Germans won because they used the skeleton keys of small political groups and lightning military strokes, masking the new warfare with armies of conscripts. Britain lost because after 1927 she failed to develop her armoured divisions and cast out the five "brains" (Fuller, Hobart, Pile, Broad, and Martel) who could have developed them into a powerful force. What he could not write in 1939 was that French politics and morale were bad and that it was not only the failure to understand modern war but also the lack of backbone in France that allowed the Germans to punch through. In 1935 Liddell Hart had suggested that Britain supply an air expeditionary force (the Advanced Air Striking Force of 1939), but too little time had elapsed for it to be made effective in 1940.

In 1941 *The Current of War* blended the three themes of actual war, prewar policy, and mechanized mobility. About half the book was composed of articles that had appeared in the years 1922 to 1940 by the republication of which he sought to justify his prewar position and to salvage his reputation, while at the same time pointing once more to the long lessons of history. The last was a theme that he took up again in 1944's *Why Don't We Learn from History?* and put more concisely than he had in *The Fog of War*. It was a good question, though it appears that since the Second World War ended it needs to be asked less frequently as more people are aware of what has happened in the twentieth century, the age of total war.

Yale University published in 1947 his first book-length treatment

* The memorandum of 9 September is in *The Current of War*, pp. 153-156. *Grand Strategy*, I, is not, according to H.M.S.O., likely to appear before 1966 at the earliest. But in the meantime a summary will be found in Michael Howard (ed.) *The Theory and Practice of War* (1965), to which Norman H. Gibbs has contributed Chapter X, "British Strategic Doctrine, 1918-1939."

of the atomic bomb, *The Revolution in Warfare*. Taking a long look at the evolution of warfare from 1500 to 1945 he once again urged its study while at the same time saying that nations living in glass houses should not throw nuclear weapons. Moreover, it was increasingly important that people should understand that it was not merely the devastation of each other's industrial capacity that was the way to victory, but to see that war was only a means to an end, *peace*, which had to be preplanned. A very considerable section of the book was devoted to an analysis of the use of airpower in the war. He concluded that it had failed as a shock weapon and that thereafter its decisiveness was vitiated by spatial considerations. Ironically, when the atom bomb appeared to fuse all warfare into a real trinity, scarcely any airpower at all was necessary for its use. These ideas he was still digesting when in 1950 there appeared *The Defence of the West: Some Riddles of War and Peace*.

The new book was originally conceived as two. The first part consisted of a series of essays on various aspects of the Second World War in which he carried out his expressed belief that supposition was always of interest and often of value.* He examined why France fell in 1940, the North African campaigns, Hitler's failure in Russia, D-Day, unconditional surrender, and resistance movements. In all of these essays he was provocative, and in many his line of thought diverged from that of many others. His little piece on the dangers of resistance movements might well be reread by those engaged in fomenting guerrilla warfare today. In some of the pieces, of course, he reverted to old themes, such as when he pointed out that if Hitler had had tracked vehicles in Russia instead of merely wheeled ones, he might have won. But in the main, these opening chapters emphasized the old themes of surprise, unorthodoxy, mobility, and the lessons of history. In the other sections of the book, he dealt with riddles of the immediate future such as bombs and home defence, how good are the Russians, the time factor, current military problems, and the need for a single unified Service. He felt that the military in the decade 1945-55 were just as hidebound as they had been in 1900-18 as far as new weapons and new ideas were concerned, and that as a result they tended to stick to the safely conservative, while ignoring the fact that modern civilizations were far easier to defeat than the primitive Chinese. Thus he called upon

* *Strategy,* 160.

statesmen to awake and look to their battlements, for in the coming catastrophe they would not be allowed a second chance in which to recover from the initial blow. The solution for Britain he deemed to be the creation of a high quality, highly mobile, armoured and airborne force blessed with a secure, but detached, political base. He then launched into a devastating analysis of the cost of conscription in terms of inefficient manpower bought at the expense of new quality weaponry. While generally arguing that the West, as he used to say Britain, must convince the aggressor that he cannot obtain a quick victory, he called strongly for conventional forces, saying especially that "armoured forces have not had their day because *they have not yet been tried*," the idea being that truly armoured divisions had not yet been used. The armoured warfare of the 1939 war was carried out by units of which only one sixth were tanks, while the postwar armies were no better and loaded down with chains of command, etc., which vitiated their potential mobility. And he concluded by pointing out that "the limitless destructiveness of the [atomic bomb] forms its own practical limitation." The concentration of thought in the West has been, he said, too much on preventing war and not enough upon limiting it.

This was the theme he took up again ten years later when after editing a study of the Red Army and completing his monumental history of the Royal Tank Regiment, he returned once again to the broad field of modern strategy. In *Deterrent or Defence?* he collected a series of pieces that had appeared over the years in which he had pleaded against the use of the nuclear deterrent and for conventional arms to counter conventional attacks. That he should take such a stand was not merely based upon his own long-term evaluations, but also upon the European awareness that the American policy of the nineteen-fifties was likely either to see Europe devastated or overrun, but hardly saved. Since, with the introduction of the H-bomb and the loss of the American nuclear monopoly, defence against atomic attack was becoming impossible, it was increasingly necessary for the West to be able to meet a conventional ground attack, for the Russians might by that means be able to undertake a strategic surprise. The defence, he argued, was stronger than the attack by a ratio of 7:1, but useless if it could be outflanked. If war was to return to the level of ordinary men, then once again gas became a possible weapon and the gas-proof tank an antidote.

Nerve gases, night maneuvers, seapower, an international military force, and disengagement were all means by which various levels of hostility might be overcome and peace restored or prolonged. As much as it is possible to judge so recent a work, it is provocative and destructive in its thought, while at the same time carrying to the present themes that he forcefully argued before the Second World War, a conflict that in the end did much to vindicate his ideas.

Like most long-lived critics, he has suffered from the difficulty of writing new pieces without sounding like a tired trumpeter of well-worn ideas. It is both to his advantage and to his misfortune when one sits down to read and analyse the work of a lifetime. Yet Liddell Hart comes off pretty well from such an examination, and the trend of modern events seems more and more to garland his reputation as his works stand the tests of time. It is notable that one of his strongest critics in 1940 became one of his most prominent supporters. In *The Saturday Review* of 3 September 1960, Senator John F. Kennedy, then a presidential candidate, accepted the aging Britisher's anti-Dulles thesis that limited aggression should not be met with unlimited force. Upon Kennedy's assumption of the Presidency there came about what has been called "the second Liddell Hartian revolution."

Seen properly against the background of the time in which he worked, Liddell Hart presents acutely the dilemma of the thinker in military affairs. He sought both the proper defensive posture for Britain and one that she could afford. But few in 1940, least of all his natural enemies at home, were willing to see this, and he became a discredited scapegoat for the disaster he had spent so long trying to persuade people to prepare to avoid. Basically Liddell Hart was correct in his teachings and if he was swayed by the events of his time and on occasion led astray, who has not been? He was cast into the shadows in 1940, and it seems strange that of distinguished and universally read writers, he received comparatively little honor in his own country until the 1960's.

In the same tradition was Capt. J. R. Kennedy, who also attacked the government's policy in the middle and later thirties and pointed to the lesson that the development of armaments followed upon the heels of the causes that created wars and not vice versa. In fact, he claimed, disarmament was more dangerous than being armed, for it created widespread unemployment.* Kennedy became a noticed prewar critic, though he confined himself primarily to Army problems, as opposed to Capt. M. D. Kennedy, his contemporary, who was an expert on Japan and the Far East. J. R. Kennedy made a stinging exposé of the lack of readiness of the land forces in his *This Our Army* (1934) and followed it in 1936 with *Modern War and Defence Reconstruction*. Both were really tracts for the day.

### CRITICISMS

Countering Liddell Hart's articles in *The Times* of 25-27 October 1937, in which he called for more defensive money to allow the base to be made secure, was the book, *Imperial Defence: A Problem in Four Dimensions*. This appeared in 1938 from the pen of the Fullerite Major-General H. Rowan-Robinson. Rowan-Robinson had been the author of a number of articles in the *Journal of the Royal United Services Institution* in the twenties and of two books from the artilleryman's viewpoint in 1928: *Artillery Today and Tomorrow* and *Some Aspects of Mechanization*. He had then called for the application of machinepower (Fuller's "mechanical muscle") to the movement of guns, but he balked at the idea that the answer to the tank was another tank. Such a view led ultimately to the development of the tank-destroyer, the turretless tank of World War II.

In *Imperial Defence* he followed the Clausewitzian school and supported dynamic attack. He pointed out that the Empire faced three-dimensional warfare affected by the fourth—time. In order, then, to deal with this situation it was essential to have a small decisive war cabinet, a Ministry of Defence to control the three armed Services, a Ministry of Static Defence to manage anti-aircraft defences and air-raid precautions, and a sharp increase in the number of naval small ships at the expense of battleships. He postulated that the first aim of British strategy had to be control of the air and that for this it was essential to develop Imperial air communications as a means of providing for mobile Imperial air defence, which should include, he said, air supply and paratroop units. In this

* "The Masque of Imperial Defence," *The Nineteenth Century and After,* CXV (March 1934), 257-267.

he was, of course, echoing the work of the Warren Fisher Committee and the Empire Air Mail Scheme, which was then leading to the vast extension of Imperial Airways' routes and to the development of other services by British Airways, while the airborne aspects were a reflection of the work being carried on in Russia and Germany, but ignored in England. Rowan-Robinson called for tanks to be developed as weapons of opportunity and not merely of assault as the First-World-War-minded saw them, and for the Cardwell system of linked battalions to be abandoned and replaced by a system of long- and short-term enlistments with, as the Reserve grew, the reduction of the Territorial Army to cadre status. He further supported the establishment of a National Register of all persons of military age from which volunteers should be drawn. His more specific recommendations, like his broader ones, all reflected both current thinking within and without the Establishment of the day and measures actually in work.

If Liddell Hart was the representative of the European school, Rowan-Robinson was the spokesman of the Imperial, for he was not touched by the taint of Fascism that rendered many of Fuller's essentially valid ideas suspect, and that caused him to be ignored when his kind of war was actually fought in the nineteen-forties. Both Liddell Hart and Rowan-Robinson had ideas of merit and each reflected the thought of the time. It is ironic looking backwards to see that, immediately after the First World War, British strategic thinking concentrated upon a war against Japan, traditionally friendly, and neglected the possibilities in Europe, where the Peace of Versailles was bound to need adjustment. The troubles of 1939 to 1942 arose from a failure, until too late, to keep a world view. What upset British planning was when Japan joined with Germany and Britain faced the reality of a war both in the Far East and in Europe. It was to meet this revised situation that Rowan-Robinson called for a larger strategy and an improved means with a wider focus than merely of a war against Germany.*

---

* For some interesting contemporary comments upon the ideas of dynamic defence and of dynamic attack on an imperial scale, see the articles by R. T. Clark in *The Nineteenth Century and After*, CXXV (January 1939), 66-72, and CXXV (September 1939), 270-278; also Lt/Col. Clive Garcia, *Planning the War* (Harmondsworth, 1941) and Stephen King-Hall, *Total Victory* (New York, 1942).

## V. W. GERMAINS

The other strong critic of the Liddell Hart school, Victor Wallace Germains, was an Austrian specializing in the Hapsburg Empire until shortly before the First World War, when he began to write in English under the name "The Rifleman." He came back to the scene with an article in *World Today* of September 1927 called "Is the Super-tank a myth?" This was followed later by "Common-sense and Secrecy in Naval Design" and by "Mirage and Mechanization," the latter appearing in *The Edinburgh Review* in July 1929. He wrote a number of articles in the early thirties along the same themes, but it was not until October 1937 in *The National Review* that he really began to pick up speed with "The Case for Conscription." He followed this in the December issue with "The Cult of the Defensive," in which he attacked Churchill for saying "Earth stops bullets and bullets kill men." He said that the theory that modern arms conferred special advantages on the defence was one that constantly cropped up, but that had led to overwhelming national disaster for those who believed in it. It had started at the Battle of Gettysburg when it had cost Lee the South's only chance of winning a decisive victory. Germains went on to cite examples to support his offensive-minded ideas, but failed to note that in most cases the winners were well-trained troops operating under a carefully defined plan. Germains complained that those who preached the defence *über Alles* had had little or no command experience. "The learned doctor of war" held too much sway in peacetime in all armies and the only counter to him was a really learned C.I.G.S. Further, while motorization favoured the attack as well as the defence, the problem still remained of knocking out the machine gun. He concluded that the soothing doctrine of the increased power of the defence was just the line the politicians wanted as the danger to the Empire grew. But once again he spoiled his point by concluding with the remark that Japanese air raids on Chinese cities had failed to knock them out, and that "the scientific critics" had no policy—a veiled slam at the Hore-Belisha purge of the top generals advised by Fuller and Liddell Hart.

In April 1938 he attacked mechanization as being costly in men and money; the lesson of industry was that machines redistributed the labour of men. It was useless, he said, to mechanize five British divisions to help the French as this could not be done in secret, and the Germans would, therefore, merely counter it. All the mechanization of the British army was doing was to provide light-weight divisions, when the thing that really won wars was heavy artillery. Freedom of maneuver in France would only be obtained by fighting for it and winning. Thus the decisive fighting would still be done by normal infantry divisions, and armour would only be used to exploit the gap made by them, or be used for raiding or for countering an enemy breakthrough. Perhaps his thinking is most clearly shown at the end of the article, which had already made use of naval examples, when he said that the only counter to a foreign 35,000-ton battleship was a 40,000-ton British one with a higher speed and heavier armament. His views were put even more clearly in *The National Review* of September 1938, when he said that the only people who wrote about war were discredited generals, "the learned wiseacres," and politicians trying to blame others for their own mistakes. By May 1939 he was pressing for a mass national army raised by conscription as opposed to the Territorial Army system then, in fact, being augmented by the draft. In the June issue of the same magazine he blamed most of the British Army's troubles on public apathy, the rise of "scientific military criticism," the evolution of the academic military mind, and upon J. F. C. Fuller for starting all the folly with his talk of the science of war. For good measure he also threw in the "Mrs. [Mary Baker] Eddy" airpower school of Groves and Churchill with their belief in the opening knockout air strike.

Germains was a continual critic who kept up a steady two-articles-a-year fire upon the Fuller and Liddell Hart school. In many of his pieces there were some valid criticisms, but in many also there were some remarks that smacked too much of the military mind that led to the stalemates of the First World War for his works to have lasting value.*

* A rather inadequate appraisal of Germains will be found in E. M. Earle's *Makers of Modern Strategy*, pp. 382-383. His own writings mentioned here are to be found in "Is the Super-tank a Myth?," *World Today*, L (September 1927), 347-352; "Commonsense and Secrecy in Naval Design," *World Today*, LI (January 1928), 162-165; "Mirage and Mechanization," *The Edinburgh Review*, CCL (July 1929), 123-138; "Some Aspects of the Present Military Situation between France and Germany," *The English Review*, LVII (16 December 1933), 609-616; "Mechanics of 'Mechanization,'" *Royal Engineers Journal*, December

EVALUATION

In 1951 Liddell Hart summed up the principal points of his thought and teaching as reviving the offensive through armoured warfare and the strategy of the indirect approach. These subjects occupied him heavily in the twenties, but he began to develop counters to them in the thirties as it became obvious that Britain and the democracies had to find a way to confront an increasingly aggressive Hitler. This line of thought led him to conclude that "victory" was a futile goal, and that stalemate, preferably without war, was in fact the ideal at which to aim. But if war came, then it had to be fought with the end in mind—future peace. His other great contribution, he felt, was in the propagation of truth through the use of scientific historical study. If there was resistance to his military teachings, he concluded that there was even more to the truths that he tried to disseminate.

Today historians are becoming aware of their own inbred prejudices and leanings, as well as of their experiences and backgrounds. Where Liddell Hart is concerned, the fact that he was a quiet, diffident infantryman has coloured his work, as have his natural neatness and desire for efficiency. He has the Englishman's capacity

1929, pp. 582-591; "The Raising of the New Armies," *The National Review,* July 1936, pp. 74-85; "The General Staff and the Army," *The National Review,* April 1937, pp. 439-449; "The Army in War (Essential Tactics and Equipment," *The National Review,* June 1939, pp. 759-766; "Kitchener at the War Office," *Contemporary Review,* CXLIX (June 1936), 687-695; "The Case for Conscription," *The National Review,* CIX (October 1937), 474-482; "The Cult of the Defensive," *The National Review,* CIX (December 1937), 757-763; *ibid, Living Age,* CCCLIII (February 1938), 498-502; "Quart Measure and Pint Pot," *The National Review,* CX (April 1938), 453-464; "Some Problems of Imperial Strategy," *The National Review,* CX (June 1938), 738-748; "To Be or Not to Be," *The National Review,* CXI (September 1938), 342-350; "The Vital Need," *The National Review,* CXII (May 1939), 604-607; "The Army in War," *The National Review,* CXII (June 1939), 759-766. After the war started he became quite popular for a couple of years, but then faded away. He also wrote *The Struggle for Bread: A Reply to "The Great Illusion" and Enquiry into Economic Tendencies by "A Rifleman"* (London, 1913); *The Gathering Storm, Being Studies in Social and Economic Tendencies by "A Rifleman"* (London, 1913); *"The Truth About Kitchener* (London, 1925); *The "Mechanization" of War* (London, 1927); *The Kitchener Armies; The Story of a National Achievement* (London, 1930); *The Tragedy of Winston Churchill* (London, 1931); *Austria of Today with a Special Chapter on the Austrian Police* (London, 1932); *Colonel to Princess* (London, 1936, a novel); with Buhet, Gil, *Couverture de Francois Crozat* (Paris, 1950); and *Crusoe Warburton* (New York, 1954).

to appear lazy, while actually thinking out some important point as his mind constantly roves over problems ranging from strategy to the waste of water in dripping barracks' faucets.

General Chassin has said that Liddell Hart had a more global view of strategy, but what he really means is that the English pundit had a wider view of war than did Frenchmen in the nineteen-thirties. For an actual knowledge of global conditions, Fuller seems to have had a broader vision. Liddell Hart never travelled outside Europe between the wars nor before the First World War.* On the other hand, he was not so optimistic as Fuller about the effects of bombing. Fuller today admits that, like many others, he vastly overrated the psychological effect of bombing and the counterforce provided by trench-warfare veterans in the population. It was his fear of a collapse of morale that made him espouse civil discipline and caused his connection with the Fascists. In this he was genuinely doing what he felt was best for Britain, and he has suffered since because of his loyalty. Liddell Hart parted with Trenchard (with whom he was associated while Fuller hardly ever met him) in the latter thirties over the failure of the deterrent and the danger to its base in the face of superior German forces. While Fuller, like Trenchard, expected the air blow to be decisive, Liddell Hart came to see that it could be parried and might well take a long time to make itself effective. But both Liddell Hart and Fuller advocated the small professional armoured force, the former including infantry, the latter not.

Whereas Fuller of the older generation concentrated upon the development and limitations of weapons, Liddell Hart, his disciple and peer, saw beyond the machine to the leadership and the tactics it used. That this was so may have been due as much to the accidents of age and assignments as to inbred differences and education. In the twenties they kept closely in touch and aided each other's cause, Liddell Hart, for instance, suggesting that Fuller be Milne's one-man operational research centre. In 1938 they were both to have served on the new War Office advisory panel on strategy proposed by C.I.G.S. Viscount Gort and his Deputy Sir Ronald Adam as a counter to Hore-Belisha's acceptance of Liddell Hart's proposal, first put forward in 1920, for an operational research

* His first visit to the United States was made in 1952. In 1965-66 he was visiting professor at the University of California, Davis, and but for illness would have delivered the 1966 Harmon Memorial Lecture at the U.S.A.F. Academy.

organization. It finally bore fruit, but without either Fuller or Liddell Hart, in the Second World War.

These two men have, then, tended to complement each other's work, with Fuller concentrating upon the tactical and Liddell Hart upon the strategical. But while it is clear that *Strategy* will become a classic work which, as the *Frankfurt Allgemeine Zeitung* said on 31 October 1955, makes its author not only the Clausewitz of our age but also one who is read, the same is not nearly so clear about Fuller. It would be hard to pick one of his works, unless it is *The Second World War* or *Armoured Warfare*, which will remain in print and be read in the ensuing decades. Fuller is an original thinker, but his political slants have blemished his brightest works. His *Decisive Battles* is a monument, but few will sit down and read the whole of it or draw from it clear lessons to match those set forth so simply in *Strategy*.

However much today we may look back on the operational researchers, Richmond, Fuller, and Liddell Hart, with feelings of sorrow that they did not succeed, we must also recall the climate of opinion in which they worked. This is set forth in great detail in my *Armed Forces in Peacetime*. It was an age of economy, an era in which a serious attempt was made to return to the budgets of the good old days before the First World War despite the fact that the pound sterling was worth far less than in 1914. It was a period in which it was much more important to do things neatly whether in budgetting or on maneuvers, to observe the rules, than it was to ask the reason why and to initiate changes. Thus these men did operate in the wilderness.

Yet in some respects were they so terribly different from the others of their day? Liddell Hart is the only one of them I have had the pleasure of meeting. I saw him once in 1938 in a restaurant in London and still remember the rather awed tones in which I was told who he was. In 1959 he kindly entertained me at his home in Medmenham. Except for his military bearing, he acts far more the part of a scholar; precise in action, but rather halting in speech. Asked to criticize a written work, he is thorough and precise, with a reputation for helping young writers. Fuller remains today sprightly, incisive, and just as outspoken as he was forty years ago. The impression of Richmond left by his friends and photographers is that of a more than usually attractive British sea dog. But one feels that he did not really develop his mind in scholarly terms until after his appointment at Cambridge. These three men were inevitably in many respects of the old school because of their up-bringing, and they made on occasion the same mistakes that others have made, before and since, in judging individual weapons. Nevertheless, they made significant contributions to the evolution of modern warfare and to the historical profession with their analytical studies of the art of war. How different and far less modern were the developers of British airpower, who too rarely had their doctrines subjected to public debate.

*Book Two*

# Theory in Practice: The Exponents of Airpower

# Chapter VI — The Heavenly City of the Airpower Philosophers: The Bombing Deterrent, Politics, and Defence — Theories and Effects

As a nation we distrust theory. We learn very quickly from experience, and are obstinately unwilling to learn in any other way. Experience is a costly school, but it teaches nothing false.

SIR WALTER RALEIGH *

It is with grateful apologies to Carl Becker of Cornell University and his *Heavenly City of the Eighteenth Century Philosophers* (New Haven, 1932) that this chapter must commence. For much as the eighteenth century French publicists destroyed one faith only to create another, so the British apostles of airpower led themselves and their followers up an equally fascinating logical canyon. An examination of the process, the ideas, and the results of this crusade is an interesting excursion into human mentality and into the influence of politics upon doctrine. Just as the older Clausewitzians had come to regard the battle as the sole purpose of armed forces, so the airmen came to hold that the logical objective was the national will. They believed that the threat of a gigantic knockout air strike in the opening, and probably the only, days of war would keep the peace. Yet they failed to carry through in providing the means by which this blow could be delivered if war did break out. Their deterrent was neither operable nor, as it turned out in the late thirties, credible to anyone but themselves and their political leaders. And they credited to their opponents powers the latter were not intending to utilize. Yet in analysing this process, readers

* *The War in the Air,* I (1922), 260.

*119*

must remain aware of the fact that the very battle between the airmen and the older Services tended to make for extreme statements that were not supported by the working majority in any of the Services.

The quotation from *The War in the Air,* the official air history of the First World War, at the beginning of this chapter puts the development of air theory in proper perspective. Distrusting a philosophical approach, British airpower began before 1914 on a perfectly practical and logical basis. Each of the two older Services developed an air arm for the campaigns it supposed it would fight. Thus the Royal Naval Air Service was designed to co-operate with the Fleet and with other naval detachments, while the Royal Flying Corps started out as an extension of the reconnaissance function of the cavalry. It was from this latter development that the term "strategic" air offensive sprang. Originally aeroplanes were envisaged as being attached to corps and divisions with the job of scouting the other side of the hill. At Army Headquarters, however, there was to be a small detachment whose job was not tactical, but strategical information. Its pilots would range away from the Army on independent surveys. The creation of the endless Western Front restricted this freedom, but the idea was revived in 1917 when an independent air offensive came to be considered to counter German attacks on England and to outflank Allied generalship in France, which seemed unable to fight a decisive action.

The heritage of the strike-force theories of the interwar years is to be found in the pragmatic development of British air forces in the 1914-18 war. By the end of that conflict most of the basic doctrinal materials were available, though the lessons of experience were not so clear as the official historian thought.*

---

* Except where otherwise noted, the sources for this discussion are Sir Walter Raleigh and H. A. Jones, *The War in the Air* (London, I [1922], II [1928], III [1931], IV [1934], V [1935], VI [1937], and Appendices [1937]); Sir Frederick Sykes, *From Many Angles* (London, 1942); Andrew Boyle, *Trenchard —Man of Vision* (London, 1962); Norman Macmillan, *Sir Sefton Brancker* (London, 1935), and Basil Collier, *Heavenly Adventurer* (London, 1959). Sir Walter Raleigh, Professor of English literature at Oxford, was appointed to write the air history in 1918 and died of typhoid in 1922 contracted while visiting the Middle East to study the battlefields. H. A. Jones, Head of the Air Historical Branch of the Committee of Imperial Defence, took over. Both of these men fell heavily under the influence of Lord Trenchard as did the third of Trenchard's official biographers, Andrew Boyle. As a result, the work of Sir Frederick Sykes, the real founder with Sir David Henderson of the Royal

Under the impetus of Winston Churchill as First Lord and the advice, official and otherwise, of Admiral "Jackie" Fisher, the Royal Navy began experimenting with bombs in early 1912. Cmdr. C. R. Samson and Lt. Clarke-Hall dropped 100-pound dummy bombs and made the necessary calculations to produce a primitive bombsight. Bombing by the R.F.C., however, did not begin to be considered until the winter of 1913-14 and was not made use of until closer to 1915.

The story of the development of the strategic air offensive is not only a tri-Service tale, but it is also inextricably mixed up with one of the least publicized jealousies of the period 1912-22—that between Trenchard and Sykes. This in itself in its middle phase appears to have been part of the greater battle between the soldiers and the politicians, between "the donkeys" and "the frocks" as they have been popularly called. On the one side were Trenchard's friends

Flying Corps, has been carefully slighted. Sykes's most important memoranda of 1918, when he had superseded Trenchard as Chief of the Air Staff, are not included in *The War in the Air,* while in Volume VI, which covers the year 1918, Sykes is mentioned but twice, Trenchard more than twenty times.

*The War in the Air* suffers from one other difficulty: it includes naval material, but much of this was incorporated from notes prepared by the naval historical branch after the death of Sir Julian Corbett in 1922. In addition to the sources dealing specifically with the British side of the First World War, wider-ranging sources include the works mentioned in *Armed Forces in Peacetime,* the many reviews of Andrew Boyle's volume including the long article by Air Chief Marshal Sir Basil Embry in *Stand-To* (Cambera, Australia), VII, No. 4 (July-August 1963), 11-15; Wesley Frank Craven and James Lea Cate, *The Army Air Forces in World War II* (Chicago, 1948-58), General of the Army, H. H. Arnold, *Global Mission* (New York, 1949); H. A. Toulmin, Jr., *Air Service; American Expeditionary Force* (New York, 1927); General Mason B. Patrick, *The United States in the Air* (New York, 1928); various biographies of and writings by General William Mitchell; Hilary St. George Saunders, *Per Ardua* (1944), and the same author with Denis Richards, *The Royal Air Force, 1939-1945* (1953-54), Sir Charles Webster and Noble Frankland, *The Strategic Air Offensive against Germany* (1961), W. R. Clark, "Strategic Bombing," *Stand-To,* VIII (January-February 1963), 1-15; the approximately 200 studies of the *United States Strategic Bombing Survey* of Germany and Japan (Unlike the British strategic bombing survey, these have been published; Webster and Frankland used both the British and the American reports.); the RAND Corporation studies, some by Bernard Brodie listed in the RAND Corporation Index and consolidated in his *Strategy in the Missile Age* (Princeton, 1959); Hilton P. Goss, *Civilian Morale Under Aerial Bombardment, 1914-1939* (Air University, Maxwell, Alabama, 1948); and an unpublished master's thesis by Eugene Emme, the historian of the National Aeronautics and Space Administration, *"German Air Power, 1919-1939"* (State University of Iowa, 1949), not to mention Douglas H. Robinson, *The Zeppelin in Combat* (1961), which studied the world's first strategic air offensive.

Sir William Robertson, the Chief of the Imperial General Staff, and Sir Douglas Haig, the Commander-in-Chief in France, and on the other Sykes's patron Sir Henry Wilson, Robertson's successor, and Lloyd George, the Prime Minister. These frictions were further entangled in the general skein of the conflict between those who believed only that the First World War could be won on the Western Front by a Clausewitzian battle to the death and those "amateur strategists" such as Lloyd George and Winston Churchill, joined later by Field Marshal Smuts of South Africa, who wished to strike decisively in some less bloody manner and more effective place.* The careers of Sir Frederick Sykes and of Sir Hugh Trenchard indicate how all these factors affected the creation of the post-1918 British deterrent theory.

### Sir Frederick Sykes—Organizer of the Royal Flying Corps

It has been said of Sir Frederick that he was one of the few who shaped the early growth of British airpower and deserved an honourable place in the history of the Royal Air Force, though few today have heard of him.† Born in 1877, Sykes was educated in France and spoke French and German fluently. Late in his youth he went to Ceylon to learn tea-planting, but in 1899 at the age of twenty-two he volunteered to serve in the Boer War. Joining the Imperial Yeomanry Scouts, he was wounded and taken prisoner. After the war he was granted a commission in the 15th (The King's) Hussars. In 1903 he was seconded to the West African Regiment at Sierra Leone and on the voyage out met Lt. P. R. C. Groves, who was long to remain a friend and assistant. The next year Sykes made use of his six months' leave to return to England and take courses that would make up for not having attended Sandhurst—musketry, artillery, signalling, transport, veterinary work, topographical surveying, and one at Farnborough in which he obtained his ballooning certificate. In early 1905 he rejoined the regiment in India and there first met Sir Douglas Haig, who was then Inspector-General of Cavalry in India. As a result of his good work

---

* The principles for such action were laid down by Churchill in *The World Crisis*, II, *1915* (New York, 1923), 36-37; see also pages 1-18.

† An appreciation of Sir Frederick by Air Marshal Sir Robert Saundby, former Deputy Commander-in-Chief of Bomber Command under Sir Arthur Harris in the Second World War, was published in *The Aeroplane* (15 October 1954) at the time of Sir Frederick's death.

on maneuvers, Sykes was called to the Intelligence Department at Simla. At the order of the Chief of Staff he wrote *A Military Handbook of General Information on India*, which was designed to be used by Territorials when, as happened in 1914, they were sent out to take over from the Regulars. On leave in England in April 1907 while awaiting the results of the Staff College examinations, he was sent by the War Office to Germany to observe the annual maneuvers. Though in this first examination he failed, on his second he was successful and was posted to the Staff College at Quetta. He acquired a motor car, and as no one could repair it, he took a short course with the Engineers on motor mechanics during the Christmas recess. In 1910 he was head of the directing staff for the June Indian Army cavalry maneuvers, a task in which he made use of his experiences in Germany in 1907. He was shortly posted to rejoin the Hussars, then in South Africa, where he again conducted maneuvers. In August 1910 Sykes was, however, granted home leave to study aviation. Shortly after his arrival the Director of Military Operations at the War Office, Henry Wilson, later C.I.G.S., suggested that Sir Frederick should go to Germany so that he could pass the examination to obtain an interpretership in German and employment by the Directorate. This he did.

After reporting at the War Office, Sykes found time to study aerodynamics at the University of London and took flying lessons at Brooklands, obtaining Royal Aero Club Certificate No. 96 in June 1911, some five months after the Air Battalion, Royal Engineers, had been formed. In 1912 when Brigadier David Henderson * was Director of Military Training, Wilson sent Sykes to ob-

* Sir David Henderson, 1862-1921, has remained one of the shadowy figures in British flying history. After passing through Sandhurst, he joined the Argyll and Sutherland Highlanders. A student of his profession, he was Kitchener's Director of Military Intelligence in South Africa, October 1900 to September 1902. In 1904 he published *Field Intelligence: Its Principles and Practice* followed in 1907 by *The Art of Reconnaissance*. In 1911 at the age of forty-nine he obtained his wings and was soon called to serve on the aviation subcommittee of the Committee of Imperial Defence as he was almost the only high-ranking Army officer with aeronautical experience. In July 1912 he was appointed Director of Military Training at the War Office and transferred in September 1913 to the newly created post of Director-General of Military Aeronautics. From the outbreak of war in August 1914 until October 1917 he was General Officer Commanding the Royal Flying Corps, except for the month in late 1914 in which he took over the First Infantry Division. He died soon after the end of the war. He was one of the better officers of his day, but like his colleagues lacked the necessary ruthlessness when involved in the political situation existing in the later years of the war.

serve the French air force and its aeroplane trials at Rheims. As one of the very few officers who had obtained wings, Sykes not only served with Henderson on the aviation subcommittee of the Committee of Imperial Defence in 1912, but also was the natural choice to draft plans for the Royal Flying Corps that the subcommittee recommended. When the Military Wing was formed in 1912, he was given command with, he says, an oral promise that he would keep it in wartime.* In January 1913 he was promoted lieutenant-colonel. He worked hard and saw to the production of official textbooks, regulations, etc. As the official history notes, that the R.F.C. was ready for war in 1914 was "due to his foresight and initiative." †

Just before the Cambridgeshire maneuvers of September 1912, the General Staff issued a Sykes-inspired memorandum emphasizing that, although aircraft would probably have several wartime duties, their primary one would be to obtain information. In this they would be closely allied with the cavalry, whose work they would complement, but not usurp. The aircraft's advantage was that it could cover so much more territory in so much less time than the horse.

In these years immediately before the First World War, Sykes got to know the First Lord of the Admiralty, Winston Churchill. Upon occasion they spent weekends together discussing airpower in future wars.‡ After the war Churchill seems to have been less enamoured of the careful Sykes, whose views on strategic bombing he had opposed in 1917, than he was with the heroic leader of the Royal Air Force, Trenchard. In retrospect it appears strange that Churchill, so much the "Easterner," should have been so taken with such an ardent supporter of Haig's as Trenchard. But this may have been due in part to Sir Winston's love of heroes and his

* Sykes, *From Many Angles*, p. 89. This was not so improbable as the Royal Flying Corps, Military Wing was then only envisaged as a small ancillary to the British Expeditionary Force, not as a major unit in itself. Though the Committee of Imperial Defence in 1912 thought of a third Service sometime in the future, without the war it is unlikely that it would have come into being in anything like the short span of time that it did.

† The early work of organizing the R.F.C. is covered in moderate detail in *The War in the Air*, I, but Sykes complains in his own book that the records he left behind at Farnborough when Trenchard took over the home base in August 1914 had all disappeared by 1941. One wonders if this was accidental, coincidental, or intentional.

‡ Sykes's ideas will be found in the *Journal of the Royal Aeronautical Society*, XVII (July 1913), 127-139, and XVII (April 1914), 86-101, and in *The Manual of Training of the R.F.C.* (1913).

fascination with machinery, an attraction that could even at times be a distraction, and in part to the fact that both he and Trenchard were opposed to Sykes's ideas.

In early 1914 the first of the differences of opinion between later high-ranking air officers began to become apparent. Maj. W. S. (later Brigadier-General Sir Sefton) Brancker,* writing for Director-General of Military Aeronautics Henderson, opposed Sykes's desire to obtain standardized designs so as to get aircraft into mass production. Each side had a point: Brancker that aircraft were not developed enough for standardization, Sykes that units were inefficient when equipped with many different machines and that production to replace training and operational wastage was hampered by lack of standardization. In typically British fashion a compromise was arranged in which two squadrons were homogenous and two contained mixed bags of aircraft. At this point Sykes regarded Brancker as his greatest rival.

In June 1914 Sykes brought the whole Military Wing, R.F.C., together on his own initiative. At Netheravon they held the final practices and training for war. As both *The Morning Post* on 19 June and *The Daily Telegraph* on 4 July pointed out, the unit was being organized not only to obtain information but also to fight to get it. Sykes was quoted as foreseeing a struggle for mastery of the air in the future and that bombing would have psychological implications for a whole nation, which might well be brought to its knees by a much smaller force than that traditionally employed. Moreover, he predicted, according to his memoirs, that the aeroplane "may prove of the greatest service to such a nation as ours with a temperamental dislike to military service."

Apart from the work of those actively engaged on the Service side of military aviation, others connected with aeronautics had been thinking about the subject. They were the lawyer J. M. Spaight, who will be taken up later, and that most notable student

* Sir Sefton Brancker, 1877-1930, was a jovial monocled artilleryman who entered Woolwich in 1894 and left two years later as "Top Gunner." He served in a number of artillery posts, passed through the staff college in India, learned Tibetan, and joined the Royal Aero Club in 1910, but did not obtain his Certificate, No. 525, until 18 June 1913, though he had already flown as an observer. Like Sykes he had qualified in German. He was appointed G.S.O.2 to the Directorate of Military Aeronautics in August 1913. After the war he succeeded Sykes as Director-General of Civil Aviation and was killed in the crash of the airship *R101*.

of air affairs F. W. Lanchester. Neither Lanchester nor those in the Service owed anything to the Italian pundit Giulio Douhet.*

### THE GENESIS OF AIRPOWER THEORY

As early as the end of 1914 the basic theory of air warfare had been laid down in England by Frederick William Lanchester (1868-1946). A distinguished, independently minded automobile manufacturer whose *Aerial Flight* (1907) was a standard designer's textbook, Lanchester was a charter member of the official Advisory Committee for Aeronautics of 1909 (now the Aeronautical Research Council).†

His major contribution to airpower theory is *Aircraft in Warfare: The Dawn of the Fourth Arm*, published in January 1916 and composed of articles that appeared in *Engineering* in autumn 1914 and early 1915. Lanchester's view was that in addition to the three existing parts of the army—infantry, cavalry, and artillery—there was now a new arm.

In his Introduction to *Aircraft in Warfare* Major-General Sir David Henderson noted that the aeroplane was a new force with new functions, yet with few restrictions upon its development. He was wise enough to recognize that no rule of thumb for the allotment of aircraft to armies existed, but that the only safe line was to proceed on consideration of the services they were required to perform and how much of the available resources could be devoted to these duties. It was, he said, a matter of relative value and not of relative numbers.

Lanchester himself suggested that the great difficulty for a theorist was that the aircraft of the day were undeveloped and in limited numbers. Nevertheless he proceeded to make a valuable contribution to the analysis of their potential. As the title suggests, he saw aircraft primarily as an arm of the surface forces, but with the secondary role of protecting these forces against other air forces. Where the airship was concerned, he quietly presented the case against the lighter-than-air machine for all work but long-range sorties not in the face of the enemy. As early as 11 September 1914

* For this point, see Appendix C, pages 257-259.

† See P. W. Kingsford, *F. W. Lanchester: The Life of an Engineer* (London, 1962). On 9 May 1957 the Royal Aeronautical Society heard the first Lanchester Memorial Lecture.

in an article entitled "Strategical and Tactical Uses of the Aeronautical Arm," he drew the parallel analogy between the air arm and cavalry, pointing out that horsemen were used both for divisional and for independent strategic duties directly under Army headquarters. Since aircraft had far greater mobility and range, they were naturally fitted for this detached role (which studies of the American Civil War were beginning to consider just before the First World War). Lanchester next produced what he called the *N-square law*, which could be applied to either the moral or the material, but not to both at once. He said, "The fighting strength of a force can be represented by the square of its numerical strength." In looking at the Navy, he said that if the units of the whole varied in strength, then the total power of the Fleet would be *"the square of the sum of the square roots of its individual units."* The advent of modern firepower having made battles no longer a matter of man against man owing to the ability to concentrate firepower, it was more than ever necessary to study the principles of war. He believed that while the N-square law applied roughly on land, it had absolute qualities at sea owing to the lack of variables. Much of what followed in the next few articles was devoted to a mathematical analysis of military actions presaging the RAND Corporation approach today in the United States. By page 96 of *Aircraft in Warfare* he was dealing with the real problems of airpower.

Lanchester held that bombers would have to be armed and escorted by fighters because the enemy was bound to protect his materials, oil, and stores with fighters. He predicted that incendiary bombs would be used to set factory debris afire after high-explosive bombs had done the initial damage. As for rockets and aerial torpedoes for use against airships, these would have no future as the "inflated beast" was even in November 1914 obsolescent. (It seems quite probable that these articles of Lanchester's influenced the First Lord, Churchill, against the Admiralty airship programme.) As for airpower affecting surface tactics, he predicted that it would not—until sufficient quantities of machines were available to demonstrate the real capacities of aircraft. Up to late 1914, at least, it appeared that aircraft had strengthened the defence more than the offence by enabling the defence to observe the enemy's concentrations. Defence had the tactical advantage of prepared ground, the offence the strategic asset of the selection of the objective. But the attacker had lost the old veil of secrecy due to air observation, and this tended to produce the stalemate then ensuing in France, which was accentuated by fielding masses of men who were able to man long lines in great depth under the shield of a preponderance of artillery. Aircraft tended only to deepen the defensive line and make it more difficult for the offensive to be launched. When this was accomplished, control of the air became a vital factor, for the side that lost control of its own air space would be unable to concentrate and take the offensive while, when on the defensive, deprived of its visual senses, it was always liable to be surprised. Put simply, Lanchester argued that as long as the defensive side could oversee the attacker's rear areas, he could have little chance of making a surprise attack, but even if he did, the very depth of the defensive positions would make its success doubtful. Lanchester's thinking was very advanced and when he concluded that it was doubtful whether an army that had lost its eyes could continue to fight unless it had a superiority in defensive weapons, he was anticipating what would happen in the Second, but not in the First World War. As he saw it in 1914, given the existing stalemate, the two air fleets would have to battle, as naval groups had before them, for supremacy.* Trenchard translated these conclusions into the unrelenting offensive.

In one of the last articles, that of 4 December 1914, Lanchester dealt with "An Independent Air Fleet and Its Duties." This force, he said, should have as its duty the seeking out and destruction of the enemy, perhaps forcing him to fight by attacking a vital point. Basically the air fleet should have sufficient speed and ceiling to match its opponent and ideally should be composed of homogeneous types, preferably of the same design. In order to make full use of the N-square law, it should attack as a unit. (In November 1914 Kitchener ordered the R.F.C. to learn formation flying. It was first used operationally in 1915.)

In retrospect, it seems quite probable that Lanchester's work was read by Trenchard (through the influence of Henderson) and communicated to Haig. Lanchester's ideas can be seen reflected in the papers that Trenchard wrote for Haig as his air adviser. This is especially so in the case of the use of the D.H.4 by the Independent Air Force of 1918 and in Haig's earlier request that a fourth of

---

* I have placed the text of this section in Appendix A so that it may be compared with Trenchard's Memorandum of 22 September 1916, which is Appendix B.

these machines should be fitted as fighter-escorts rather than as bombers. In its day the D.H.4 was faster than the opposing fighters and had a very good ceiling, but that advantage did not last long. Sykes also appears to have been familiar with Lanchester's works, which was only natural as he was Henderson's Chief of Staff in the early days of the war.

On the question of the development of aerial battleships, Lanchester seemed to feel that these would come, though they would be single-seaters, simply because the need to concentrate could not be accomplished with a large and unwieldy swarm of smaller planes. Moreover, said Lanchester, the bigger ships were apt to be faster and able to climb higher.* But, said the automobile engineer, where command of the seas could be world-wide, command of the air could be only local owing to the lack of key positions from which decisive control could be exercised. In Europe, he felt, the great powers would seek supremacy over their own territories in peacetime, and peripheral bases sufficient to deter hostile aircraft on the outbreak of war. In war the role of the air arm would be to maintain control of the skies at home and over the Army and Navy units abroad. This air Service was not a new kind of navy nor an independent service to which large-scale, extra-battlefield duties might be assigned, but rather a Fourth Arm. In peacetime the air Service would require about 5,000 aircraft if it were to be the equivalent of one per cent of the number of bayonets in the Army. It would have to guard against accidents because of the importance given to casualties other than in war. And most important, while for obvious reasons Lanchester tended to favour the Royal Aircraft Factory, he urged the need of a continuous policy in peacetime in order to

---

* Sykes, p. 224, writing in 1941, noted that, unless unlimited production capacity was available, there were advantages in a large number of smaller high-speed aircraft, which could be more rapidly turned out and manned than a comparatively few large and complicated machines. The latter suffered also from the fact that their production had to be more concentrated and was thus more vulnerable to bombing. Moreover, the handling of large machines required not only larger crews, but also longer training for both air and ground staff. The large long-range bomber needed long-range escort fighters. But, he added, the big, well-armed and armoured bomber was the most effective weapon for retaliatory defence and for offensive uses. It must be remembered that he wrote this just when Bomber Command was going into action with Lancasters and Halifaxes. Webster and Frankland, *The Strategic Air Offensive against Germany, 1939-1945* (1961) would only agree on smaller high-speed aircraft such as the Mosquito.

maintain strength through a vital aircraft industry. He was correct about accidents and about the industry.

When he came to some areas of an air force's work, Lanchester could not say much as there was too little experience to go by. But he did reckon that if bombers were concentrated in time over their target they would lose fewer craft to anti-aircraft fire from guns sited outside the target area as the losses to these would be constant and not dependent upon the numerical strength of the attackers. (This approach was adopted over France in November 1915 and over Germany from 1942 on.) In this line then, he predicted that bombers of the future would carry but one large bomb and make but one run over the target. But as so much of air development was still at the threshold, what he predicted would be a revolution in warfare. For, when sufficient aircraft became available, the new technique of war would be to maintain a continuous attack upon all points of strategic importance so as to create a virtually impassable zone a couple of hundred miles deep in the rear of the opposing army, one that would both strangle the defence and make retreat impossible. This would enable a bloodless victory to be won, for it gave the enemy no choice but to retreat early, surrender, or be annihilated.

In November 1915 Lanchester wrote that just because Zeppelin raids on Britain did not for the moment pay the Germans, there was no reason to assume that other raids would not follow; therefore, it was essential that defensive steps be taken in 1915 and not when the next raids commenced. Britons, he said, had to fear such an act of war, which could overcome the fire-fighting apparatus of London, for neither fighters nor anti-aircraft guns could beat off all aircraft without a stupendous effort. Once the enemy could overcome the fire brigades, he could wreak havoc out of all proportion to his efforts. "It is futile to attempt to disguise the self-evident fact that a serious attack on the capital city of an enemy containing in its heart the administrative center both of his Army and Navy in addition to the Headquarters of his Government, cannot be regarded other than as a legitimate act of warfare. No international agreement or convention can make it otherwise." To bomb London, he wrote, was not unethical but in fact the duty of an enemy government, which should not neglect any act that would enable it successfully to prosecute a war. Conversely, measures of defence had to be proportioned to the incentive to attack. If this held true, then one form of defence for London was to remove the Government from it, an idea officially investigated from 1924 to 1937.

When, held Lanchester, a wanton raid of no military value was delivered, then it had to be answered at once with an appropriate reprisal. Thus the Government should not reside in London in peacetime, for an enemy air fleet might well open a war without warning by a surprise blow. There was no proof yet in 1915, he wrote, that adequate defence against air attack was impossible, but that contingency might have to be faced. Nevertheless, he suggested that measures of defence should include a vigilant air force, fire-proof city construction and town-planning to limit conflagrations, a well-equipped fire department, and an active aircraft industry out of range of enemy aircraft and defensible (i.e., located, say, at Belfast) with due recognition given to the tremendous importance of a steady daily output of machines. As the aeronautical arm was not a matter solely for the Army or the Navy but for the Nation, he joined the general cry of the time for a thorough overhaul of the air forces, which led in 1917 to the agreement to create the Air Ministry and the Royal Air Force.

In a footnote written in November 1915, Lanchester said significantly:

> The power of reprisal and the knowledge that the means of reprisal exist will ever be a far greater deterrent than any pseudo-legal document.

Unlike the American air force, the R.A.F. seems to have lacked a sense of historical investigation and retrospection. The very power of Trenchard coupled with his enigmatic nature, the disproportionate glory assigned to the dogfighters of the First World War, and the subsequent fight to save the independent air force, all seem to have overshadowed the way in which doctrine came to be created. Moreover, men seldom like to acknowledge their mental indebtedness to others. The result has been that Lanchester has been slighted. Far more than the overrated Douhet he, and others to be mentioned, seems to have provided a basic handbook on the use of an air force, even devoting a chapter to actions of the naval air wing.

It is too easy in the pursuit of intellectual trends to claim that men were under the influence of some individual of whom they may never have heard, when in fact in their own backgrounds the materials were present that could be mixed into the particular ideas of survival that they preached or appeared to be operating under. But in Lanchester's case, there is much less speculation. He was, after all, a distinguished engineer. His work with the Advisory Committee for Aeronautics placed him in constant contact with Captain Murray Sueter of the Naval Wing of the Royal Flying Corps * and with Henderson of the Military Wing, as well as with Colonel Mervyn O'Gorman, the head of the Royal Aircraft Factory at Farnborough, and with others such as Capt. Geoffrey de Havilland, designer for the Royal Aircraft Factory and for the Aircraft Manufacturing Company. How much Trenchard read is, unfortunately, not indicated to us by his biographer. But, as mentioned earlier, it seems fairly safe to assume that Henderson brought Lanchester's book, if not his articles, to Trenchard's notice. Sykes and Groves, too, must have read them. F. W. Lanchester himself, however, seems to have remained one of the forgotten men of British aviation.

He has been far outshone by Sykes, Groves, Smuts, and by Marshal of the Royal Air Force Lord Trenchard himself.

### TRENCHARD—MYTHICAL FATHER OF THE R.A.F.

Born in February 1873 of a respectable middle-class family that went bankrupt, Hugh Trenchard attended various private schools where he lived an isolated and uninterested life. Finally through the traditional crammer's efforts he entered the Army on the third try as a militia candidate, for which the requirements were lower than for Woolwich or Sandhurst. He placed eighth from the bottom of the infantry list in 1893 and was shortly gazetted to the second battalion of the Royal Scots Fusiliers in India. The unpromising schoolboy at last found a sense of belonging and began to blossom. He took fierce pride in his regiment, but his ambitions appeared to rise no higher than his organization of a polo team. The last-named brought him two gifts—a knack for organization and a chance contact with a subaltern named Winston Churchill.

He spent other of his spare time reading biographies of men of action whose drive to the top he dreamed, Mittylike, of emulating. It is said that he read on the quiet, for Army officers did not read books, and that he enlarged his knowledge this way. What else he

* Officially the R.N.A.S. did not come into being until 1914; before that it was part of the R.F.C.

absorbed besides the standard schoolboy's love for heroes in the Henty fashion we are not told. After a hernia operation he developed an acute dislike for illness and it took him a great while to treat those who were sick with sympathy. On the other hand, he was of his time and class in considering sport more healthy than church-going. When the war in South Africa broke out, Trenchard pestered his colonel, then went over his head to get there. But as a proper officer he would never in his life admit that the leadership of the British army in the Boer War was incompetent. By the time Tren-chard reached South Africa the frontal attacks against concealed Boers in natural positions had been replaced by more mobile and flexible tactics. So Trenchard found himself detailed to form a mounted unit, an offensive polo force. Moreover, he was restricted in training only by general orders and was free, not for the last time in his life, to develop new methods of warfare. Unfortunately he was seriously wounded in one of his early engagements and was sent back to England. But sheer determination got him back to South Africa, where he became a troubleshooter for Kitchener, a contact that soon got him promoted to major. In 1903 he found himself in the usual postwar military quandary and opted to become Assistant Commandant of the South Nigerian Regiment. Always somewhat of a lone hand whose philosophy was that if everyone detested you, you must be on the right track,* he enjoyed the challenge of in-dependent command in West Africa, where he was able to play the Hentyan role to the full. Respect for pompous superiors was not his strong point, though he later learned to be more subtle in handling persons he regarded as incompetent or obstructive. At the same time, he developed a great respect for the use of force and sought never to employ it except upon the battlefield. In 1910 illness again dogged him and he was shipped home with an abscess on the liver to add to the weak lung punctured on the veldt and the partially paralysed hand that made writing so difficult that most of his minutes in later years were typed by a secretary.

Once again restored to health, he was posted to his regiment at Londonderry, where he soon became bored with routine peacetime soldiering. In February 1912 he applied for a post with the mounted branch of the Colonial Defence Forces in Australia, New Zealand, or South Africa. In May he sought service with the Macedonian

* He told Wing/Cmdr. Norman MacMillan that criticism made him and that he learned never to pull his punches. (*Great Airmen* (1955), 147-157.)

Gendarmerie. Suddenly in the spring a chance letter from a former colleague in Nigeria who was learning to fly in the infant R.F.C. suggested a novel escape. Trenchard at thirty-nine applied for three months' paid leave and went off to Weybridge to become a pilot. After one hour and forty minutes of flying time he got his wings (Royal Aero Club pilot's certificate No. 270) and then proceeded to the Central Flying School at Upavon. He was soon made an instructor and later adjutant of the unit. Again his organizing abilities came to the fore. He could not help but be noticed by the Director of Military Training at the War Office, Brigadier David Henderson, author of books on reconnaissance. While at the school Trenchard made the acquaintance of other rising important men such as John and Geoffrey Salmond, Sefton Brancker, Hugh Dowding, and Edgar Ludlow-Hewitt, all of whom played key roles in the interwar and early Second World War R.A.F. He also came to rival Lt/Col. Frederick Sykes, the dapper commander of the Military Wing, R.F.C., for whom he developed an instant dislike and disrespect. Though he is credited with being a very good judge of men, he had the natural sports-oriented career officer's dislike of certain types. In sharp contrast was the able and articulate Sykes, by now something of a politician, a staff officer more than a regimental one, with a notable career. Sykes earned more aversion than he deserved at first sight while in the ensuing years conflicting ambitions and interest made him and Trenchard the deadliest of rivals, those for supreme command. In 1914 Trenchard was a simple soldier with the rigid military caste outlook on moral values and a belief that politics was another sphere of activities quite detached from military life. In the field he was to belong throughout the war to the *offensive à outrance* school of the day.

On the outbreak of war Trenchard proceeded to Farnborough and on 12 August took over the base depot from Sykes, who was off to France. There Sykes would be Henderson's Chief of Staff of the Royal Flying Corps. Before they departed, friction between Trenchard and Sykes apparently came into the open. In later years Trenchard complained to his biographer that Sykes was uncivil. Sykes, however, had been working night and day in the heat getting the organization overseas. It does not seem unreasonable to believe that when an ancient major, adjutant of the Central Flying School, appeared to take command, the peacetime commandant of the Corps, whose promised position had just been usurped by a friend of Field Marshal Lord Kitchener, the newly appointed Secretary of State for War, should be rather quick in handing over and departing, for he was afraid that the war might be over before he could get there.

Additional cause for friction probably existed in Trenchard's pique at finding that Sykes had taken all the aircraft with him. Sykes notes that this was the wish of the General Staff and of the Committee of Imperial Defence, who also thought the war would be short. Moreover, it had started before the R.F.C. was up to strength. At this point it seems a little premature of Sir Walter Raleigh to say of Trenchard in command at Farnborough, "the Royal Flying Corps had found its destined Chief."

When by October it became obvious that the war was not going to be won at once, the call went out from the commander of the B.E.F., Sir John French, for an immediate increase in the R.F.C. At the same time Sir John asked for the new units to be organized, trained, and equipped in exactly the same manner as the squadrons then in the field. These plans were naturally supported by Sykes as they reflected credit upon his prewar work. They were opposed at home by Trenchard and Brancker, now Assistant Director of Aeronautics (Henderson was still Director, though also commanding in France). Trenchard proposed that instead of keeping the Headquarters Wing and one Wing with each Army, which Sykes had developed with Henderson in furtherance of the intention of the C.I.D. subcommittee in 1912 that eventually a third Service should be created, the R.F.C. should be distributed at Corps and Divisional level. On 18 November the Army Council adopted the Trenchard-Brancker view and so notified Henderson, who replied to the contrary for he was aware, says Sykes, of the danger of the R.F.C. being dominated by generals ignorant of how to use it.

On 22 November Henderson was given an infantry division and Sykes was promoted colonel and placed in command. This did not suit Trenchard's plans, and he took advantage of his acquaintance-ship with Kitchener to call this fact to the Secretary's attention. Whereupon Kitchener, declaring that he needed Henderson to carry through the planned expansion of the R.F.C., reinstated Sir David in command on 20 December but left Sykes in his new rank. Meanwhile, on 18 November Trenchard had arrived in France with a new Wing, which allowed the distribution on 25 December of one Wing to each Army. Trenchard's went to Haig's First Army, while a small nucleus of a third Wing remained at G.H.Q.*

The very first meeting between Trenchard and Haig seemed to weld a bond between them, and thereafter the taciturn Lowland Scot, the future Field Marshal, leaned heavily upon Trenchard for air advice and often, indeed, sent in "Boom's" thoughts as his own, an old military and official habit.

In command of the First Wing, Trenchard developed many of the characteristics that he was to use so effectively later, though often in more restricted form. He constantly visited his squadrons, inspiring his men with his own force of character and at the same time picking their brains for shortcuts, economies, efficiency, and new ideas. But as far as has been revealed, he, unlike Sykes, was much like his contemporaries; as a general he remained behind the lines and never flew operationally,† though he was often flown to visit his units.

Trenchard is credited with initiating debriefings as a means of finding out as much as possible from the men who actually went over the lines. Yet he remained a soldier in his approach towards operations. He believed in the offensive and that the air arm was solely an offensive weapon. He was not matured or educated enough to see that superior results might be obtained with better training and that no campaign could be waged to the hilt all the time.‡

* The fact that the accounts given of this incident by Jones, Sykes, and Boyle are quite dissimilar lends strength to the suggestion that politics rather than military necessity governed these changes in command. Sykes was Trenchard's junior in age, but not in acting rank, and had far more experience of the air service. Whether, as Boyle states, Trenchard accepted command of only one of the three wings on Henderson's assurance that Sykes would never command the R.F.C. is open to doubt. True, he hated Sykes, but would that have caused him to deny himself command in the field? Was this statement not, perhaps, a later invention to further blacken Sykes's reputation to the advantage of Sir Hugh's?

† This was again one of the difficulties of the Second World War. Very few higher officers flew on operations and so most lacked experience of actual conditions. The reason for this was the fear that such a man might be captured (or killed) much to the advantage of the enemy. But such a risk was probably outweighed by the insights to be gained from even one trip over enemy territory. See the comments upon this by Webster and Frankland, I, 53, n. 1; 427, n. 2; and by D. C. T. Bennett, *Pathfinder* (London, 1958), 162 ff. This was less true in the American Army Air Force, where quite a number of generals flew.

‡ One wonders how much British adherence to the concept of the continuous offensive was due to their experience of colonial wars in which casualties were rarely heavy, the advantage of firepower with the European troops, and in the Anglo-Saxon psychology of superiority over the natives an inestimable moral

Rest and regrouping, training and practice were essential to success. Those in charge of aircraft production at home, Brancker and later Sir William Weir, Sir David Henderson on regaining control over the air defences of Britain, and even the stolid C.I.G.S., Sir William Robertson, all complained that Trenchard's casualty rate was too high.* Trenchard may also have forgotten that Lanchester was talking of the future and not of the present in his comments upon air superiority. The French commander of the day, Commandant du Peuty,† was more willing to recognize that even air forces might have to go on the defensive. In fact, despite the impression that the sky had no barriers, aircraft radius of action was an effective one. Fighter sweeps could gain air superiority in a local area and offensive methods had to be employed to do so. But such action could not be undertaken indefinitely with the resources then available without reckless expenditure of men and materials. Moreover, when air superiority was lost, neither side collapsed, vital secrets were not exposed, and the war did not end.

In December 1914 Henderson went on sick leave and Sykes remained in charge of the R.F.C. in France with Trenchard under him in command of one Wing and Robert Brooke-Popham of the other. This situation lasted until 26 May, when Brooke-Popham succeeded Sykes as Chief of Staff a few days after Henderson returned from sick leave in Britain. But Kitchener came to realize that what Sykes had pointed out in his memorandum of 30 October 1914 was true: the Director of Military Aeronautics was the crucial post in the organization and Henderson could not continue in France. After Lloyd George became Minister of Munitions, Henderson was recalled and on 19 August 1915 Trenchard was raised to the command of the R.F.C. in France.

Once again the position of Sykes is obscure. It is stated in the official history that he was brought back to England and that after

advantage. The British tommies' magnificent disregard of the odds stems, no doubt, from a long tradition of overcoming adverse ones. This ability did not encourage good generalship.

* Robertson in *Private to Field Marshal* (London, 1921, 224) said of Trenchard's losses in 1915 that they were caused by his sending his boys into action too young with the result that their recklessness caused unnecessary loss of life. See also *The War in the Air*, II, 325; III, 293, 339-340.

† Interestingly though Boyle makes a good deal of him, French aviation history seems largely to neglect Commandant du Peuty. Not even his first name seems to be easily available.

that the Admiralty asked for his services. Sykes says that a few days after Henderson returned, he (Sykes) received a letter from the War Office saying that the Admiralty had asked for his services to survey and report upon the organization and operations of the Royal Naval Air Service at the Dardanelles.* It seems most probable that some reshuffle in the R.F.C. was desirable. No doubt Brancker objected to the return of Sykes to the Directorate of Military Aeronautics as the two were unlikely to see eye-to-eye. Pressures were being put upon Kitchener by Brancker and Trenchard, and in these maneuvers the role of Henderson is unclear. But it is obvious that Sykes, though he had met Kitchener in India, was not of the clique. Therefore, the need to move him laterally out of the way. The Dardanelles was regarded by Kitchener as a diversion, but Churchill, the First Lord of the Admiralty, thought it vital. Thus it was possible to shunt Sykes off to another appointment that Churchill could persuade him was important, though he himself resigned as First Sea Lord in May. At any rate, Sykes proceeded to the Mediterranean, took stock of the situation, reported back, and on 24 July was appointed to command the Royal Naval Air Service (R.N.A.S.) in the Eastern Mediterranean with the rank of wing captain. It was while there that he directed raids against the Turkish capital of Constantinople, feats that he considered the first operations of an independent air force. In early 1916, upon completion of the withdrawal from Gallipoli, Sykes was returned to the War Office, the Admiralty expressing appreciation of his services. He was soon posted to convert the Fourth Mounted Division into a cyclist unit and then to organize the new Machine-Gun Corps. He was not again associated with the development of air warfare until he was appointed Chief of the Air Staff in 1918.

In only a year and a few days after the war began, Trenchard found himself raised from adjutant of the Central Flying School to General Officer Commanding the R.F.C. in France, from major to brigadier-general. His wartime contribution to the Royal Air Force of the future was to create the fighting traditions so essential to the morale of a military service and to keep them alive in peacetime.

---

* Churchill has nothing to say of this in *The World Crisis, 1915*, written after the war while Trenchard was Chief of the Air Staff. Nor does Corbett mention it. Boyle says that when in the spring of 1917 Smuts investigated Sykes as replacement for Trenchard as Chief of the Air Staff, no one knew why Sykes had been removed in 1915, while Robertson actually supported Sykes for Chief of Air Staff.

Discipline and organization were his forte; strategy was not. He was later to become known as the father of the R.A.F., a title that, with reason, he disliked.

Trenchard was never at his best very articulate; in fact, he was in this respect, again, perhaps typical of the officers of his generation. Maurice Baring, the scholar who became his secretary and remembrancer in August 1915, possessed the great advantage of being not only an interpreter, both of languages and of Trenchardian rumblings, but also a master of prose.* Later he was succeeded by Christopher Bullock and the small brains trust at the Air Ministry in which S/Ldr. MacKay and S/Ldr. Jack Slessor served. Perhaps Trenchard was not in the popular sense of the word an *intellectual*. But he occupied a dominating position and was not only the spokesman for but also the executor of both policy and doctrine, and his influence upon the Royal Air Force and its predecessor cannot be denied. Much of this may have been due to force of personality and to a more-than-average organizing ability; that it has not been heretofore given sufficient limelight has been due to the nature of his position, to his own abhorrence of personal publicity, and to his failure to tell the inside story. Yet in the 1920's he controlled the future destiny of England, and in the thirties his disciples ruled. If Liddell Hart and Sir Thomas Inskip had not pressed for defence of the home base so that the bombing offensive could be launched safely, England might well have been Nazified in 1940. The truth is that until almost 1944 the deterrent striking spear was only a shaft with neither war tip nor launching arm, and even thereafter it did not have the power, by itself, to be decisive.

The British first used tactical bombing deliberately in the battle of Neuve Chapelle of March 1915. Trenchard followed this in September with an ambitious short-range programme in conjunction with the battle of Loos.† It was from the pattern of these attacks at Loos, some of which went forty miles behind the German front, that Trenchard would conduct the operations of the Independent Air Force in 1918.

In introducing the section entitled "The Policy of the Strategic

---

* Baring's autobiography is *R.F.C., H.Q., 1914-1918* (London, 1920). In 1930 this work was reissued by another publisher with the title *Flying Corps Headquarters, 1914-1918.*

† Boyle, *Trenchard—Man of Vision*, p. 149, errs in saying that the Loos action was the first use of tactical raids in land warfare. Antedating Neuve Chapelle were Italian operations in Libya in 1912 and French in France in 1914.

Air Offensive," in *The War in the Air,* II, H. A. Jones says the strategic air offensive is fundamental, axiomatic, and founded on nothing more than the principle of the offensive. "The moral effect of aircraft attack is so great that those who are attacked from the air always call for protection." As aeroplanes cannot be scattered over the face of the earth, they must be used to carry the war to the land of the enemy and keep it there. "The air war becomes a test of nervous endurance. The nation which keeps a stiff upper lip, and whose air service adheres to its determined offensive, of course will, in the end, secure the greatest measure of protection from the air for all its various activities." This was written in the middle twenties when Trenchard was Chief of the Air Staff, but it introduces a section in the official history dealing with the evolution of air doctrine in 1915. At that time and for most of the rest of the war, Army G.H.Q. viewed the battleground in France as the testing place of moral forces. At the same time, as noted earlier, the term "strategic" simply meant operations carried out beyond the limits of Corps work, but still within the Army zone. That is not what strategic meant after 1923.

In the autumn of 1915 Trenchard and du Peuty of the French Air Force discussed strategic air offensive policy and came to the conclusion that the best way to protect Corps aircraft engaged on reconnaissance and spotting duties was to fight the enemy and to subdue him away from aircraft co-operating directly with the Army. Thus, by early 1916 there were created two fighting Wings whose sole duty for the rest of the war was attrition of the enemy fighter force.* Their losses were more than double the German.

At the same time as these discussions were taking place, unity in equipment was making possible changes in tactics. On 25 November, nine aircraft bombed military buildings near Achiet-le-Grand and showed that groups of aircraft did not offer exaggerated targets to anti-aircraft guns, as Lanchester had said they would not. The Third Wing was also experimenting with another conception, a basic principle of war—the concentration of force with all aircraft attacking one target. This tactic was introduced into the R.F.C. in January 1916. By March 1916 as many as twenty-three bombers and eight escorts could attack a single target in formation.

The year 1916 was destined to be one of disappointment. The

---

* After the Somme, Trenchard issued a memorandum containing his views. This will be found in Appendix B.

Dardanelles were evacuated; Townshend surrendered at Kut; the Turks pressed close to the Suez Canal; the Western Front bled profusely in the unproductive battles on the Somme, while at home agitation for a change of government and of the organization of the air Service mounted. It was intended during early 1916 that Trenchard should go home to relieve Henderson, who would reassume command in the field. But German air raids on the Midlands prevented this. At the same time the Army-Navy quarrel over aeronautical procurement was leading towards a full-dress inquiry and the institution of various Air Boards under Lords Derby, Curzon, and Cowdray. To head off some of this agitation, the Government decided early in 1916 to make Henderson a member of the Army Council. It seems clear today that another force militating against Trenchard's transfer was Commander-in-Chief Haig's desire to keep his air adviser with whom he was so much in sympathy. And so for two more years Trenchard remained as General Officer Commanding.

In the battle of Verdun the French showed that offensive fighter patrols could keep the enemy busy enough that bomber raids could cross the front and penetrate unmolested to local targets. But this was not to hold true, despite Trenchard's beliefs, in the longer raids when the enemy decided the target was worth defending, with fighters withdrawn from the reach of Allied offensive patrols as Lanchester had predicted. The Trenchardian insistence on the offensive led to high casualties (30 to 50 per cent per month), and these losses were attacked in the House of Commons. Coupled with the logistical difficulties and the cries for home defence, Noel Pemberton-Billing's remarks in Parliament helped create the Air Board and ultimately the Air Ministry when German raids on London were renewed in daylight in mid-1917. With the soldier-of-the-day's disdain for politics, Trenchard failed to understand the significance of these developments. He thought Pemberton-Billing, sometime owner of the Supermarine Aviation Works, a nuisance, but that was all.

### The British Operational Origins of Strategic Bombing

Apart from the few spasmodic raids on Constantinople conducted by the units attached to the Dardanelles operation, little had been done on the British side with long-range bombing other than by the

Royal Navy in direct connection with its own problems. Except for the Zeppelins, neither side in the West had any machines suitable for strategic raiding until about 1916. The Admiralty requirement for a long-range bomber was published in December 1914. The Handley Page o/100 first flew in December 1915 and began to become operational the following September. It could carry sixteen 112-pound bombs.

Though Trenchard in June 1916 dutifully put forward a scheme for more bombers, including a ten-squadron long-range striking force, he was not in favour of a strategic force operating independently, but only of a tactical. He feared that while the French and the Royal Naval Air Service dissipated the air effort in long-range raids against enemy munitions centers, the Germans would gain air superiority over the Western Front. His antipathy to the naval effort was increased not only by his failure to acquire naval pilots and equipment to aid in his own continuous costly offensive, but also by the arrival in the spring of 1916 of naval aircraft at Luxeuil, near Belfort, to undertake long-range work.

Even before the war the Royal Navy had thought in terms of carrying the war to the enemy. The outstanding example of this was Fisher's Baltic Plan to land Russian troops on the Pomeranian coast under the protection of the Royal Navy so as to strike directly at Berlin. Churchill, ever the proponent of aggressive ideas, supported a number of these schemes designed to hit the enemy where he was least expecting a blow, with the consequent greater psychological effect. The Royal Naval Air Service had in the early days of the war made a number of notable, if puny, raids into Germany including the attack on Friederichshafen, the home of the Zeppelin constructors. But most of its efforts had had to be concentrated upon helping the Fleet, covering coastal waters in which U-boats were a nuisance, and from July 1914 to February 1916 conducting the air defence of Great Britain. As soon as it was relieved of that task, its commander, Rear-Admiral C. L. Vaughan-Lee submitted to his superiors a memorandum calling for bombing of German industrial targets as part of the campaign against U-boats and in aid of the blockade. What Vaughan-Lee was advocating was an extension of the policy already initiated by Wing-Captain C. L. Lambe in command of the Dunkirk Wing, R.N.A.S. He had in November 1915 obtained approval for a bombing offensive to strike at German airfields and Zeppelin sheds from which attacks upon England were being made. Lambe's offensive took some time to organize, and it was not until 20 March 1916 that an Anglo-French force was able to attack German air bases in Belgium as a reprisal for a German raid on Dover and Ramsgate on the nineteenth. Intermittent raiding by the Dunkirk Wing brought retaliation upon Dover and Dunkirk on 19-20 May. This in its turn raised the question of counterattack, but as most of the enemy-held towns within reach were in Belgium, it was eventually decided that these tactics would have to be dropped until raids against Germany itself could be undertaken. In the meantime, standing patrols were instituted to fend off future German raiders. Lambe noted in June 1916 that it was obviously inadvisable to start a bombing offensive unless one had the pilots and machines to run it day and night, and the necessary fast fighters to prevent retaliation by day.*

The Luxeuil Wing came into being to strike at German steelworks in the Saar basin. Much of its force was dissipated through the Admiralty's lending an ear to Trenchard's pleas for more aircraft in support of the Somme battlefront, which was starved by the failure of production in Britain. The result was that by September Trenchard had received sixty-two of the seventy-two aircraft allotted to the naval bombing force. The most marked effect of these raiders was the creation on 8 October 1916 in Germany of a unified air command and Home Defence organization. The R.N.A.S. irritated the Germans enough to strengthen their defences, while achieving little material damage. Once again a surprise in force had been thrown away by premature action as at the Dardanelles and with the tanks.

The differences between Trenchard and the Admiralty appeared at almost every point and came to a head in the summer of 1917 when discussions were taking place as to the types of aircraft to order for 1918 and to their roles. Trenchard and Haig argued against twin-engined aircraft and night bombing, but their case was undermined by Captain Vyell Vyvyan of the R.N.A.S. pointing out that Trenchard knew nothing about the twin-engined Handley Pages, which had in fact a lower loss rate than Trenchard's own

---

* It was believed that nothing could be done about hostile aircraft at night, which was certainly the experience of Lambe's bomber force. Trenchard, too, called for night bombing of enemy back areas in early 1916, but the R.F.C. was so poorly trained that no raids could be undertaken until courses in night-flying were started that spring.

D.H.4 single-engined bombers. The R.N.A.S. at Dunkirk had found that one Handley Page with a crew of three could carry as much bombload for fifty-four gallons of petrol per 100 miles as six D.H.4's using six engines, twelve crew, and 120 gallons of petrol. Moreover, a naval study showed that night bombing was more effective than day, though the latter had a higher psychological value, for there were more calm nights than days, defences upon the ground were more inaccurate, and fighter opposition negligible, while aircraft could operate at a lower altitude carrying more bombs and dropping them more accurately. It was while these discussions were in progress that the Germans made their daylight Gotha aeroplane raids on London, and these had dynamic political effects.

The immediate military result was to order reprisal bombing after the raid of 4-5 September 1917. That this new offensive, which began on 17 October, was undertaken with D.H.4's was due simply to the unexpected accident of the Russian Revolution, which made fifty such aircraft previously allotted for the Eastern Front available. The effect of the few attacks undertaken upon German industrial cities further augmented the clamour in Germany for defences and diverted German strength from the Front. But in these operations the bombers did not always get through, and in recognition of this the newer programmes of procurement of 1917 and 1918 called for 25 per cent of the bombers produced to be armed as escort fighters. In some cases casualties were very heavy, as when on 31 July 1918 No. 99 Squadron lost ten out of twelve aircraft to forty attacking fighters. Writing later, the official historian (H. A. Jones) noted that "the success of day raiding depended upon the efficacy with which formations could be kept." * Several of the daylight raids proved to be devastating in their morale effect owing to the breakdown of the German warning system and the subsequent high casualties incurred, notably at Cologne on 18 May 1918, at Düren on 1 August, and at Bonn on 31 October.

By February 1918 the reprisal raids were having enough effect that the King of Spain on behalf of the Germans raised the question of limiting bombing. The British General Staff drew up the reply

---

* The same thought remained uppermost in the minds of the commanders of Bomber Command early in World War II, until it was conclusively shown that cannon-armed fighters were more than a match for machine-gun equipped Wellingtons, formation or no. The U.S. 8th Air Force had to learn this for itself again in 1943.

of the London government citing the German General Staff as their authority for saying that the sole criterion as to the legality of bombardment was whether or not the place attacked possessed at the moment military value for the enemy. Who could say what was an undefended town? To make this limitation would obviously hamper the freedom of action of the new strategic bombing force that was then being considered.

In the various manipulations in London towards the end of 1916 connected with the dissolution of the old Asquithian government, the Air Board had been partially involved. When it moved in January 1917 into the Hotel Cecil, it co-opted Sir William Weir, the knowledgeable Scottish industrialist, to handle air procurement. Weir's ambition was to gut the industrial heart of Germany by long-range bombing, for with his experience he knew where the sinews of war lay most exposed. It was Weir who persuaded Lord Cowdray, the third head of the Air Board, to develop a strategic striking force as a counter to the U-boat. And Weir could work with Trenchard because he was familiar with air problems and could meet the leader of the R.F.C. in France upon his own ground. Trenchard's hesitancy to endorse any sort of long-range effort was based upon his concern not only with Haig's offensives, but also with the mutinously low morale of the French. But even more, Trenchard regarded it as a lesson of war that once reprisal bombing was undertaken, it should never be allowed to drop off, for that would enable the enemy to undertake a campaign of his own. At the same time, he was well aware that German air raids on Britain were a form of indirect approach designed to create public clamour and to pull off aircraft from the Western Front. In his view, the only way to stop the attacks was to completely knock out the Germans on the Western Front. Here again Trenchard reflects the military mind. While recognizing the game the enemy was playing, he wished to ignore political considerations and make the problem very simple by launching a massive offensive over the trenches.

THE FORMATION OF A UNIFIED AIR COMMAND AND STAFF

All through the war there had been growing a difference of opinion both within the Cabinet and between the politicians and their military advisers as to the conduct of the war. The first moves of those who stood for all-out conduct of the war had been to gain power. This had been accomplished in December 1916 when Lloyd George succeeded Asquith as Prime Minister. But Lloyd George's position was far from secure despite his dictatorial powers, even after he was able to bring that other great "amateur strategist" Winston Churchill into the Government as Minister of Munitions on 16 July 1917. This meant that the Prime Minister had to move slowly and tread warily. The removal of Kitchener had already antagonized a number of influential persons. His death in the sea was politically fortunate for the Lloyd George group. The U-boat campaign and the action taken to revamp the Admiralty, which would culminate in late 1917 in the removal of Jellicoe from his post as First Sea Lord, was another policy fraught with domestic perils. Relations between Lloyd George and the War Office were also becoming strained owing to the natural doubts that he as an "Easterner" had about the forthcoming Passchendaele offensive that Haig was opening in mid-1917. This led to friction with C.I.G.S. Sir William Robertson, culminating in his dismissal on 18 February 1918. Lloyd George never felt quite strong enough to attack Haig directly and so had to concern himself with ways of limiting his power as it became increasingly obvious that the Field Marshal's only solution to the stalemate on the Western Front was yet another bloody offensive in a campaign of attrition. All of these currents were thus present when the Germans made their first daylight aeroplane raid on London on 13 June 1917.

In this they achieved complete surprise. As a result, the casualties were greater than in all the previous Zeppelin raids put together. The Gotha appeared to be a weapon "of indefinite possibilities." A few hours later a Cabinet meeting was held at which Robertson, of all people, proposed and the Cabinet accepted a vast increase in the number of aircraft being produced. At the same time he plumped for a fully independent ministerial Air Department, much to the amazement of Haig and Trenchard, who firmly regarded the R.F.C. as an Army unit. Even so, Trenchard continued to think of the air offensive that had been anticipated by the order for an additional ten bombing squadrons in the late 1916 programme as designed solely to aid directly the Army in its offensive. On 21 June the Cabinet agreed to consider increasing the R.F.C. from 108 to 200 squadrons and definitely approved this on 2 July with the provision that there should be a similar increase in the R.N.A.S. Of the

increased force, forty squadrons were to be for a long-range bombing force. On 7 July, just after the defending fighters called over
from France had been sent back, there was a second German daylight raid on London. Though 187 fighter sorties were flown against
the two raids in June and July, only one Gotha was brought down.
One result of this was that by June 1918 London was protected by
469 guns, 622 searchlights, and 367 aeroplanes manned by 10,060
officers and men.

When he was told on 13 July to look into providing airfields for
the new forces sanctioned by the Cabinet, Haig replied that he
could see no reason to increase the R.F.C. beyond the needs of the
Army in France and that he did not view the long-range bombing
force as of other than secondary importance. He did, however,
demand ten additional bomber squadrons for operations against
enemy airfields. He was informed that the employment of the new
striking force would depend upon the military situation and upon
whether or not the Air Ministry was formed. Haig's attitude must
be presumed to be that of Trenchard, who habitually wrote Haig's
air statements. If this was so, then Trenchard, with reason it is
true, must be judged myopic in his vision. As Field Marshal Lord
Wavell pointed out in his *Allenby*, a squadron or two on the
Western Front made far less impact than a similar number of new
aircraft would have had in such a theater as Palestine.* Moreover,
if Trenchard's policy was to clear the air so that his own army
co-operation machines could move freely over the battlefield, what
better way to erode his opponent's strength than to compel him
to withdraw squadrons to defend the Fatherland? This would
create a situation in which the advantage of choice was with the
attacking British bomber squadrons, whose numbers would be out
of proportion to the fighters and anti-aircraft units required to
protect Germany against their sporadic intrusions. In fact, H. A.
Jones notes that study of the German daylight raids of 1917 lent
support to the postwar doctrine that a nation might be forced to
sue for peace through an air offensive.† In other words, that a war

* (London, 1941), p. 210, n. 1.
† *War in the Air*, IV, 155. It may also be noted in passing that Jones felt that
the German raids on England were justified simply in military terms in that
12,000 personnel were held to oppose raids that rarely exceeded thirty aircraft,
while at the same time the cost of the anti-aircraft shells fired against the Germans
often exceeded the damage their bombs did! And the official historian went on
to say: ". . . and if what has been said is well-founded, the power of the air

could be won by an indirect approach. After the war this was, in fact, to be Trenchard's booming theme.

On 15 June 1917 Trenchard prepared for Haig a memorandum on methods for preventing air raids upon England. Four possible courses of action were available: to capture the coast as far as Holland; to land people at night equipped with explosives to destroy German aeroplane sheds; reprisals; and standing patrols. He stated the advantage of reprisals: "The German population is more easily moved by having their own country touched than the English population." This could be done at first and at once by a few machines using bombs and leaflets—"and single machines would have a greater chance of getting through and back without being seen"—because the German commander has assured his people that the more distant towns are safe. Such words would have a greater effect and make it likely that he would withdraw some of his aircraft to protect them. But, said Trenchard, the only aircraft that could be fitted to do this work were some D.H.4's in England, and to organize more long-range bombing squadrons would take time. But

> Another disadvantage of reprisals is they would only lead to further reprisals from the enemy. We must be prepared, if reprisal methods are to be adopted, to carry it through and outlast the enemy. They would always defeat us at reprisals unless we put forth our whole energy and this would seriously interfere with the supply of machines necessary for artillery work.*

He concluded by noting that ten co-operation squadrons requested a year ago still had not been supplied.

In England the immediate aftermath of the raid of 7 July was the establishment of committees. On 11 July, while Lord Cowdray and the Second Air Board were trying to decide what should be done, the War Cabinet was establishing a committee of two to do the same thing. The Lloyd George-Smuts group was in fact Field-Marshal Smuts's alone. Cowdray later met with Smuts and proposed

weapon to call into being interminable defensive activities, which might become so elaborate as to be almost intolerable is emphasized. In other words, the aeroplane is an offensive weapon, and the advantage in war will go to that side which exploits its offensive qualities with trained imagination and the most determined mood. . . . The only defence in the air likely to be effective in the long run is an offensive more powerfully sustained than that conducted by an enemy." (IV, 158)

\* *The War in the Air,* V, 481.

that a unified air service be established after the war, but that while the conflict lasted the Air Board should be provided with a staff so that it could make policy and have control of the "surplus aircraft fleet." This latter was a paper group based on predictions by Sir William Weir that there would be an over-all surplus of 3,000 machines in 1918.

Meanwhile, on 9 July, Henderson had handed Smuts a note in which he had called for the creation of a unified air force if the war was likely to last beyond June 1918. But he made the mistake in this piece of demanding that the new Service should be free from "amateur advice." Smuts had several advantages. He belonged to none of the English political parties. He was not involved in any of the internecine Service rivalries. And he had witnessed the raid of 13 June. He was impressed in the latter case by the psychological rather than the physical damage created by the Germans. Moreover, his mind was open for he had only arrived in England in March, fresh from his victorious campaign in East Africa. There and in the South African War he had been imbued with ideas of mobility. Almost immediately Smuts came to the conclusion that as far as Home Defence was concerned the only immediate steps that could be taken were to strengthen the gun barrage and to organize formations of fighters to attack enemy bombers.

The far more important result of his deliberations was revealed to the Cabinet on 17 August. Starting from Henderson's practical, historical, constitutional, and administrative memorandum of 19 July, Smuts stated:

> 5. The time is, however, rapidly approaching when the subordination of the Air Board and the Air Service [to the Army and the Navy] could no longer be justified. Essentially the position of an Air service is quite different from that of the artillery arm. . . . It is a weapon, an instrument ancilliary to a service, but could not be an independent service itself. Air service on the contrary can be used as an independent means of war operations. Nobody that witnessed the attack on London on 11th July * could have any doubt on that point. Unlike artillery an air fleet can conduct extensive operations far from, and independently of, both Army and Navy. As far as can at present be foreseen there is absolutely no limit to the scale of its future independent war use. And the day may not be far off when aerial operations with their devastation of enemy lands and destruction of industrial and populous centres on a vast scale may become the

---

\* *The War in the Air,* VI, 4, gives the date as 7 July.

principal operations of war, to which the older forms of military and naval operations may become secondary and subordinate. The subjection of the Air Board and service could only by justified on the score of their infancy. But that is a disability which time can remove, and in this respect the march of events has been very rapid during the war. In our opinion there is no reason why the Air Board should any longer continue in its present form as practically no more than a conference room between the older services, and there is every reason why it should be raised to the status of an independent Ministry in control of its own war service.*

Smuts then went on to point out that in the future the war would increasingly become one in which the dominant side would be the one that could produce machines to replace the dwindling supply of men. Therefore, it behooved Britain to carry "the air battlefront . . . far behind on the Rhine" so that such continuous pressure would be a serious factor in bringing about peace. He also pointed out the advantages of using air power to obtain overwhelming results in areas such as Palestine, where the enemy's communications were precariously based upon a solitary railway line. He ended with comments upon the practical means of bringing a unified air service into being, including the establishment of the Air Staff to which were to be posted not only the best air brains then available but also frequent additions of officers fresh from combat to keep the staff up to date.

On 24 August the War Cabinet set up a secret Air Organization Committee to bring these recommendations into being. There were, of course, dissentients, notably at G.H.Q. in France, where the files were filled with unsigned memoranda arguing against the creation of an Air Ministry. They were summarized on 15 September in Haig's reply † to the C.I.G.S.'s informatory letter of 24 August. Again it must be presumed from what we know that this was the work of Trenchard. He called for practical examination by experienced officers of "theories which are not in accordance with practical experience." His general conclusions were that the Germans were favoured in their operational position, while the British would be at a severe disadvantage. The bulk of the note was concerned with the disadvantages to the Army commander of losing control of his air force. But once again these comments overlooked the need to provide for the air defence of Britain, the arsenal from which Haig

---

* *The War in the Air,* Appendixes, p. 10.
† The text is printed in *The War in the Air,* Appendixes, pp. 14-18.

would derive the liberal "means of gaining and maintaining supremacy in the air. . . ." In fact, while he had been considering all these evils, the Germans had attacked London on the night of 4-5 and on 6 September Smuts had noted "that in such cases the only proper defence is offence. We can only defend this island effectively against air attacks by offensive measures, by attacking the enemy in his air bases on the Continent and in that way destroying his power of attacking us across the Channel. . . ." On 18 September he followed this with a memorandum that shocked the Cabinet by pointing out that British air strength was declining just as German was rising. This called not only for efforts in the air but also at home on the production front. He noted that Trenchard was right in Haig's memorandum of the fifteenth in noting that the 106 squadron programme of December 1916 was still unfulfilled and that it needed the same priority as the shell programme of 1915. However, Smuts could still call for a major independent air offensive for 1918 as the production figures were still optimistic, though they were not to remain so as engine supplies fell rapidly below estimates. As a result of these papers, the Cabinet appointed an Aerial Operations Committee to deal with priorities. Composed of the Ministers most concerned, including Churchill of Munitions, the new body first moved to get the Cabinet to change its name to the War Priorities Committee, with power to control the production of all munitions. So a full three years after the war started, Britain finally obtained the administrative organization for conducting a modern, three-dimensional industrial war. But the Germans collapsed before its full momentum could be used operationally.

No sooner had the War Priorities Committee been established than Admiral Mark Kerr, then on loan to the Air Board, produced a memorandum showing that Germany was building a strategic bombing fleet (known in Germany as the *Amerika* programme).* This persuaded the Cabinet that there should be no more delay in getting an Air Ministry and an executive Air Staff. So Smuts was appointed to head the Cabinet Air Policy Committee. But although these steps were taken and the necessary legislation passed by Parliament in November 1917, politics involving the resignation of Lord Cowdray and his replacement with Lord North-

* Printed in full in Kerr, *Land, Sea and Air* (London, 1927), pp. 287-291. In fact, the *Amerika* programme was designed to counter the threats of large-scale American aircraft production, of which very little ever reached Europe.

cliffe's brother Lord Rothermere, prevented the Government from laying down any definite policy by which the new Air Ministry, which came into being in January 1918, might formulate operational proposals. (And it may be said that in 1936 the Air Ministry took up from this point.) The operational proposals were not, in fact, laid down until the Sykes-Weir memorandum of 23 May 1918, nor finally accepted by the Cabinet until 10 July.

The interplay of politics and experience at this point in late 1917 is worth noting. Smuts and Lloyd George had their doubts about the activities on the Western Front. They wished to weaken Haig's position while at the same time seeking a way to break the stalemate in the mud. Smuts was a Boer and had led commandoes. Lloyd George was a nonconformist who belonged to the anti-Western Front group known as "the Easterners." If they could get an independent air force, perhaps they could really have control over one offensive and make a success of it. It was against this independent policy that Churchill objected in his memorandum of 21 October 1917 in the midst of the Cabinet sessions on the conduct of the war in 1918.

In Section IV, Paragraph 19, Churchill, the old Easterner, pointed out that the most important of all the mechanical factors available was the Air Offensive. Owing to the fact that there were no flanks to be turned on the Western Front, the Germans were striking under the sea and causing the British to put twenty times the effort into parrying this as the Germans put into the attack. But a better method of conducting the war was to strike not at communications, but at enemy bases. This was where air predominance came in. It could either paralyse the enemy or force him at least to devote a proportion of his resources to the defence of his bases and communications. But, said Churchill, all air attacks had to be related to the main battle, for no air offensive was going to win the war by itself. Moreover, terrorization of the civil population was unlikely to compel a government to surrender, for familiarization with bombardment, the use of dugouts, strong police, and military control should leave national fighting power unimpaired. The British experience showed that air attack actually tended to make the population more combative. The true object of air attacks was military targets and not civilian populations, though it was inevitable that the latter would suffer some losses. "The supreme and direct object of an air offensive is to deprive the German armies on the

Western Front of their capacity for resistance." He then proceeded to advocate the establishment of a proper air general staff to draw up an air war plan under which the proper material could be procured. It seemed to the Minister of Munitions that at that date the true object of the air offensive was the enemy fighter base, and after it had been destroyed, then the rear could be attacked and possibly parties landed there.* In his stint as Secretary of State for War and Air, 1919-21, Churchill, who believed in battle as a means of destroying enemy forces, refused to sanction a strategic bomber force; † this refusal was in line with his memorandum and with reality. At the time, of course, he belonged to the school that felt that the R.A.F. was not long for this world, and he had delivered himself of the dictum that civil aviation would have to fly by itself for the Government would not aid it.

Once again, with the appointment of Trenchard as Chief of the Air Staff, the exact pattern of events is obscure.‡ When the secret Air Organization Committee was established in August 1917, Henderson was appointed to help Smuts with the foundations of the Air Ministry and the R.A.F. In October Henderson was deprived of his seat on the Army Council and was removed as head of the R.F.C. This once again placed the ambitious Brancker a mere temporary appointment away from supreme command of the R.F.C. To his chagrin he found that the appointment was to go to Major-General Sir John Edward Capper (1861-1955), an Engineer who had commanded the Balloon Factory

* *The World Crisis, 1917-1918* (New York, 1927), II, 309-310; and also in *The War in the Air*, V. Churchill had been a strong critic of air affairs until he returned to the Cabinet (C. G. Grey, *The Aeroplane*, 15 April 1955, pp. 471-472).

† Groves, *Behind the Smoke Screen* (London, 1934), p. 168. On 3 September 1940 Churchill found himself Prime Minister of an embattled Britain and was compelled to say that the bomber was the only means to victory. His doubts were, however, amply reinforced by the poor results achieved by Bomber Command. In 1939 Churchill wrote in *Colliers* (CIII [17 June 1939], 114), "Bombs Don't Scare Us Now."

‡ The historian is all too often at the mercy of men's memories and interests. It is notable that neither Lloyd George in his own *Memoirs* nor his biographers, notably Frank Owen in *Tempestuous Journey*, provides any depth to these incidents. In his biography of Smuts, Professor W. K. Hancock is less than interested in these events. In an attempt to resolve some of the difficulties, I wrote in April 1963 to the ailing Lord Beaverbrook and asked for his help, but he died a year later before any answer other than to refer to his books, which I had already exhausted, was forthcoming. This leaves the danger that events may have had motives ascribed to them that did not exist, the actions taken having been merely ordered in haste amongst other distractions.

at Farnborough from 1903 to 1910 and, after commanding the 24th Division in France from 1915 to 1917, had come home to the post of Director-General of the Tank Corps. Capper was not enamoured of being General Officer Commanding (G.O.C.) of the R.F.C., so upon Brancker's protesting this appointment to the pliable Lord Derby, the Secretary of State for War agreed that Capper should be liaison officer between the War Office and the Air Ministry when the latter came into being. Major-General John Salmond was brought back from France to be Director-General with a seat on the Army Council. This suited Robertson, but his plans were upset by the Kerr Memorandum, which finally decided the Cabinet on an independent air force. This decision, however, while it ensured Brancker's posting early in 1918 to the United States to get him out of the way, also left the politicians with a further problem. Who was to fill the new post of Chief of the Air Staff? Sykes was then with Sir Henry Wilson at the Supreme War Council in Versailles; Robertson was still C.I.G.S. To the Press lords, Northcliffe and Rothermere, there seemed but one choice. They were anxious to oust Lloyd George, but after Northcliffe's public rejection of the Prime Minister's confidential offer of the Air Ministry, his brother Rothermere had taken it. These two persuaded Trenchard that it was his duty to take the post as he was the best and most experienced man for the job though Haig wrote at the time, "To repeat, Trenchard's proper sphere is in the Field, but he must be placed in a position so that he can get his requirements met from home." He was replaced in France by Sir John Salmond. In fact, Trenchard wanted to be both C.A.S. and G.O.C. in France. Lloyd George and Churchill are singularly quiet on this appointment, while the official history merely says that Trenchard's recall showed how importantly the Government regarded the new post. Strangely, too, what about Henderson? He had been a brigadier-general when Trenchard was a major. Was Henderson, now made an additional Member and Vice-President of the Air Council, considered superior to Chief of the Air Staff? If this is so, why did he resign when Sykes was appointed a few months later?

The newly established harmony in the air did not last long. On 28 January 1918 the Germans bombed London again. Not only did they drop 2,200-pound bombs, but one 660-pounder burst in the air raid shelter in the basement of Odhams Printing Works, killing thirty-eight and wounding eighty-five persons. Its effects were to be multiplied in the ensuing years. The last of these attacks did not come until 19 May. In Whitehall Trenchard, not in the first place happy with the way in which he had been dragooned into the position of C.A.S., now found himself increasingly at loggerheads with the Secretary of State. A believer in the rigid military code of conduct and discipline, "Trenchard soon found Rothermere acting much as Lloyd George had in interviewing young officers to find out what was actually happening." But it was something more fundamental than this which caused a parting of their ways. Trenchard had been an opponent of the independent third Service, and with stubborn consistency he continued to carry the torch for his cause even when he was Chief of the Air Staff charged with carrying out a fundamental change of policy. The puff that destroyed the last illusions that Rothermere may have had as to the uniqueness of Trenchard's status amongst airmen was Trenchard's memorandum of 18 March, with its demand that all the air force should be sent to France to support Haig in opposition both to Rothermere's desire to send some of it to help the Navy in its campaign against the U-boats and to the Cabinet's programme for an independent air offensive against Germany. Trenchard even went so far as to tell Rothermere what the lines were between the political and military spheres of action. This allowed Rothermere to point out that Trenchard was not his only adviser and that moreover the Chief of the Air Staff was supposed to provide plans, none of which had so far been received. The next day, upon the receipt of Rothermere's reply, Trenchard tendered his resignation. He later said that he did it rather than split the air Service asunder. But judging from the fact that the Cabinet spent a good deal of the next two weeks pondering the problem as well as facing up to the consequences of the German break-in on the twenty-first of March, it would not be unreasonable to suggest that Trenchard perhaps hoped to seriously embarrass the Lloyd George Government. It was rumoured at the time that an Asquithian plot involving Robertson and Jellicoe as well as Trenchard aimed at upsetting the Unionists, who had dared to dismiss the three Service chiefs within a matter of months.* Once again the Cabinet had a dilemma in the form of a deadline. The

* Jones dismisses the whole incident as unpleasant politics and devotes scarcely a line to it. Collier in *Heavenly Adventurer*, p. 80, and Norman MacMillan, *Great Airmen* (London, 1955), p. 153, shed new light on this incident. Mac-Millan talked with Trenchard about it. Boyle gives a version more favourable to Trenchard, as a good biographer should.

new Royal Air Force was scheduled to come into being on 1 April. Smuts was appointed to investigate; he concluded that Trenchard should go and that Sykes was the only man who could succeed him. He did.

In the meantime, the idea of an inter-Allied staff had grown in late 1917 into the Supreme War Council at Versailles. The British military delegation was headed by Sir Henry Wilson; he chose Sykes to head one of the three subdivisions, the "M" Branch dealing with Allied and enemy manpower, aircraft, munitions, and transport. In mid-February 1918 Wilson replaced Robertson as C.I.G.S. Early in April Sykes visited London to collect some needed information. Lord Milner, the new Secretary of State for War, asked him to stand by, and on the eighth he was promoted major-general and two days later made Chief of the Air Staff.

The dissolution of the old clique soon followed. Brancker had already been posted on a mission to the United States; Trenchard's resignation was accepted on the thirteenth, Henderson's followed, and Rothermere went on the twenty-fifth. The most difficult problem arose over the future of Trenchard. Lloyd George ordered the new Air Minister, Weir, to find Trenchard a job. He was offered the command in France again, but declined to relieve Brooke-Popham in the middle of the battle then raging. Eventually, he was persuaded to accept the face-saving role of commander of the Independent Air Force.*

Henderson returned to the Army and was eventually appointed an area commandant in France in the closing months of the war, then posted to the embassy in Paris to help with peace-making. He was described by Sir Walter Raleigh as "a white man, a good friend, and an honourable enemy, high-spirited and sensitive—too sensitive to be happy among those compromises and makeshifts which are usual in the world of politics. The first chief of the Royal Flying

---

* This should have been called the Long-Range Striking Force or the Strategic Bomber Force or the like, for the Independent Air Force (I.A.F.) became a bone of contention between the British and the French. After the war it became thoroughly confused with the idea of an independent air service. The plan was, of course, that this was to be an offensive force free from the crippling control of generals, but making Trenchard the head of it merely played into their hands. We have not been told whether this matter was at the heart of the Trenchard-Rothermere quarrel; if it was, then the generals won, for Trenchard was one of the principal opponents of the idea. Sykes's Memorandum of 1 June is obviously simply an official note for the French (Sykes, *From Many Angles,* 542).

Corps was a loyal and simple soldier." * As to why Henderson resigned on the appointment of Sykes, we can only speculate. If it was
true that Henderson and Trenchard had wanted Sykes out of the
way in 1915, then his prodigal return was a victory they could not
avert. Moreover, Sykes had a strong ally in Sir Henry Wilson, the
C.I.G.S., and the two of them had political influence. It may be
suggested that Henderson outranked Sykes and could not, therefore,
serve under him; but if this was true, then he should not have
served under Trenchard, either. In view of his early death, it may
well be that he was tired of the struggle, prepared to take a rest and
await the next throw of the dice.

The differences between the first two Chiefs of the Air Staff had
not decreased by 1918. Trenchard was a taciturn, inarticulate, fighting infantryman. He was a battlefield general who was not enamoured of paper work. His war service had all been on the Western
Front or in England, and he belonged to the Haig-Robertson camp.
His successor was a cavalryman, fluent in English, French, and German, an able administrator often on the staff. He had served in
France, the Eastern Mediterranean, England, and on the staffs in
Whitehall and Paris. Moreover, he liked and understood politicians
and belonged to the Henry Wilson set. In many respects Trenchard
and Sykes represented the difference between the old Victorian
soldiers and the new modern officers. These differences and rivalries
were to continue after the war when Trenchard reassumed the post
of Chief of Air Staff and Sykes was made Controller-General of
Civil Aviation. The bitterness between them continued until Trenchard's death in 1956, two years after Syke's death.

Once in control, with Weir as the new Secretary of State, Sykes
proceeded to organize the new Independent Air Force. His difficulties were political, logistical, and military. The French argued
against the idea of an independent force operating from behind the
battlefront in France,† production at home was hampered by tech-

---

* *The War in the Air,* I, 445.

† The description given in *The War in the Air* (VI, 105-106) of the second
meeting of the subcommittee of the Supreme War Council dealing with this
problem on 31 May 1918 appears intended to make Sykes look foolish. But reread today it may be interpreted as an example of the military mind of the day,
wedded to the offensive and the view that the only place in which the German
should be beaten was on the battlefields of France. Sykes replied to this view at
the time by stating that once the necessities of the armies in the field had been
met, the balance of aircraft resources were to be devoted to bombing squadrons, "a

nical difficulties and by the need to make good the wastage caused by the German March offensive, while the new commander of the Independent Force, R.A.F., to give it its proper title, tended to employ it against targets within the Army zone.* But a principal reason for the failure of the Independent Air Force was the supply difficulties that occurred at home, due especially to the failure of engine production to come up to expectations, lack of priority for aircraft production, and the comb-out of men to make up for the losses in March. On top of this, there were in London all the confusions and uncertainties of a new Service and a new Ministry.

Weir recommended that Sykes be raised to the rank of lieutenant-general, but was unable to overcome the opposition to such a move.† Sykes himself recalled P. R. C. Groves from the Middle East and made him Director of Flying Operations. So recklessly had the R.F.C. been kept on the offensive that pilots were going into action with less than twenty hours solo flying, while the rate of losses was four British casualties to every German brought down.‡ One of the first moves was to raise the solo hours to fifty.

In June Sykes submitted a notable memorandum, which is not mentioned in the official history. In this he reviewed the present and future for the War Cabinet, starting by saying, "In the next war the existence of the British Empire will depend primarily upon its Air Force. The giant aeroplane of today will inevitably develop in striking-power to something analogous to an aerial dreadnought. But even the present aeroplane, if produced in sufficient number, could on the outbreak of war quickly secure success for that Power which possesses undoubted aeroplane superiority." He deemed it probable that in 1928 one thousand bombers would be able to deliver five hundred tons of bombs at a blow, while, when it was recalled that the essence of air attacks was surprise, no nation could afford to dis-

statement," says Jones, "which prompted General Duval to retort with Gallic irony that he would be grateful to any authority who could establish the limit of what was necessary to a battle. The great commanders, he said, had always solved this by putting into the battle every resource they had." Liddell Hart's *Strategy* demonstrated the falsity of this statement, at least in the way Duval meant it.

* For the operational history of the Independent Air Force, see *The War in the Air*, VI, 118-174, and Appendixes.

† According to Frank Owen's *Tempestuous Journey* (New York, 1955, p. 479), King George V opposed promotions for Rothermere and Weir. Presumably he was influential in blocking that of Sykes also.

‡ Sykes, 220; *War in the Air*, V, 469 n.

regard the menace of the future, said Sykes. "It is imperative that the first line of the force of the future shall always be on a war footing. The existence of such a force ready to strike is undoubtedly our surest means of defence. When peace comes the temptation to drift will be great, but if again we fail, retribution will be swift and final." * Under the influence of the *Report of the Committee on Aerial Transport (Cd. 9218),* which he had helped draft, he called for the formation of an air reserve to keep the aircraft industry in business. "In formulating strategy the first consideration is to weigh any new factors which may have emerged. There are three factors: the national aspect, the air, and the submarine. This war, unlike previous wars, is in the fullest sense a war of nations. . . . The success of armies or fleets depends upon the energy and the *moral* of the nation supporting them." He then talked of the possibilities of a "strategic direct long-range air offensive," and pointed out that such attacks would have a three-fold effect. They would dislocate the German munitions industry, deal a heavy blow at the U-boats, and bring about far-reaching moral and political effects in Germany. Such attacks would bring the best and most rapid return for the expenditure of national manpower, material, and money.

By the end of the war the basic ideas that were to govern the central part of Royal Air Force doctrine in the interwar years had already been circulated and embodied in Cabinet memoranda. Immediately after the Armistice, Sykes drew up a scheme for the peacetime composition of the R.A.F.† Its key sentence was:

> Highly specialized air forces are now essential components of all fighting efficiency, and aviation also provides a distinct and separate striking force of tremendous potentiality. Before a formal declaration of war it may be possible to deal a paralysing blow at some vital nerve centre. . . .‡

This was a theme that was to be developed by P. R. C. Groves in 1922 and adopted by Trenchard and the Royal Air Force.

* The text is given in Sykes, pp. 544-554.
† This document of 9 December 1918 is given in Sykes, 558-574.
‡ It may be pointed out that writers such as H. G. Wells and others before the First World War had said this. Sykes was apparently the first to include it in an official paper after it had become a (practical?) possibility.

# Chapter VII—Airpower in the Interwar Years

During the war British strategic bombing policy developed from a combination of logic, practice, and politics. After the war, logic and politics continued to exert a strong influence, but practice was sadly lacking, with unfortunate results. By the time the Second World War came neither the men nor their equipment were ready to carry out what had long been the axiomatic role of the Home Defence Air Force. And if the test of a military Service is, as it must be, its ability to wage war, and if Trenchard was "the Father of the R.A.F.," he cannot escape the blame for this failure.

The importance of the German daylight raids of 1917 on the making of wartime British strategic bombing theory has already been noted. The influence of the attacks did not stop there. They were the basis for many assumptions about the effectiveness of bombing that dominated British policy-making in the interwar years. And because the Air Force was so offensive-minded, there was a failure to admit the other side of the coin, that in the First World War the defence had eventually mastered both the day and night bomber. In each case this had been achieved when sufficient forethought, direction, effort, and money had been made available. Faced with this challenge, the attacker had either to swamp the defences with a three-to-one preponderance or to adopt a new and more indirect approach—that was the lesson of the First World War. The Second re-emphasized this in the Battles of Britain, of Germany, and of the Atlantic. In 1918 both sets of weapons used in aerial warfare were immature, and this misled the airpower school into making the statement that the bomber would always get through. But as the Second World War showed, even if the bomber did get through, it took a great many bombers to achieve even major damage in pre-atomic days. As is so often true in technological evolution, just when the revolution in aircraft design and manufacture was taking place in the thirties, when aircraft were exceeding the capabilities of sound-location, radar appeared to provide a detection device that has served and will continue to do so after the warning of the use of a major deterrent is taken over by electronic satellites. At the same time radio-telephone enabled ground controllers with an overall view to run air battles. In this the British excelled as the German fighter commander has noted.*

But there is also another factor to be considered. On the ground in 1914-18 morale was shaken because death was apparently being dealt out by a piece of wizardry that was impervious to assaults by the Government. After all, in 1915 it was only three years since the Home Secretary had assured the House that any low-flying offender would be dealt with by the local policeman, whose attention was called to the fact.† And as is the way with that indefinable mass known as "the public," and not infrequently largely the Press, much more fuss was made about the casualties from the German air raids than about those from the Western Front or from the public's actions. In World War I only 1,414 British persons were killed and 3,416 wounded, in air raids, one third of them by British anti-aircraft fragments! In the same period 2,099 were killed and 42,544 were injured in traffic accidents. In 103 raids the Germans dropped 270 tons of bombs on land, and these did about £3,000,000 worth of damage. Rats annually did £70,000,000 worth! The daily cost of the war was £7,000,000, and this went on for fifty-one and one-half months.‡ The casualties in Germany from air raids were 720 killed, 1,754 injured, and damage to property was estimated at £1,175,000. Moreover, both the Germans and the British thought that they were engaging in accurate bombing, though on the British side at least the German effort was branded as "frightfulness" or "baby-killing." It was not until 1936 that Air Commodore L. E. O. Charlton, an officer who revolted against air policing in Iraq in the late twenties,

---

* Adolf Galland, *The First and the Last* (New York, 1957), p. 20.

† *50 H.C.Deb.5s.*, p. 227, 12 March 1913; see also my *The British Rigid Airship, 1908-1931: A Study in Weapons Policy* (London, 1961), especially Chapters VI and XV on decision-making.

‡ L. E. O. Charlton, *War over England*, pp. 15, 21; Fuller, *Machine Warfare* (London, 1941), p. 100.

pointed out in *War over England* that bombing *was* indiscriminate, noting that the Germans needed fifty tons at night to accomplish what they did with twenty in daytime. But it was the Spanish Civil War that showed how haphazard bombing really was. That this was not realized earlier may be attributed to the fact that the R.A.F.'s only peacetime experience of bombing was either over training ranges or in Iraq and on the Northwest Frontier, where conditions were untypical as there was no air or anti-aircraft opposition.* Even in the latter part of the Second World War, when Pathfinders and the Mark XIV gyro bombsight were available, sixty Lancasters sent against the old Zeppelin factory at Friederichshafen hit the target with only *9 per cent* of the bombs dropped.† Yet from the highly limited experience of the First World War, incredible computations were made that were from time to time up-dated as the size of the largest air force within striking distance, first the French and then the German, increased.

Nevertheless, Air Commodore Robert Brooke-Popham ("Brookham"), later Air Marshal and Trenchard's Chief of Staff in 1918, said that little was done with bombing in the war due to lack of bombs, of aircraft to lift them, of bombsights, of trained aircrews, and of properly trained ground crews. But, he said, its *moral* effect was far greater than that of shellfire; and he quoted German letters to support this thesis, though failing to note that troops in the trenches were under much tighter disciplinary control and better trained than were civilians with their loved ones about them. He mentioned that incendiaries were great weapons as they scattered and set extensive fires, but were little used. He also pointed out that accurate bombing in big wars would be impossible due to anti-aircraft fire, yet bombing was no good at all unless aimed against objectives of political, strategical, or tactical significance.‡

Not only those within the Air Force and its adherents but even

---

* This was once brought out in a cartoon that I recall seeing years ago. It showed two instructors sitting beside a beer barrel filled with eleven-pound practice bombs, but with one about three feet away in the ground. One officer is turning to the other and saying, "Smith seems to be a bit off his aim today."

† W. J. Lawrence, *No. 5 Bomber Group, R.A.F.* (London, 1951), pp. 139-144. See also the relative sections of Webster and Frankland, *The Strategic Air Offensive against Germany* (H.M.S.O., 1961). Bombing errors were sometimes as great as *thirty miles.*

‡ "The Air Force," *JRUSI,* LXI (February 1920), 43-70. By March 1919, Brooke-Popham was a member of the Council of the R.U.S.I. representing the R.A.F. amongst the 5,160 members.

noted soldiers such as Field Marshals Sir William Robertson, Earl Haig, and Generalissimo Foch foresaw that strategic bombing, as it came to be called, would probably be inevitable owing to the economic nature of modern war. "Wully" Robertson warned in his memoirs that air attack on populations might backfire psychologically by exasperating the victims (and in the Second World War it called forth not only countercampaigns by both sides but also seemed to strengthen the will to fight), especially as the enemy would be able to roam much farther afield than London, and that much greater attention would have to be paid to applying science to defence.*

Much of the early argument about the use of strategic airpower was confused by the limited range of the actual machines available and by the logical danger of carrying arguments to extremes, especially in Parliament. In the First World War the restricted radius of action of aircraft meant that they could usually bomb only supply lines in back of the front and not armaments factories.† These practical limitations upon the actual use of aircraft failed to be carried over to the Disarmament Conference of the early thirties, where endless hours were wasted in technicalities. The aircraft the British used for tribal police work could hardly have been used in a European war even if they could have been gotten there, while the whole argument about police bombing was a purely British political furor. As with naval disarmament, pure ratios were meaningless unless related to each nation's strategic needs.

Having their own experience to work on, guided by Britain's particular strategical needs and bossed by the determined "Boom" Trenchard, the Royal Air Force worked out its own doctrine. But because Trenchard laid down in his famous memorandum of 1919 (*Cmd. 467*) that the Independent Air Force must come first with only side assistance for the other two Services, tactical doctrine on co-operation was neglected except in the staff college and in the few squadrons assigned to the Navy and the Army. These were commanded by young men in junior ranks, and the accusation was

* *Private to Field Marshal*, pp. 350-351. *Lord Riddell's Diary of the Peace Conference, 1918-1923*, p. 269, 21 January 1921, notes that Foch's conversion to the idea that the Germans might at any moment launch an all-out air blow was a great fillip to General P. R. C. Groves, whose contribution to this story is discussed later. It also appears to have converted Trenchard at about the time Douhet's work appeared in Italy.

† In the United States a factory is called a plant, whereas in England plant refers to the equipment within a factory.

made that they were manned by cast-offs. Army Co-operation went through vicissitudes and had mostly to be relearned from the Germans in the Second World War and then brought to operational perfection by the Second Tactical Air Force under Air Marshal Sir Arthur ("Mary" [Maori]) Coningham. Apart from punitive work on the Northwest Frontier, at Aden and in Iraq, Army Co-operation was limited to reconnaissance over Salisbury Plain and not to attack work. The one major contribution to the field did not come until Wing/Cmdr. (now Marshal of the R.A.F. Sir John) Slessor wrote *Air Power and Armies* in 1936, and it was mostly an examination of the limited use of tactical air forces on the Western Front. Naval Co-operation doctrine was badly snarled up in the whole controversy between the Air Ministry and the Admiralty over the ownership of the Fleet Air Arm and of coastal patrol aircraft that began in the First World War and continued into the Second, after being sidetracked by Richmond as mentioned earlier. The role of Coastal Command was virtually ignored, and no such organization existed from 1919 to 1936.\* Trenchard, as might be expected, wanted to bomb only military objectives, though he said that in air warfare the moral effect was to the physical not in the old Napoleonic ratio of three to one but of twenty to one.

### The Road to an Official Peacetime Deterrent Policy †

After the Khaki election in late 1918, Prime Minister Lloyd George was able to reform his Cabinet. The sometime First Lord, infantry Colonel, and Minister of Munitions, Winston Churchill, became Secretary of State for both War and Air. It was the intention of the Prime Minister that the Royal Air Force should be disbanded and mere wings once again allotted to the land and sea forces. But amidst the many distractions of the Peace Conference and the aftermath of war, he could not keep tight control over the Air Minister.

---

\* For the Sykes proposals for a peacetime air force, see my *Armed Forces in Peacetime,* p. 149, and on the Fleet Air Arm, pp. 226-233. Also Captain A. F. E. Palliser, "The Effect of Air Power upon Naval Strategy," *JRUSI,* LXXII (May 1927), 339-357, and *United States Naval Institute Proceedings,* LXXXIX (March 1963), 46-53.

† In addition to the sources already mentioned, the interwar development of the R.A.F. and its doctrine are discussed in Sir Robert Saundby, *Air Bombardment* (New York, 1961); Sir Charles Webster and Noble Frankland, *The Strategic Air Offensive against Germany* (H.M.S.O., 1961); Basil Collier, *The Defence of the United Kingdom* (H.M.S.O., 1957), and in my *Armed Forces in Peacetime* (London and Hamden, Conn., 1963).

Churchill appointed Trenchard Chief of the Air Staff again, and Sykes was persuaded to become Controller-General of Civil Aviation.

Why Trenchard was appointed remains something of a mystery. Chiefs of Staff are not normally replaced after an election. Sykes intimates that he was pressed to take Civil Aviation as it was to be the more important division of the Air Ministry in peacetime. It appears equally likely that he was ousted. He and Churchill had not agreed about the strategic bombing programme, and though they had known each other before the war, their friendship appears to have cooled. Trenchard the hero had more appeal to Churchill, especially after his mutiny-breaking actions at Southampton early in 1919. It also seems highly likely that he was appointed as someone known to be opposed to an Independent Air Force. If the R.A.F. was to be broken up and returned to the older Services, who better to do it than the man Rothermere had kicked out? Moreover, his reappointment would do something to atone for the setting aside of more distinguished soldiers. A rereading of Trenchard's famous Memorandum, *Cmd. 467,* gives evidence of this train of thought.

> The principle to be kept in mind in forming the framework of the Air Service is that in the future the main portion will consist of an Independent Force, together with Service personnel required in carrying out Aeronautical research.
>
> In addition there will be a small part of it specially trained for work with the Navy, and a small part specially trained for work with the Army, these two small portions probably becoming, in the future, an arm of the older services.
>
> It may be that the main portion, the Independent Air Force, will grow larger and larger, and become more and more the predominating factor in all types of warfare.

The bulk of the Memorandum is innocuous in that it deals primarily with the organization of the air services and not with their role. Like many political documents, it seems designed to be used on either tack. Obviously a man appointed Chief of Staff was not, unless specially pledged to do so, going to scrap his own position even in this case if he could have.

In the summer before *Cmd. 467* was issued, the British Government published *Cmd. 384,* the *Report of the American Aviation Mission*, dated 19 July 1919. The gentlemen who wrote this document had interviewed a number of prominent Allied politicians and officers including Sykes, Trenchard, and Foch, as well as aeroplane builders such as Caproni of Italy, Douhet's patron. Two of their conclusions seem relevant in explaining why Trenchard changed his mind from his antagonistic stand in 1918 to whole-hearted support of strategic bombing by 1921.

> 2. That Great Britain has come to consider the dominance of the air as at least of equal importance with that of the seas, and is frankly and avowedly planning a definite policy of Aerial development to that end.
> 3. That any future war will inevitably open with great aerial activity far in advance of contact either upon land or sea, and that victory cannot but incline to that belligerent able first to achieve and later maintain its supremacy in the air.

These conclusions reflect a blend of those ideas of both Sykes and Trenchard that have already been noted. But the significance of the open avowal of these thoughts, and especially their support by Foch, seems to have been overlooked for some months. For it was not until late 1920 or early 1921 that Foch's support of them appears to have given them in England the equivalent of a papal seal of approval.

If an Independent Air Force had such great power, why was it reduced in *Cmd. 467* to two squadrons? Did the Ten Year Rule of August 1919, decreeing planning on the basis of no major war for ten years, really require that? Why were the orders for really long-range bombers (the Handley-Page V-1500) cancelled and no specifications for such a type published by the Air Ministry until 1932? Is not the answer that in 1919 Trenchard was still not weaned away from the Army Co-operation view of the air arm? And was not it politically dangerous, if anyone had really the time to consider the problem, to abolish the R.A.F. overnight? The best thing instead was to reduce its power to insignificant proportions. It may not be quite fair to suggest all these points, for it is true that a great deal had to be done to establish the Service on a peacetime basis, for it had been virtually non-existent in 1914. Nevertheless, the point is that the Chief of the Air Staff of the day was not then an open supporter of the counterstrike-deterrent force that he was soon to champion.*

* From what has been said so far, it seems highly doubtful that the Italian theorist Giulio Douhet had any influence in England. It is possible that he did in 1921 as noted later. Otherwise it was not until the second edition of his *The Command of the Air* in 1927 that a copy was acquired by an English Service institution, the R.A.F. Staff College at Andover. For a further discussion of the Douhet problem, see Appendix C.

Trenchard was fated to build. So he brought his organizational powers to bear once again and created a new Service that played upon the Government's desire for economy and a return to 1914-level Estimates. Using the Henderson-Smuts-Sykes structure, he ruthlessly slashed off all squadrons that did not have an active role to play and concentrated instead on laying the foundations for the Air Force of the future manned by a well-trained and disciplined ground staff and an elite flying group. By 1921 the programme had resulted in almost no front-line air strength in Britain itself and in jibes about "the Royal Ground Force." But in overseas operations the new Service was proving that, apart from Army Co-operation work, it could save money in policing primitive open areas. It was in this establishment of the R.A.F. as an independent third Service with an independent role in Empire control that Trenchard made a real contribution.

It was in these years immediately after the war that once again the term "independent" created confusion. It is rarely clear from contemporary literature whether writers were referring to the bombing force that Trenchard commanded in 1918 or to the third Service. No doubt this confusion was at the root of some of the bitter disagreements and misapprehensions as to the nature and functions of the R.A.F. Nor must it be forgotten that all through the twenties the two older Services sought to recover their air arms, despite official recommendations to the contrary. In *Cmd. 467* Trenchard had promised them that they should, but not until the R.A.F. was fully recognized as an independent Service. Yet it is also possible to read *Cmd. 467* from an opposite point of view and to interpret it as paying lip service to the Independent Air Force idea, while really planning to return the air arms to the older Services. Trenchard wanted this, then. Churchill as a politician no doubt ensured that the document was sufficiently vague that it could be interpreted either way as the need arose. But it certainly was the Government's intention up to 1922 to abolish the R.A.F.

In order to gain support for their Service, Air Force officers gave a number of lectures and published articles explaining the nature and function of airpower. Typical of these was a lecture to the Royal United Service Institution in 1921 by Group Captain (now Sir Adrian) Chamier, a most competent staff officer. He pointed out that any nation that adopted a defensive strategy was at a disadvantage; defence was justifiable only on the grounds that it protected the base until an offensive could be mounted and that it prevented popular clamour. But, he said, the power of the weak in the air to delay attack was non-existent, for an inferior Air Force could not withdraw without exposing the whole country to air attack; thus it could not play the role of a fleet-in-being. (But Fighter Command did succeed on the defensive in 1940.) Like the Navy, the Air Force had to be ready on a war footing the day war broke out so that by offensive action it could provide a defensive barrier behind which the reserves could mobilize. He then pointed out that the Army's role in war was to defeat the enemy's forces in the field and so force him to sue for peace; the Navy's to defeat his fleet and blockade him; while the Air Force's role was first to attack enemy airfields and then to destroy his will power by assaults on his cities. As there were no lines of communication in the air, "an unremitting offensive aimed at the enemy's air forces is our one legitimate strategical objective." * Chamier later left the R.A.F. and became the director of the Air League of the British Empire. But his importance here is that he obviously, along with "Brookham," reflects thinking at the Air Ministry, and that stemmed mostly from Trenchard.

These early pronouncements and others like them were gradually leading to a major campaign that bore fruit in 1922 and 1923. After the Chamier lecture the next step came with the annual Royal United Service Institution Prize Essay, whose topic for 1921 was "The Influence of Aircraft upon Problems of Imperial Defence."

Flight/Lt. Charles MacKay produced the winning, very wide-ranging essay. He started by analysing the problems of peace and then proceeded to call for minimum Home Defence Forces while favouring "a ruthless offensive" against enemy aircraft and homeland targets, which would make the public force the Government to withdraw all aircraft from other fronts and use them for home defence.† But the trouble with MacKay's highly optimistic article was, as Air Commodore L. E. O. Charlton pointed out later, that it was funny that when anyone else had bombers or submarines, they were useless, but ours are always divinely safeguarded when we use

---

* "Strategy and Air Strategy," *JRUSI*, LXVI, 1921, 641-661.

† *JRUSI*, LXVII (May 1922), 274-310. MacKay also won the Gordon Shephard Memorial Prize Essay, *ibid.*, pp. 622-641. He died of angina pectoris in late 1928, and his widow and child received £105 per annum pension (Ira Jones, *An Air Fighter's Scrapbook* (London, 1938), p. 178).

them.* Yet belief in one's equipment, doctrine, and commander is an essential attribute of the fighting man and is necessary to overcome the actuarial logic of warfare. Servicemen are gamblers, and when they write they are much like experts on bridge: they presume that the opponent will have certain assets and will act in a particular way. They often fail to recall that every challenge will produce a response; the reply to the threat of an actual bombing is dispersion and protection as in Britain and Germany in 1939-45.

Sir Frederick Sykes told the Lees-Knowles audience at Cambridge University in 1922 that wars would open with counterblows delivered by aircraft against the centers of civilian population, industrial, and military targets. The immediate reserve for the Air Force would come from civil air transport, which would supply both aircrews and consumers to maintain the aircraft industry.† His arguments were based soundly upon maritime precedents that had been used in Britain for guidance from 1910 onwards and upon the developments already mentioned; but like other writers, he looked too far into the future. In 1924 organized British airlines employed only 118 persons in all, and the orders for aircraft averaged only 7.2 multi-engined landplane transports annually in the first ten years after the war; of these Handley-Page built all but eighteen.‡ Until 1922 the industry received no orders from the R.A.F., which was living off war-surplus aircraft and spares while at the same time being drastically reduced in size.

It was, in fact, the intention of Bonar Law and Lloyd George that the Independent Air Force should be abolished. The Secretary of State for Air had ceased to be a member of the Cabinet when that portfolio left Churchill's hands in March 1921. But as America abandoned Europe and the French became more adamant about reparations and the prostration of Germany, and as a crisis loomed ahead, Englishmen suddenly became aware of the fact that while the French Air Force had only ninety miles to go to reach London, the British had two hundred to cover to hit Paris. Moreover, the Gauls had over one thousand aircraft, while the first-line home

* *The Air Defence of Britain* (London, 1938), pp. 41-42. For his obituary, see *The Aeroplane*, 25 April 1958, p. 563.

† *Aviation in Peace and War* (London, 1922), pp. 100-102.

‡ Peter W. Brooks, *The Modern Airliner: Its Origins and Development* (London, 1961), Chapter II. De Havilland built thirty-three single-engined transports, Vickers a few, Supermarine thirty-three flying-boats, and Short Brothers twenty-five flying-boats, 1918-28.

defence strength of the R.A.F. was *twenty-four aircraft,* just two squadrons of which might possibly be able to reach Paris and return.* It was this situation that led to a press campaign.

## P. R. C. GROVES (1878-1959)

Brigadier-General Percy Robert Clifford Groves was the son of a member of the Public Works Department in India. Educated at Bedford, he joined the King's Scottish Light Infantry (K.S.L.I.) in 1899, served in the Boer War with the West African Regiment, with the Territorial Army in its infancy (1909-1912), and joined the Royal Flying Corps in 1914 with the rank of Captain. In the next four years he served with distinction in France, at the Dardanelles, and in the Middle East. In April 1918 on the formation of the R.A.F. he was brought back to London by his friend Sykes to become Director of Flying Operations at the Air Ministry. In this position he oversaw the work of the Independent Air Force in France. From this post with its acting rank of brigadier-general he went as the British Air Representative to the Paris Peace Conference, just as Trenchard came in as Chief of the Air Staff again in London. He retired in 1922, after heading the Inter-Allied Air Commission on Disarmament. He remained active in his post as air correspondent for *The Times* and in air affairs through the Air League of the British Empire and was recalled in September 1939 to be Deputy-Director of Intelligence at the Air Ministry. He held this post until April 1940, when he was seconded to the Foreign Office for the rest of the war. Afterwards he retired to South Africa, and died in 1959.

In his position as head of the air disarmament team, he had long been pressing upon the authorities the necessity of waking up to the fact that the Germans were using their restriction to building and operating only civil aircraft as a front behind which they were developing aircraft with which they could strike a quick and deadly blow against the Allies. This was an idea he and Sykes had suggested in the Memorandum of 9 December 1918. And they had been inspired by the Japanese opening gambit in 1904. As Foch, the soldier of the day, had been against airpower, it was a tremendous help to Groves when the Generalissimo openly switched sides. In fact, from

* For the full story, see my *Armed Forces in Peacetime: Britain, 1918-1939,* pp. 147-190.

then on he was voluminously quoted as though God had said that the next war would begin with a devastating aerial blow.

Agitation came with the publication in *The Times* and *The Daily Telegraph*, the two most respected papers in London, from 21 March 1922 of a series of articles by Groves. Before the end of the year they had been collected into a book, which was already in a second edition. *Our Future in the Air: A Survey of the Vital Question of British Air Power* * had a profound impact. In it Groves pointed out that modern war was a matter of areas, and not of fronts, with morale the new target. If Britain could not afford to maintain adequate defences in peacetime, then she must maintain a striking force, as the next war might well be won in the opening days, when civilians would not be immune. But, said Groves, Britain had virtually no aircraft industry, while the state-supported French industry was turning out 150 military machines a month, not counting production for air transport. (The French airlines had knocked the British out of the air in March 1921, forcing the English Government to provide subsidies.) Britain could not get by with a small professional Air Force as she had for years with the Army. Moreover, civil aircraft could easily be converted to military uses.† Thus Britain must have airpower or disaster, civil air transport or conscription. On 24 March Groves wrote, "It is an axiom that in the last analysis national policy is dependent upon the armed force behind it. An obvious corollary is that the effectiveness of policy is often proportional not merely to the force behind it, but to the readiness for action of that force." His tactics were compounded of fact and the big scare, but he also joined with Sykes in blasting the Air Ministry and Trenchard. He scathingly pointed out that Trenchard had said that civil air transport was useless in war, but that at the same

---

* In 1935 Groves published a second work with this title, which was based upon four articles in *The Observer* carrying the message that Germany was potentially dangerous; but it is not at all the same book, a fact bibliographies have overlooked.

† This problem plagued disarmament discussions and led to the French proposal in 1932 that all civil aviation be internationalized. The German Dornier and Heinkel bombers of early World War II were originally flown as transports. The development of internal bomb bays to obtain higher performance caused a divergence between civil and military design in the late thirties that continued for twenty years, but the development of atomic and airborne missiles that can be carried in detachable pods has once again revived the transports as potential bombers. In recent Russian machines even the civil versions carry a bomber's glassy nose.

time the Chief of the Air Staff worried about the German air trans-port companies of the twenties.* He accused the Air Ministry of having conducted an archaic militarist policy that had virtually ruined the aircraft industry, then on the verge of bankruptcy, by its failure to obtain foreign markets for it, thus creating unemployment at home.

For Britain the danger in being unarmed was that it was only in circumstances where one side was unprepared that the knockout blow might win the war in the first few days, said Groves. That Britain lacked air doctrine was not entirely the fault of the Secretary for Air as the Air Council had only three military members—the Chief of Staff, the Director-General of Supply and Research (Brooke-Popham), and the Air Member for Personnel (Rear-Admiral C. F. Lambert, R.N.). The Controller-General of Civil Aviation (Sykes) was also a former Army officer, but his views perforce had to be op-posed to those of the R.A.F. Moreover, the Air Council lacked liaison with other Services, neglected foreign developments, and re-fused to accept outside advice.

Groves maintained that Trenchard was intolerant and did not care for some officers, especially those who disagreed with him. More-over, he was an Army man, while the R.A.F. itself contained many former R.N.A.S. personnel who had not been involved in either the R.F.C. or the Independent Air Force but in Naval Co-operation. On the civil side was the fact that from 1919 to 1924 the Secretaries (Churchill, Guest, and Hoare) were Army men, though Churchill had been instrumental as First Lord of the Admiralty in establishing naval flying and had flown himself. But it was not until May 1923 that the Secretaryship was raised to Cabinet rank. Up to then Lloyd George and Bonar Law had refused this on the grounds of expense, though in reality because they wished to disband the separate Air Force.

The proper aims of British air policy, said Groves, should be to build a Home Defence Air Striking Force "as a deterrent," to pro-vide the Army and Navy with specialized flying arms, to create R.A.F. forces to handle areas (such as the Middle East) where they could more cheaply replace the older Services, and to maintain and de-velop the aircraft industry. He pointed out that bombers would

* See my *Britain's Imperial Air Routes* (London, 1960; Hamden, Conn., 1961), pp. 60, 89.

have to be escorted by fighters, which was done over the lines in France, but not on longer raids.*

The argument about escort fighters was an old one. The realities of combat had forced each side to begin to protect its scouts and then its bombers as these attempted to operate over the lines on the Western Front or to penetrate beyond them. With the peculiar illogic of the military mind, it was argued that once bombers could be passed through the fighting zone, then they would have a clear run to their target. It was also posited that attacks on enemy airfields near the front line would keep his fighters grounded. It was not always made clear by British air commanders that when the enemy found his planes under attack on his airfields, he would withdraw these out of range while at the same time gaining the advantage of being able to attack bomber forces that had been forced to shed their escorts. This happened in the R.A.F.'s conduct of the Battle of Britain and in Northern France in World War II when the Germans withdrew their fighters beyond Spitfire range and rose to fight only when they chose to do so. In the First World War, all of this was becoming obvious, and the seesaw of arguments can be seen in the procurement programme for the Independent Air Force. Haig, for instance, demanded that 25 per cent of the new bombers assigned to operations for 1918 should be fitted as long-range fighters, and at one time the proportion rose as high as twenty out of sixty-five squadrons with an additional one fitted with a quick-firing gun in the French manner. Trenchard himself appears never to have been highly in favour of escort fighters and requested in late 1917 that all of the fighters for the I.A.F. be assigned to the main Army-affiliated R.F.C. His argument was that the type of fighter needed could not yet be determined. But after the war he regarded the fighter as a panacea for civilians and imposed a psychological barrier against the long-range fighter that hampered its development far more than did the technical problems. Not until 1943, when the drop-tank-equipped Mustang (P-51) finally proved that the long-range fighter could match the short-ranged interceptor if proper tactics for its use were created and new concepts of relay escorting introduced to meet its special needs, did bombers on deep-penetration

---

* In the Second World War this was forced upon both the U.S.A.A.F. and upon the R.A.F. for both day and night penetrations. (See Jones, VI, 171, and Webster and Frankland, II, 75 and 139, n. 2)

flights have suitable protection. Again, this may be taken as a reflection of offensive-mindedness. It would have been acceptable if the bombers could have been designed and made immune to interception and if Home Defence could have been assured by ground defences alone.

Entering into the Groves-Trenchard controversy was the fact that Groves was in the Sykes camp. But unfortunately for Groves and Sykes, they played into Trenchard's hands and strengthened rather than weakened his position. The wheel of fortune had twice made Trenchard Chief of the Air Staff. With a congenial but disinterested master of visionary powers in 1919, he was able to consolidate his position. Admiral Beatty made the mistake of launching a campaign to recover its own air arm for the Navy. This backfired when Earl Balfour, the sometime Conservative Prime Minister and founder of the Committee of Imperial Defence, ruled upon investigation that the R.A.F. had a diplomatic role to play that neither of the other Services could fulfil. Thus the airpower prophets won their game because the spectre of French belligerence frightened Downing Street and combined with anti-Lloyd George forces waiting in the wings. Balfour also said that only the Air Force could defend the nation against air attacks.

Groves was opposed by *The Morning Post,* but supported by the other big dailies, as well as *Flight, The Aeroplane,* and technical periodicals. Undoubtedly he was effective, but all the above-mentioned forces, when combined with the natural consumption of war stocks as well as the scare caused by the Chanak crisis with Turkey helped play their part, so that, like many successful agitators, Groves achieved his end because he voiced public opinion in a telling, authoritative, and informed way at an opportune moment, when national prestige needed repolishing.

Groves reinforced his arguments with a second book just when the 1930's rearmament of the R.A.F. was announced in July 1934. This was *Behind the Smoke Screen,* in which he continued the attack upon Trenchard, whom he accused of having censored *The War in the Air,* Volume III, by H. A. Jones.* But what delighted Groves

* *Behind the Smoke Screen* (London, 1934), pp. 123-134. It is interesting how Jones's writing reflects the environment in which he worked; see, for instance, *War in the Air,* VI, 85 ff. And, of course, the reverse was true; Jones and Raleigh, with their evidence and conclusions, influenced R.A.F. thinking and tactics. See also my comments on p. 120 n.

was that despite this supervision, it was evident that Trenchard's Independent Air Force had never been anything more than a tactical support force and not really a strategic one. Moreover, said Groves, Major-General M. M. Patrick, Chief of the Army Air Service, U.S.A., stated in his memoirs that when he visited Trenchard at his headquarters in 1918, the Englishman told him that he had fought for several years against an Independent Air Force, but that it had been forced upon him.* But despite this, the Chief of the Air Staff soon wholeheartedly adopted the striking force doctrine and made it R.A.F. dogma, perhaps in part because the Service was constantly striving to find a *raison d'être,* and, being young, wanted something different than merely being the auxiliary of the older Services. Perhaps also because once a Jove-like Foch had adopted the idea that the next war would be an air war, Trenchard suddenly saw the light and became as ardently for a striking force as in 1917 he had been against one.

Groves was supported in his ideas by S/Ldr. A. A. Walser, who wrote (in *The Nineteenth Century and After* in 1922 and 1923) articles that gave a broad analysis of the air problem and of Imperial strategy. Like Groves, Walser called for immediate strikes against civilian centers as soon as war broke out. But he also was more broad-minded and desired the relation of sea and air strategy, noting that henceforth Britain would have to maintain both.† Walser was a Clausewitzian thinker who in his second article pointed up the lessons of the First World War but used lessons of the German side, where the effects of the loss of air superiority were more clearly shown. He made the point, which had validity in the Second World War, that as British generals had not had to operate without air support, they did not realize what it could mean to have the sky open and rear areas intimidated. While Walser foresaw anti-aircraft techniques keeping pace with the development of aircraft and ground forces equipped with anti-aircraft mounted upon tank chassis, others felt that because anti-aircraft had not been decisive in the late war, it would not be effective. Walser helped Sir Edgar Ludlow-Hewitt, in 1939 Air Officer Commander-in-Chief Bomber Command, to write the first R.A.F. Service Manual.

Many English officers read the American doctrinal writer, Maj.

* *Behind the Smoke Screen,* pp. 136-139.
† *The Nineteenth Century and After,* XCII (September 1922), 349-361; XCIII (April 1923), 598-611.

William C. Sherman, U.S.A.A.C., in whose *Air Warfare* (1926) they found confirmation of Groves and of the French ace René Fonck, whose view was that Paris could be annihilated in two to three weeks by aircraft carrying two-ton bombs. Sherman, however, noted that strategic bombing in the First World War was indiscriminate and unhumanitarian, hitting civilian rather than military objectives, but that this achieved the intended effect.* He argued that the best restraint would be fear of reprisals and that a power that had not a retaliatory force was asking to be annihilated. Walser recognized this in suggesting that part of air defence would have to be the creation of the correct civilian morale to resist bombing.

Moreover, it must be remembered throughout these discussions that a deterrent that is not credible, or dreadable, to an opponent serves no useful purpose, while if those who possess it have an implicit and ungrounded faith in it, it is much more dangerous to themselves than to the enemy. The realization of the impotence of Bomber Command in September–November 1938 was a very distinct shock to British statesmen and does much to help explain the policy of appeasement at Munich. Yet even after that date, the Air Force persisted in thinking that Bomber Command could be made into a decisive weapon. However, in 1938 Air Commodore L. E. O. Charlton pointed out that it was still a common fallacy that bombing could be accurate. He noted that against isolated targets crack crews managed no more than 18 per cent hits, while less experienced ones would, as the war showed, do much less well.†

The importance of these theorists is their interplay upon the making of national policy. As Liddell Hart once remarked with a good deal of truth, "It has been the victorious nations who have most often suffered worst from successful but shortsighted strategists who could not see beyond the last battle." ‡

INSIDE OFFICIALDOM: VICTORY THROUGH SCAREPOWER

In November 1921 the Committee of Imperial Defence (C.I.D.) asked the principal service experts to report upon the problem of

* *Air Warfare*, pp. 210-214.
† *The Air Defence of Britain* (London, 1938), pp. 48-49.
‡ "The Limitation of Air Warfare," *The Defence of Britain* (London, 1939), p. 194. In this case Liddell Hart himself did not go far enough, for he might have added that victorious nations, alas, tend to ignore the strategists altogether.

possible future air attacks.* Their committee reported back to the C.I.D. in 1922, accepting the conclusions of the Air Staff that France as the aggressor could drop 1,500 tons per month on England (versus the German total of just over 300 tons in the whole of the 1914-18 war) flying on only twenty days and using only half her aircraft. London itself could expect to receive 150 tons in the first twenty-four hours and 110 tons in the next day with the rate thereafter dropping to 75 tons per diem for an indefinite period. At the same time the committee warned that the morale effects of such an attack would far outweigh the physical. This report greatly upset the C.I.D. and the Cabinet, to whose attention Balfour called it. By 1923, when the Salisbury Committee on the fate of the R.A.F. was sitting, the Air Staff appreciation had raised French capabilities to 84 tons per twenty-four hours. Meanwhile on 3 August 1922 Lloyd George had announced the formation of a Home Defence Force of twenty-three squadrons (fourteen bomber and nine fighter). (There were then only twenty-eight in the R.A.F. and all but seven overseas.) This was followed on 25 June 1923 by Baldwin's announcement that the force would be raised to fifty-two squadrons, or a "force of sufficient strength adequately to protect us against air attack by the strongest air force within striking distance of this country." This scheme was due for completion in 1928, but was still incomplete in 1935.

After the authorization of the fifty-two squadron force, Trenchard called a meeting at the Air Ministry on 19 July 1923 for some "enlightenment," he said.† He started out by stating that the staff college studies generally agreed with his own division of the new force into twenty-four squadrons of day bombers and fifteen of night, with thirteen fighter squadrons, though admitting that one staff college appraisal had called for twenty-four fighter squadrons. The meeting was then led into a discussion of the differences between day and night fighters in which the Chief of Air Staff was

---

* Franklyn Johnson, *Defence by Committee*, provides some information here, but the bulk comes from *The History of the Second World War, Civil Series* volumes: T. H. O'Brien, *Civil Defence* (H.M.S.O., 1955); C. L. Dunn, *The Emergency Medical Services* (H.M.S.O., 1952-53); R. M. Titmuss, *Problems of Social Policy* (H.M.S.O., 1950); and also Sir Charles Webster and Noble Frankland, *The Strategic Air Offensive against Germany* (H.M.S.O., 1961) and Basil Collier, *The Defence of the United Kingdom* (H.M.S.O., 1957).

† The minutes of this meeting are reprinted in Webster and Frankland, IV, 62-70.

challenged upon a number of occasions as to his facts by Air Vice-Marshal J. M. Steel, the Deputy Chief of Air Staff.* But when this discussion was about over, Trenchard began to hit home on the idea that in a war against the French it would be no good merely meeting and holding them "all along the line," but rather that as in a soccer game defence did not win, only the attack won, and he thought that in a counterbombing war the French would "probably squeal before we did." "The nation that would stand being bombed longest would win in the end." Having it put this way to him, Air Vice-Marshal Sir Philip Game, then Air Officer Commanding India, said that naturally he would put all his money into bombing as it gave positive results. Game did not think much was to be gained if the number of fighters was doubled. Trenchard then went on to point out that the attack on morale was vital as it was something that no other Service could do, but he placed the emphasis on hitting the source of supply rather than the actual weapons delivery system. The discussion then reverted to machines, and Trenchard laid down that there should not be two different types for day and for night work, but only one capable of both, as it was essential that the nation be impressed with the fact that the R.A.F. was getting to work on its new role at once. Brooke-Popham, who was then commanding the staff college, wanted a single type of fighter and a single type of bomber. Trenchard then stressed that night bombing would have to be limited to about four months a year in Europe so that day bombers were the thing and would have to carry smaller bombs than the 4,000-pounders that S/Ldr. (later Marshal of the R.A.F. Lord) Portal wanted.† The general tone for the future development of the R.A.F. at home was set at this meeting.‡

The insistence upon day over night attack forces was backed up by a study undertaken by Plans, which showed that a much higher

* Steel was at this time engaged in setting up the air defences of Britain (Collier, *The Defence of the United Kingdom,* pp. 15-16).

† A 2,000-pound bomb had been developed in 1918. It was never dropped, but an example stood outside the R.A.F. camp cinema at Uxbridge for many years. (*The Aeroplane,* 25 November 1960, p. 723.)

‡ An immediate effect of these discussions can be seen in the lecture jointly sponsored by the Royal United Service Institution and the Royal Aeronautical Society on "Air Strategy," which Wing/Cmdr. C. H. K. Edmonds delivered. In many respects this followed rather closely the July 1923 meeting at the Air Ministry, but raised serious questions as to the effective means to be employed to defeat the enemy air force and in Empire defence. (*JRUSI,* LXIX (May, 1924), 191-210.)

proportion of night attacks by the Independent Air Force than of daylight sorties had failed to reach their objectives. From then on the Air Force tended to assume that daylight operations were the only worthwhile type and, because the primitive state of night navigation was not considered, night flying was largely ruled out, and relatively little training in this was undertaken until shortly before the Second World War. This in its turn helps explain why the results of even the Regulars sent on night operations over Germany after the devastating German day-fighter attacks on Wellingtons in late 1939 brought negligible results.

It is also interesting to note that although Trenchard insisted in his memorandum of 2 May 1928 that in future wars air attacks would be delivered upon the enemy's most vital communications and munitions centres, the Air Ministry undertook little research and development in the field of long-range bomber operations as opposed to record-breaking, long-distance flights and flag-showing tours. Yet it must also be pointed out that there was a strong, but quite unrealistic, public and Service feeling that bombing was immoral. Trenchard took particular cognizance of this in pointing to the Hague draft code of rules for aerial warfare, which specifically permitted the bombing of military objectives. Moreover, he pointed out that—and the influence of J. M. Spaight shows through here—naval bombardments had damaged civilians and their property, but that this was bound to happen when military targets were situated in populous areas.*

## CONSEQUENCES

If it was the opinion of the Air Staff that bombing offensives were the best means of attack and that defensive fighters could not effectively stop the bomber getting through, then obviously the Cabinet had to take some steps to protect the general public so that they could endure the bombing duel till France collapsed. Thus at the end of 1923 the Home Office was instructed to begin preparation of a scheme for what became to be known as A.R.P. (Air Raid Precautions). In January 1924, just before it fell, the Conservative government through the Committee of Imperial Defence appointed an A.R.P. subcommittee, and with this the new MacDonald Government concurred. It met regularly to 1929, but then only

* Webster and Frankland, IV, 73.

spasmodically during the period of apparent peace and economic difficulties until 1935. The eight topics upon which it was required annually to report reflect the thinking of the time: warning, prevention of damage, maintenance of vital services, repair of damage, movement of the seat of Government, legislative powers required, departmental responsibilities for action to be taken, and the education of the public to the significance of air attack.

By 1925 the Air Staff had raised the rate of attack to 100 tons every twenty-four hours, 50 per cent upon London. From here on, the whole possible effect of bombing began to skyrocket as committees sat and attempted to make estimates of what would happen and what was needed to counter it. The whole was based upon an assumption of the Air Staff based upon a mixture of what the Germans had done in the First World War coupled with intelligence assessments of French capabilities. As these figures were secret, no one was in a position to challenge the Air Ministry's reasoning, and the vicious cycle continued.* The medical subcommittee of 1926 reported that the 1925 figures of 100 tons per day taken in conjunction with the standard casualty rate computed at seventeen killed and thirty-three wounded per ton of bombs would produce 3,300 wounded the first day declining to a steady 1,100 for the third and following days with total casualties of 50,000 injured, of whom 36,000 would have to be hospitalized for an average thirty days each. This would mean that 36,000 beds would be needed.†
Not until 1935 was the Government's fear that to talk of possible air raid precautions was likely to lead to panic overcome and *Cmd. 4827* issued with some information on the subject. Yet for years Parliament had echoed with dire predictions of the coming of hell, mathematically computed, and a whole literature already existed in print. In 1931 the Government came to regard evacuation as a military countermeasure to mass-bombing attempts to break civilian

---

* The mathematical assumptions failed to take into account the new science of probability and tended always to assume the worst case in civil defence, which was the most optimistic view of destruction where the offence was concerned. Moreover, the actual destructive power of bombs was far overrated, especially against military targets. As late as September 1944, only 5 per cent of the machine tools in the German aircraft industry had been damaged despite many attacks. (Webster and Frankland, II, 280, n. 3.) But the Air Ministry should not be too heavily blamed for a failure that even eminent scientists suffered from, as for instance the Lindemann or Cherwell memorandum of 30 March 1942 (Webster and Frankland, I, 331-336).

† Dunn, *Emergency Medical Services* (H.M.S.O., 1952), I, 4.

morale. In the years 1924-33 eighty-six subcommittee meetings discussed four hundred memoranda on this topic alone. Yet it was not until 1938 that the plans were completed and issued as *Cmd. 5837.* J. B. S. Haldane, a socialist scientist who had visited Spain, called the whole plan idiotic unless Germany gave Britain time to carry out the scheme.* It is interesting to note that the French took quite the opposite view and as early as 1927 had a law on the books for regulating the Nation at War.

The danger of secrecy in this type of planning may be shown by contrasting these early figures, based largely on the one lucky hit on Odham's printing works on 28 January 1918, with the figures of German bombing results against Britain, 1939-45. In the period from September 1939 to May 1941 in London only, there were 20,102 killed (2.1 per ton), 26,054 injured and hospitalized (2.8 per ton), and 47,046 minor casualties (5.3 per ton). To cause these, the Germans dropped 46,518 bombs weighing 9,334 metric (1.1 short United States) tons. Regardless of the size of the bomb, the number of deaths caused per bomb was only 3.7. An even more interesting statistical analysis is that which shows that in London's three main inner divisions and in four large provincial towns, the distribution of bombs was 60 per cent in open spaces, 30 per cent on buildings, 6 per cent on railway bridges, docks, and the like, about 1 per cent on air raid shelters, and 3 per cent elsewhere. Moreover, the bulk of the casualties was caused by falling buildings and flying debris and not directly by the bombs themselves.† In other words, a gigantic card house was built upon one isolated example. Yet better evidence existed. But, as far as has been revealed, no one appears to have thought to look at casualties on the Western Front as a guide to bombing. There it took many tons of shells and numerous bullets to kill one man slightly sheltered by sandbags and earthworks.

When the bombing offensive against Germany started, it was very quickly revealed that almost all of the assumptions about the ability of the contemporary air forces to deliver a knockout blow were

* Major-General E. B. Ashmore, "Anti-Aircraft Defence," *JRUSI,* LXXII, 1927, 1-15; Maj. B. C. Dening, "The Defence of a Civil Population against Air Attack," *Fighting Forces,* III (July 1926), 250-261; Rees Jenkins, "Civil Aspects of Air Defence," *JRUSI,* LXXII, 1927, 521-534 (a particularly prescient article), and Maj. C. C. Turner, "The Aerial Defence of Cities," *JRUSI,* LXIII, 1928, 692-699. Titmuss, *Problems of Social Policy,* p. 24; Haldane, *A.R.P.* (London, 1938).

† Dunn, II, 210-219.

incapable of fulfillment. Studies made of R.A.F. bombing results by Air Chief Marshal Sir Basil Embry, for instance, showed that in May 1943, when he took over anti-shipping strike forces, their average bombing error was 1,200 yards against targets whose maximum length was generally not much over 100 yards. By hard work he reduced it to an average 300 yards error giving a one in three chance of a hit versus one in twelve.*

Analyses of the effectiveness of the main bombing effort against Germany are even more devastating, for it was not until mid-1944 that the R.A.F. had the ability and the means to deliver something akin to a knockout blow at even individual cities, let alone at a whole nation. Webster and Frankland go into this in great detail in their three-volume narrative. Perhaps it will suffice to say here that for a long time the percentage of hits within three miles of the center of the target was extremely small, but that by the end of the war Pathfinders were able to lay their markers within 100 yards of the aiming point, and that some groups reduced their bombing error over German cities to an average of under 300 yards. Even the much-vaunted American daylight bombing proved very imprecise. In two U.S. Eighth Air Force raids on the Gnome et Rhône Aero Engine Factory at Le Mans, France, only seven of the 1,754 bombs dropped hit the target, or 0.4 per cent.† And this was in early 1944!

There was a second fallacy in these analyses, and that was that the defence would be so poor that highly accurate bombing would take place in daylight. Yet, as Major-General E. B. Ashmore pointed out in *Air Defence* in 1929, the defences had always made the Germans switch from day to night bombing, which was notoriously more inaccurate (twenty times so in the Independent Air Force in 1918). The Air Staff appreciation was correct really only in one respect, that the bombs would be high explosive and incendiary, but not poison gas. When the Second World War blitz came, the chaos and collapse of morale envisaged did not take place, not even in Hamburg on 24 July to 2 August 1943, nor at Hiroshima in 1945.‡

What then of the Sykes-Groves striking force theory and concepts

---

* *Mission Completed* (London, 1958), p. 221.

† Webster and Frankland, II, 293, n. 1.

‡ Martin Caidin, *The Night Hamburg Died* (New York, 1960); John Hersey, *Hiroshima* (New York, 1946); and also the *U.S.A.A.F. Strategic Bombing Survey* (1947).

of a great deterrent? The answer would seem to be that against a prepared and determined people, provided with shelters and emergency services as well as an anti-aircraft defence, which at least by its sound is comforting, morale will not crack. Moreover, to many former servicemen, bombing in the Second World War was not so bad as shelling in the First. But what, of course, becomes equally significant after such an analysis as that above is that the R.A.F.'s whole concept of defensive war through attack (two thirds of the Home Defence Force was composed of bombers) was based itself on a false premise.*

In 1925 the observation system used in the First World War was re-established in Kent and Sussex and the resuscitation of the anti-aircraft forces begun.† At the same time the A.R.P. Committee decided that if London was knocked out, Britain could not continue the war, nor could industry easily be moved out of the area.‡ Thus the Committee was led to conclude that the nation whose people could longest withstand aerial bombardment would win the struggle. Yet despite the lessons of the First World War, it was thought that in the next conflict such attack would be continuous. Here again, of course, the lessons of history were forgotten in the shadow of a highly propagandized unknown being analysed in the mists of secrecy, while the results of the next historic war were to show how fallacious these arguments were. Air attack alone has so far won no major conflict. In the Second World War Germany was crushed by massive armies and Japan was sunk by the depradations of American submarines just as much as by bombing, while Italy simply gave up when Allied forces made it opportune for her to do so. Airpower alone was not decisive in Spain nor even in Abyssinia. The very arguments over the nature of the next war, which tended to revolve about strategic airpower, caused the true role of airpower to be overlooked. Its function was, and perhaps still is, three-fold: to provide mobility and tactical support to the land forces; to co-

---

* The most blistering attack on the R.A.F. for this is Admiral Sir G. C. Dickens, *Bombing and Strategy: The Fallacy of Total War* (London, 1947; corrected edition, 1949). See also Marshall Andrews, *Disaster through Air Power* (New York, 1950); Webster and Frankland; and Fuller, *The Second World War*.

† Ashmore, *Air Defence* (London, 1929), and Pile, *Ack-Ack*, supplement earlier references here, as does briefly Lt/Col. Percy Etherton, *Adventures in Five Continents* (London, 1928), 277 ff.

‡ By 1930 20 per cent of the population of the United Kingdom lived in the London area.

operate with seapower, and to act as an independent striking force against military-economic-political targets within the enemy's defensive sphere that cannot be reached and/or occupied by surface forces.

Though in 1925 the A.R.P. (Air Raid Precautions) Committee called for tests to be conducted to determine the destructiveness of 500-pound and larger bombs, these were not undertaken until the Air Ministry was forced to do them in 1937. It is remarkable, since the Air Ministry expected an all-out assault upon London in the opening days of a new war and since their counter to this was the threat of an equally devastating blow at an opponent's capital city, that they had not considered the weapons with which such an attack was to be delivered. In part, of course, this was traceable to the fact that the destructive power of bombs, leaving aside any consideration of the probability of each one dropped doing equal damage, was as much exaggerated as was the airmen's belief in the war-stopping power of their weapon. The 500-pounder was designed only for military objectives, and the bulk of the bombs in stock in 1939 was not only old but also of the "general purpose" variety suitable for military support but not so good as blast bombs in built-up areas. It should also be noted that, although the Air Ministry thought in terms of a three-day war, they were also planning for a three-year one. Perhaps as air defence improved, a vague realization came that victory might be delayed.* As to the question of the effectiveness of a blackout, this was confused by H. A. Jones, who said that in the Great War it had been overdone.†

Though not strictly concerned with the theory of strategic bombing, the British Government's reaction to the threat of air attack is also of interest. In 1928, in the glow of the Briand-Kellogg Pact, the Cabinet placed the Ten Year Rule on a sliding basis and cut defence and Air Raid Precautions spending. At the same time the Chiefs of Staff asked for a civilian general and planning staff as the A.R.P. Committee was still concerned with "the knock-out blow." Then the Office of Works said that shelters were too costly and "the tubes" (the underground railways) too useful so that the only hope for Londoners lay in evacuation, and this concept remained a

---

* See Scott and Hughes, *The Administration of War Production*, pp. 363-367; Air Commodore Keith, *I Hold My Aim*, p. 32; and Asher Lee, "Trends in Aerial Defence," *World Politics*, VII (1954-55), 233-254.

† *War in the Air*, V, 3.

dominant part of planning down to the opening days of the war. From 1929 to 1935 the A.R.P. Committee fought within the C.I.D. (Committee of Imperial Defence) for permission to discuss publicly the problem as a means both of educating the public and of getting funds from Parliament. But, although such discussions were taking place abroad, the Government refused to countenance them at home. Official secrecy is not infrequently a cover for official lethargy.

In the autumn of 1933 Major-General H. L. Pritchard was appointed Air Raids' Commandant (designate) of London, which was still regarded as the coming battlefield. He soon submitted a memorandum based on the ideas accumulating since 1924. He demanded funds in fiscal 1934/1935 for an establishment for the London command, for full-scale tests of the destructive power of the 500-pound bomb, for an A.R.P. exercise in Hackney in 1934, for a Press liaison officer at the Home Office, and for the preparation of certain schemes in detail such as the centralization of fire brigade control as in 1918. But this was turned down as the sum needed was £150,000. Instead, the usual allotment of £20,000 was made mostly for the Chemical Defence Research Department.

But Pritchard's memo did have one important side effect: it caused a re-examination of the Air Staff's scale-of-attack hypotheses. This had envisaged war solely between England and France, a rather unlikely possibility by 1933. So in December of that year, the Ten Year Rule having just been revoked, the C.I.D. obtained permission to go ahead on a general approach since it was felt it would be many years before Germany would be a menace. At the same time the new Defence Requirements subcommittee called for the completion of the 1923 Home Defence Force Scheme, more anti-aircraft guns for London, and public air-raid education.

In June 1934 the Chief of the Air Staff furnished a new appraisal that calculated that by 1942 the Germans could, operating from Germany alone, drop 150 tons daily on England. The next year the Germans announced that they had achieved parity with Britain, and by 1937 the Air Staff were telling the planners that the Luftwaffe could deliver 644 tons every twenty-four hours and that by 1939 this figure would rise to 2,520 tons per day, one third on France, the rest on Britain, though counterattacks, the power of the defences, etc., would reduce the effective amount for Britain to 644 tons daily. Nevertheless, the first day's raid was expected to deliver 3,500 tons.* More-over, after the Germans came again to be regarded as the menace, gas was feared and the manufacture of civilian gas masks under-taken, and by 1937 production was at the rate of 150,000 weekly.† The emphasis was laid in A.R.P. on anti-gas measures because the Government could give instruction, but it did not know what to do about incendiaries or high explosives because no funds for tests with them had yet been voted (and the effects of bombing, such as they were, had not been examined). As a result of committee studies of high explosives and incendiaries, by 1938 the A.R.P. Department of the Home Office was basing its ideas of an attack on a mixture of 50 per cent high explosives and equal parts of incendiaries and gas.

Meanwhile, the Air Ministry, forgetting the lesson of naval gun-nery that war results were only about one fortieth as good as peace-time shootings, had proceeded to up its estimates of the accuracy of bombing. In 1931 it had said that 100 tons of bombs would be sufficient to paralyse public services to London.‡ By 1939 it was assumed that the maximum cohesive force, twenty-seven aircraft, could drop on a single command forty tons of bombs from 20,000 feet into a square with 440-yard sides. And civil defence measures, still partially secret in 1939, were based upon these predictions. But despite the fact that R.A.F. Bomber Command crews used in the early days of the war were the cream of the peacetime air force, the results achieved were pathetic until 1942.§

Yet a further ramification of the Air Staff's short-war theory's impact was the plan for the evacuation of the Government from London. A committee under the ubiquitous and enigmatic Sir Warren Fisher, the Secretary of the Treasury, was set up to consider

---

* The heaviest single British attack appears to have been that on Dresden on 13-14 February 1945, when only 2,978 tons was dropped, and this was very late in the war, when aircraft carried much greater loads than in 1939. Fifty-nine per cent of the built-up area was destroyed.

† See the scare article by the influential Wickham Steed, "Aerial Warfare: Secret German Plans," *The Nineteenth Century and After,* CVI (July 1934), 1-15, and the sequel, "The Future of Warfare," August, 129-130; September, 331-339.

‡ In addition to the sources already cited, see in this respect also C. B. A. Behrens, *Merchant Shipping and the Demands of War* (H.M.S.O., 1955), and C. I. Savage, *Inland Transport* (H.M.S.O., 1957).

§ Constance Babington-Smith, *Air Spy* (New York, 1959); Hilary St. George Saunders and Denis Richards, *The Royal Air Force, 1939-1945* (H.M.S.O., 1954), I; Webster and Frankland, *Strategic Air Offensive,* I.

this in March 1936. Its report was accepted by the Cabinet a year later, and by November 1937 detailed plans had been worked out. The plans themselves raised an awkward question: if the minimum time in which evacuation could be accomplished was ten days and the knockout blow might be delivered in four or less, when should the dispersion of the Government take place? If it took place just after war broke out, then not only would mobilization be hampered, but also the Government itself would be dislocated in the vital opening days. If war came as a surprise, obviously the move could not be taken beforehand, while if there was a crisis, to shift the seat of government might not only weaken the country at a crucial time, but also might precipitate affairs. These dilemmas, like many others, were only really studied during and after the Munich crisis, with the result that when war came, apart from civilian evacuations, only those official services like airlines and parts of the Admiralty not deemed essential for the conduct of the war were dispatched to the north and west. In this as in so many other cases, such as food planning,* many assumptions were made that were not re-examined. The original Air Staff calculations were based upon doubtful evidence and dogmatic beliefs that remained untested long after they should have received something more scientific in the way of examination than the rival Chiefs of Staff could give them. Thus, as R. M. Titmuss says, fears created by social, political, and scientific forces, not to mention theorists, contributed to a horror concept of the next war, and these in their turn tended to magnify the threat. The Air Ministry was guilty of multiplying the possible number of tons that could be dropped by fifty, and of assuming a proportionate increase in damage and casualties, making no allowance for those already killed, evacuated, or dispersed to hospitals outside the danger zone, and the whole based on the extremely tenuous basis of sixteen night raids on the London police district in 1917-18, on figures that the official History disputed, upon casualties caused by British anti-aircraft and upon two mathematical errors in the actual figures submitted to the C.I.D.! †

By 1937 the C.I.D. was envisioning a war opening with sixty days of bombing in which 600,000 would die and 1,200,000 would be injured, costing the nation in compensation £120,000,000. The Home Office had plans laid for mass burials in lime as it could not afford

---

* R. J. Hammond, *Food*, II (1956), 153-160, 317-324.
† *Problems of Social Policy*, p. 12.

£300,000 a month for coffin lumber alone. In 1936 Lloyd's and the other insurance companies refused to accept war risk insurance, and in April 1937, despite the fact that it had made a handsome profit on it in the First World War, the Government voted not to provide insurance against air attack. This was backed up by the investigations of a committee that supplied a new multiplier from those much-worked-over 1917-18 figures—£35,000's damage per ton of bombs dropped. And at the time of Munich this report, and its remarks about the destruction of 500,000 houses and damage to 1,200,000 in the first year of war, was accepted. All of this only reinforced the Government's belief in the 1924 premise that bombing would cause a collapse of morale and that, therefore, maintenance of order would become a problem. So 17,000 regulars were detailed to reinforce the police along with 20,000 reserve constables, primarily for use in London. It was not until after the Ministry of Health had issued local officials with 1,000,000 extra burial forms that the Government came to its senses, looked at the lessons of Spain, and began to drift back to reality.

A word must be said for the civil and military servants who handled planning and the making of hypotheses. They were largely working with the unknown. They were mostly junior personnel who lacked broad experience or a wide vicarious knowledge through books. They were persons affected by the general movements at the time, and they were handling materials marked "top secret" and so could not even discuss them with other officials without carefully obtaining clearance, so that they were denied even the chance to obtain the advice of those wartime members of the Government who were still alive. It was only in 1935 that a prescient Air Minister insisted that Churchill, then out of office, be asked to sit on the Air Defence Committee and to give it the benefit of his already large acquaintance with military matters. And this led to another interesting reflection of the image of the military intellectuals, the quarrel—so pointedly discussed by C. P. Snow in *Science and Government*—between Sir Henry Tizard and the official scientists in favor of radar and Professor F. A. Lindemann, Churchill's adviser, who opposed its development.

In this dispute over radar and other countermeasures in the few years immediately prior to the Second World War, most of the elements of intellectual controversy were present. The dispute not only involved a matter of life or death for the nation, but also had its origins in psychological and personal factors as well as in differences between insiders and outsiders, solid civil servants and freely enterprising directors. Each man felt he was right and was prepared to stake his reputation upon his judgement. But who was to judge between them?

For the civilian politician, the military scientist poses a double problem. Not only does the technician deal with an obscured subject using a strange language often interspersed with figures, but he generally has a highly trained brain and several learned initials after his name. Moreover, the arguments of both sides deal with something that may or may not happen or may or may not be possible. Faced with this dilemma, the Minister will either tend to side with the man he knows the best or make the the least expensive decision—unless, of course, there is sufficient pressure brought to bear upon him to do otherwise. Tizard's difficulty was that Lindemann was Churchill's protégé.

## OUTSIDE CRITICS

If what has been related above reveals a little of what was going on within Government circles, it must not be forgotten that outside them there was also activity. Apart from speakers in Parliament, there was Ashmore's plea in his *Air Defence,* countered by J. M. Spaight, an Air Ministry civil servant given to legalistic writings on air problems, in *Air Power and the Cities.** Oliver Stewart, until 1962 editor of *Aeronautics,* was writing copiously, attacking the weakness of the R.A.F. as was C. C. Turner; both contributed many articles to *The Saturday Review.* This magazine came under the influence of Lady Houston,† and became more and more violent against the Government till upon her death it expired. Turner, for instance, emphasized the point that though in the 1931 air exercises of the 112 attacking bombers, 84 were adjudged destroyed, these results were highly exaggerated.‡ That this many were brought down was surprising considering that in pre-radar days it was possible as late as 1935 for a visiting French squadron to be missed

---

* (London, 1930). See pages 000-000.

† Lady Houston was a remarkable character much noted for shaming the MacDonald Government by supplying £100,000 so Britain could enter the last Schneider Trophy race and for sponsoring the first flight over Mount Everest.

‡ *Britain's Air Peril* (London, 1933), pp. 101-104.

by its British escort, which only landed at Northolt after the visitors.* This showed how easily the bomber could get through, especially when the best British fighters could do only 220 m.p.h., or less than the new American commercial airliners used by European airlines.† Is it scarcely surprising then that on 10 November 1932 Stanley Baldwin told the House of Commons that the bomber would always get through? ‡ Of course, he had to do so or repudiate his long-time Chief of the Air Staff, Trenchard, and imply his own incompetence as Prime Minister in keeping him. The nice thing about the 1931 maneuvers was that you could say that the bomber would always get through or that the defence would have the upper hand. At night or in clouds the bomber stood a very good chance, but in large part because almost no money had been spent since 1918 to find out how to stop it. Yet just before he died, M. Paul Painlevé, the scientific former French Premier, pointed out that the dangers of air warfare were exaggerated for the defence would always match the attack.§ In fact, in 1932 the French had published a handbook on A.R.P. for householders. It was not until 19 July 1934 that Baldwin announced a five-year expansion plan for the R.A.F., and it was eleven days later that he finally took the wraps off A.R.P. to the extent of consulting local authorities. But secrecy remained, and the Government denied the creation of the A.R.P. Department in the Home Office until an M.P. produced a photograph his wife had taken of the doorplate at No. 5, Prince's Street! ‖ Yet it was not until mid-1935, when the Peace Ballot was obtaining its 11,500,000 signatures, that Baldwin would acknowledge that Germany enjoyed parity with the R.A.F., though he never admitted that her aircraft were superior at that time.

Groves returned to the attack in 1934 with *Behind the Smoke Screen,* in which he lambasted the Government for basing its foreign policy on the League of Nations, while saying that British airpower had been allowed to decline due to a combination of public apathy and political and departmental opportunism. Moreover, he blamed the diminutive size of the R.A.F. upon the fact that it had been

* Boyd Cable, "Anti-aircraft Defence," *The Saturday Review,* CLIX (22 June 1935), 777.

† Oliver Stewart, "Air and the Future," *The Saturday Review,* CLV (15 April 1933), 356.

‡ 270 *H.C.Deb.5s.,* 631-632, 10 November 1932.

§ *The Saturday Review,* CLVI (11 November 1933), 489.

‖ O'Brien, *Civil Defence,* p. 55, n. 2.

the chief target of the limitation of armaments as it possessed little political influence. Once again he cried that the only defence for Britain was the threat of reprisal against the enemy.

Others who joined in the airpower chorus, though by no means always singing the same tune, were L. E. O. Charlton with *War from the Air* (1935), which contained speculations upon airpower at the Battle of Waterloo and raised the question of airborne invasion, followed the next year by *War Over England*. The second half of the latter was printed separately in 1937 as *The Next War;* in it the Battle of Britain was forecast and also the blitz, both of which Britain lost fictitiously in 1936. In 1935 Groves brought out a new book under the old title of *Our Future in the Air*, which from the vantage point of the 1960's is spoilt by the fact that in seeking to play the old theme with a new twist, he becomes arbitrary. The verdict of history is that he was wrong that long-range fighters would not prove useful, wrong that enemy fighters should not be destroyed in favour of other targets along the way, wrong that the only way to win a war is to attack the people themselves, and wrong that anti-aircraft would be inconsequential. Yet he was correct in arguing that the R.A.F. was the only Service which could defend London and the Midlands. Others, too, began to attack A.R.P. as did Charlton, G. T. Garratt, and Lt/Cmdr. R. Fletcher in *The Air Defence of Britain*, a Penguin published at the time of Munich. Professor J. B. S. Haldane, who had been on the Cabinet aerial defence committee from 1924 to 1930 and was an expert on gases and ventilation in mines, pointed out in *A.R.P.* (1938) that in Spain not only was high explosive fifty times more effective than gas, but that gas was not used there because the density of persons was not great enough and the weight of gas bombs needed too high, as compared with high explosive, to be effective, especially when it took ten times the amount of gas to poison householders indoors as persons in the open. Nor were incendiaries much used in Spain, as they failed to ignite and most Spanish houses contained little wood. Haldane attacked the British government for being obsessed with the fear of panic while taking little action to provide actual protection for the people. Yet in Spain as early as the raids on Madrid in 1937 air attacks had little effect upon morale. Moreover, as Haldane noted, the fact that even the trains ran during air attacks helped boost Army morale. Moreover, the war showed that bombing was highly inaccurate, as, for example, despite 100 raids upon them, three bridges were still intact. The lesson of the war in Spain was, he felt, that bombing civilians only prolonged the war.*

Haldane was supported by Frank Morison (Albert Henry Ross) in his *War on Great Cities: A Study of the Facts* (1937), which re-examined the Great War's air raids with the benefit of the official *War in the Air* and concluded that chemical weapons would not be used by air forces until one side became desperate, for to do so would be against human nature, indiscriminate, and liable to immediate retaliation. But at the same time he thought gas would produce panic on the Home Front sufficient to destroy the morale of the fighting forces. He further feared that a war in which a gas assault marked the opening phase would result in chaos and a new order of civilization in Europe. More concretely and with grounds for concern, Morison noted that Britain's danger lay in the fact that the A.R.P. authorities were concentrating far too much upon the dangers of the untried gas weapon and not nearly enough upon the containment of the damage that incendiaries and high explosive might do, for these were the known and legitimate weapons. But like others, Morison was far too optimistic in his belief in the accuracy of bombing, for he envisioned the first few attacks being aimed at knocking out certain ministries that would otherwise play a vital part in the war.

Vice-Admiral Sir Herbert Richmond also lent his voice to those who argued that defence against bombers was possible. As early as 1932 he had written in *Imperial Defence* that it was the peculiar mental habit of the military always to attribute to the enemy the ability to do things they themselves could not do and vice versa. Passive and active air defence was possible both in Britain and in an opponent's land, he said. Attack was only the best defence if you had the power to compel the enemy to follow your initiative and to make use yourself of the advantage gained. Since the bomber could always get through, Richmond foresaw simply purposeless cross-raiding as the end result of the deterrent strategy, while at the same time the uselessness of the bomber for home defence might make it more a liability than an asset. Properly the Air Force was only an arm of each of the older Services and was best used only when governed by a common purpose. Moreover, said the Admiral quoting someone unknown, there was a vast difference between preparing for *war* and organizing for *a specific war*. The vul-

---

* *A.R.P.*, pp. 42-75.

nerability of London was not as a capital city, that mythical Achilles heel that hypnotises political and military minds, but rather as the seat of the direction of the armed forces and as a city of 10,000,000 persons capable of starvation within forty-eight hours if the Port of London was closed. Richmond felt that the pessimism expressed by the Government and in Parliament in the thirties was not justified, for aerial attack could be beaten if measures and funds were provided to discover how. It was foolish for the Government to talk of the air threat and of a strategic deterrent without protecting the people from the consequences of such policies.

In 1935 Hitler proposed an air pact that would have limited bombing to an area 100 kilometers behind the front. Britain refused to accept this limitation though it would have been to her advantage. As Liddell Hart suggests, aggressive powers have a much more realistic idea of their enlightened self-interest than do non-aggressive democracies, for the conqueror wants to make his gains at least cost. Democracy, on the other hand, not only likes war unlimited, but costly as well.* A supporter of Trenchard's, Liddell Hart, broke with him in the mid-thirties and began to insist upon fighter defences first, bombers second.

By 1939 there was a large and controversial political literature for and against the Government and strategic bombing. As public discussion increased, more rational approaches based upon experiences in Spain began to bring air strategy back into the main stream of military thinking; "Ajax," for instance, in *Air Strategy for Britons*, pointed out that German and Italian officers viewed the R.A.F.'s reprisal bombing policy as merely an excuse to attack civilians, and even allowing for his anti-R.A.F. bias, he was correct in saying that the most effective counter to bombers was fighters and not reprisal bombing, that manpower would be the ultimate factor, and that the Empire could not be defended by the R.A.F. alone. The Second World War was to show that defence against bombers was best achieved with a combination of anti-aircraft, fighters, and deception, but what critics in 1939 did not know was that radar had suddenly made the fighter effective in cloud and at night. Though it took some time to perfect, the results were in accord with the principles of war. The weaker air force was put on the defensive, but operated from interior lines. The German bomber was first defeated by making the

* *Defence of the West*, pp. 318-320.

type of action engaged upon uneconomic, in daylight, then at night. When a new approach was tried of sending in light fast bombers individually, these were met by ground-directed, radar-equipped British night fighters.* It must be remembered that if their scores were low as compared to the German night-fighter pilots, it was because, as the technology and the techniques improved, the targets on the English side of the North Sea decreased in number while on the German side they might number one thousand or more a night. Moreover, Groves overlooked the development of both day and night long-range fighters operating in relays so as to give cover to bombers throughout their penetration. The early version of these was the Messerschmidt 110 and its successors, the 210 and 410. On the Allied side the Beaufighter was not used in Europe as a long-range escort, except experimentally, but the Mustang by day and the Mosquito by night were. The technique of interruption through intrusion was also employed.

Much the same pattern occurred where the R.A.F.'s assault on Germany was concerned. The first daylight attacks by the much-vaunted Wellingtons equipped with four-gun turrets resulted in disaster. So Bomber Command switched to night operations. Losses on these were held down by paying great attention to evasive routing, by the leisurely pace of air warfare in the early days, and by the gradual development of technological aids for use against night fighters and radar defences. But what made the strategic offensive against Germany possible was the weight of the attack. The first 1,000-plane raid on Cologne took place on 30 May 1942, in which the saturation of the German defences was achieved through the use even of operational training aircraft. Thereafter the pressure built up through the gradual accumulation of a round-the-clock bombing force in England composed of American day and R.A.F. night bombers, though this was not effective until 1944. But before they could be used fully, at least in daylight precision attacks, the German fighters had to be destroyed, and so parallel to the Battle of Britain three years later there was the Battle of Germany, which, however, the defenders lost.

Whether or not strategic bombing was successful depends rather upon whether or not the judge can steer a middle course between

---

* C. F. Rawnsley and Robert Wright, *Night Fighter* (London, 1957) and Air Commodore Roderic Chisholm, *Cover of Darkness* (London, 1957) show this shift as seen by three participants.

its proponents and opponents. On the one side there is Marshal of the R.A.F. Sir Arthur Harris in his *Bomber Offensive* (1947) maintaining that the Admiralty handicapped his work and made the war drag on because they were forever persuading the Cabinet to allow them more airpower for the Battle of the Atlantic and its corollary bombing of U-boat bases, and on the other side Admiral Sir Gerald Dickens in *Bombing and Strategy: The Fallacy of Total War*, which also appeared in 1947, arguing that what he called the Douhet doctrines of Trenchard and his school were quite wrong. Dickens believed that the following four principles should have governed British strategy: the selection of the principal objective and the concentration of all forces against that, which he regarded as the attack upon British maritime supremacy; singleness of purpose, which should have meant concentration upon the Battle of the Atlantic and not as well upon that of Germany; the restriction of the war so as not to allow massive bombing of civilians; and that the object of the war should have been a stable and enduring peace, which the bombing of civilians endangered. Essentially, said Dickens, the lesson is that new weapons do not alter the principles of war. Fuller in *The Second World War* maintains that the effort employed to build Bomber Command would have brought an end to the war much sooner if it had been put into tactical air forces, air transport, and landing craft.

Charges have been hurled by the adherents of both parties. But the truth is that the whole controversy and its consequent testing in the crucible of war is not so simple as the contenders would like to make it. Both sides were partially correct.

## CRITICISMS

To start with, it seems apparent that the development of British air doctrine was based upon Lanchester, Sykes, Smuts, the German raids, and upon politics. Douhet's influence must be heavily discounted. He may have had the same ideas, but British doctrine was largely an official flower fertilized by factionalism within the Higher Direction. As this was not much known after the war, the acceptance of airpower by Foch and at the same time the appearance in Italy of Douhet have had the appearance of making Trenchard look like a Douhetist. It has been mistakenly assumed that ideas that sounded like Douhet's were Trenchard's. In England they were not until well into the 1920's. The doctrine that Groves espoused and Trenchard adopted came from Whitehall. The examples quoted were taken from Trenchard's limited experience with an independent bombing force and upon unscientific conclusions drawn from the wartime experience of London. The Independent Air Force was never ready to bomb Berlin before the war ended in 1918. The airpower theorists felt that they had to create a startling doctrine to justify their own existence as a separate Service, and their seeds fell upon the fertile ground of public opinion in an England recently panicked by the German raids. Moreover, they had allies in Parliament and the Press, former officers anxious to see the air arm remain the R.A.F. Trenchard worked behind the scenes and directly discouraged controversy. Not only was he known to be a man of strong opinions about persons, and not only was career-mindedness dominant for much of those depression years, but also as with many others in similar critical struggles, he realized that the infant R.A.F. could not afford the luxury of a house divided against itself. Thus, if there was little public discussion within the Air Force, what Groves and his followers said outside bore considerable weight. So Britain's defence became based upon a peacetime deterrent—retaliatory bombing— and the Sykes-Groves and Trenchard schools gradually, for political reasons, became merged. But despite the soothing tones of *Cmd. 467*, inter-Service rivalries and feuds continued. And for many years doctrine outran any ability to carry it out. This was not because the designers and manufacturers could not produce the necessary material, but because they were not asked to do so. It was not until just before the Second World War that an enormous technological change took place in air material. But even with the impetus provided after 1934, it was not until well into the war that the means to try out the doctrines were at last available in meaningful quantities. And then, just when what a deterrent Air Force should have been able to do in 1936 became possible *en masse*, the atomic bomb reduced the number of aircraft and crews required to 1920 levels again.

Apart from the fact that all of the Services were embarrassed and unprepared in the first years of the 1939-45 war, it must be recognized that war, and even peace, is never so simple as military men would like it to be. To have concentrated all of the available resources to fight the Battle of the Atlantic at sea would not have won that struggle if it left the German sources of supply and training free from molestation, unless, of course, U-boats could have been sunk fast enough to convince the German High Command that they were no longer a feasible weapon. To put it simply: if a man is wielding a sword against you, the quickest way to get rid of him is to counter his blow and strike at his heart. If you have only a sword, you have to meet his blade, but if you have a pistol as well, you parry and fire. Or even fire first. Liddell Hart has pointed to the fog of war. The smoke of peacetime internecine battles also can conceal realities. And where the airmen were concerned, some of their best friends proved to be their worst advocates. A lesson of history is that each Service has its role to play. Presuming that political guidance is informed and reasonable, the armed forces must then act co-operatively so as to achieve the ultimate object, which is not merely victory, but the re-establishment of peace. This co-operation may mean combined operations by two or more of the Services, or it may entail co-ordinated attacks by various means against dispersed objectives designed to achieve the same end result. Strategic bombing was conceived originally as a defensive reprisal deterrent and as an outflanking movement. It was recognized as such when Hitler in 1935 proposed the Air Pact, which would have been to his advantage but not to Britain's as the then-envisaged use of the R.A.F. would have involved breaking a pledge with consequent unfortunate diplomatic repercussions. But as Hitler's counterdeterrent (actually largely a British fiction) placed him ahead of the R.A.F. both in numbers and in power, the pressure that the British could bring declined. Hitler's intuition failed him, though there was still in 1939 much to support his judgement that Britain would not fight over Poland; and the R.A.F. found itself at war. The deterrent worked in reverse then, with aircrews being ordered not to bomb other than strictly military objectives while most of Bomber Command's loads were limited to pamphlets and strict instructions were given that these were not to be dropped as delivered in case a bundle should damage something civilian and cause the long-delayed knockout blow!

But once having gotten into the war, what should be done with Bomber Command and its coming new four-engined monsters capable of bombing Berlin? This was a major policy dilemma and caused further conflict between traditional British policy and the war-born airpower solution. Thus, even though the events of 1940-

41 showed that the bombing of British cities had no effect upon morale, an attack had to be launched upon Germany to prove that prewar theory was right, to cause the Germans to tie down manpower in flak (anti-aircraft) defences, and to boost morale at home as well as interrupting German war production and thus stemming the flow of blood to the sword hand.

Critics of the exponents of reprisal airpower have to consider, as do others, the time, place, climate of opinion, and the availability and capability of forces both then and in our own day as both affect our judgement. The great deterrent theory in peace is much more reasonable and realizable today than it was in 1945. "Airpower over all" was the militant dream of a few theorists outside the Service and the nightmare of their antagonists. It was not the guiding opinion of all R.A.F. writers.

There are a few additional points that should be made. In the first place, the planning undertaken by the Air Ministry in the interwar years left a good deal to be desired in the way of clear thinking. Until the newly appointed Minister for the Co-ordination of Defence, Sir Thomas Inskip, asked Liddell Hart to draw up counterproposals for air defence, and then imposed this defence-of-the-base-first idea upon the Air Staff, the bomber-offensive group had had almost everything their own way. And in the laying down of specifications for new bombers suitable for carrying out the doctrine, the Air Ministry followed only the line of "the bigger must be the better." In this the Trenchard school followed steadily in the footsteps of the French *offensive à outrance* school of Field Marshal Earl Haig, Trenchard's long-time commander and friend, if not idol. But as Webster and Frankland are at pains to point out through most of their massive analysis of the strategic air offensive against Germany, the heavy bombers of the Stirling, Halifax, and Lancaster types were not half as successful in terms of operational economy, invulnerability, and crew and manufacturing requirements as the sleek, high-speed de Havilland Mosquito, which the Air Ministry had summarily rejected in its infancy. The heavy bomber force, though wielded with skill, was nevertheless a blunt instrument that long failed to be able to do what its fathers had decreed as its role. It is both curious and lamentable that the leaders of the R.A.F. neglected in the interwar years so many of the essential needs of a deterrent striking force. Though months were spent practicing aerobatics for the Hendon Air Display, until after 1930 almost nothing was done about target-finding, bombs and bomb-aiming, blind-fly-ing, night navigation, or aero-medicine, let alone actually determin-ing whether or not the force created could achieve the objectives that had been set for it. These were deficiencies for which lack of money can be but a partial excuse. Nor can the politicians be made to bear more than a section of the burden. It is true that they were niggardly with appropriations and that the Ten Year Rule was their doing, but that was the spirit of the times. They had a right to expect expert guidance from the Air Staff, but they also had the ob-ligation, when they could, to challenge its assumptions until they broke them down or were convinced. In this they were only partly helped by the other two Service staffs owing to the general rivalry for the slices of the Exchequer pie. Credit must go to Churchill, Balfour, Hankey, Salisbury, Hoare, Londonderry, Inskip, and Swin-ton for their efforts to give the new third Service a proper place in the national defence establishment. But they must also stand before the bar of history for their failure to see through the cracks in the Air Staff schemes and their equal remissness in not promoting a vital, modern aircraft industry as a necessary sinew of war. They got away with it, but only just. Many of the arguments used were fal-lacious, some correct decisions were taken for the wrong reasons. The confusion over maintaining a 1918-style "independent air force" and a peacetime one, as well as the internecine struggles with the other Services, caused far too much emphasis to be placed upon the central bomber deterrent force. Because it was politically useful, a certain amount of intelligence was brought to bear upon the question of the defence of London, but little was done about air co-operation with the surface forces, though there were writers who investigated these phenomenon.

### CONCLUSION

The development of British bombing doctrine is a casebook ex-ample of the interplay of reality and politics in the making of policy. What would have happened if the war had continued into 1919 and Berlin had been bombed, as Sir Henry Wilson urged Sykes to do even with one aircraft on 14 October 1918,* we do not know. Only a sustained campaign would have revealed the weaknesses in a re-prisal operation. But with conditions in Germany at that date, it

* Sir Charles Callwell, *Henry Wilson*, II, 136.

was probably fortunate that it did not take place, for there is little doubt that it would have elevated the status of airmen to an even more dangerously disproportioned position in the national councils. If Trenchard had been based in England as was the intention, would he have become another Sir Arthur Harris with privileged access to the Prime Minister? Or would his Haiglike stance have become even more obvious and led to his retirement in favour of a Sykes man? These are questions that cannot be answered.

But what can be noted is that Trenchard's career provides plenty upon which to ruminate. He was an unbeliever who became a convert, at least outwardly. But he brought to the R.A.F. the long-ingrained mentality of the Army of his day. And though Richmond, Fuller, Liddell Hart, Sykes, and Groves had only spasmodic influence, Trenchard had eleven years as Chief of the Air Staff, not counting three as G.O.C., R.F.C., in France. He wrote little that we can as yet see,* so we must judge his ideas and actions on the broader evidence currently available. He shows the danger of a powerful individual in a position to carry theory unchecked into action. Moreover, he tended to retain only those officers who agreed with him, and his influence in the higher echelons of the Service lasted well beyond his own tenure of office. And because he was in command of the junior Service, which many hoped to disband, he enjoyed more leeway under Churchill than the Chief of Imperial General Staff, while in later years he had to deal with junior and less experienced Ministers than if he had been First Sea Lord. More than this, not only were his aeroplanes good propagandic distractions, but in the last six years in office he acted behind the cloak of the Chiefs of Staff Committee. This body often failed to put forward papers if it could not agree upon them, thus keeping many highly controversial and doubtful issues away from the Ministers, who were not in that day likely to have a very strong interest in them anyway. Not until the two years culminating in Munich in September 1938 was an examination undertaken to see if weapons matched doctrine. Then it was found that plans called for a javelin, but that administration had provided only a stiletto, and no shield. Trenchard ensured that a disciplined and organized R.A.F. would survive. That was his contribution. But he must share the blame with the people and politicians of

---

* British official papers are not open to scholars for fifty years. Though there are exceptions in the way of technical and operational documents, this rule applies strictly at the policy-making level.

the day in not providing a well-rounded Service prepared to defend the home base, the sea lanes (though the Admiralty too heavily discounted the air menace), the Army in the field, and to maintain a credible deterrent. Was he a 1914-model man of iron in a situation that demanded someone more plastic? *

One of the constantly puzzling developments in all fields of scholarly endeavour is why no one has ever investigated any particular thing before. When Webster and Frankland's comments on the operational failures of the R.A.F. in the Second World War are considered, it seems strange that no one had taken the trouble to work out, before Robinson did so in *The Zeppelin in Combat,* how the world's first strategic air offensive had fared. Yet, as he notes, the basic materials were in *The War in the Air.* Careful study would have revealed that the Zeppelin campaign showed the utter uselessness of dead reckoning, astro-navigation (as then used), and radio bearings at night; the extreme uncertainty of target location by visual means at night; the high degree of inaccuracy of nocturnal bombing; and the gross self-deceptions experienced by flight crews in regard to where they were, what targets they had bombed, and what damage they had done. Robinson has suggested that the explanation for the British neglect lies in the Zeppelin, since airships were thoroughly discredited in England after 1918, and in the fact that the British had, after all, muddled through to victory. At any rate, it certainly is true that the R.A.F. had not learned the lessons of the last war, nor of any before it.

Because the R.A.F. was established during the emergency of war, the enabling legislation was passed rapidly without nearly the full, free public debate that occurred in the United States, where Congressional action to establish the Army Air Corps was not taken until some years after the celebrated Mitchellian sinking of battleships and wide propagandizing. In the United States British ideas were developed from the point at which they had existed when Mitchell knew Trenchard in 1917. The paramount trends in the interwar

* Since his death, the Halton Branch of the Royal Aeronautical Society has established the Trenchard Memorial Lectures, the first of which was given by Marshal of the R.A.F. Sir Dermot Boyle (the first Cranwellian to become C.A.S.) on 20 February 1958; the Prime Minister has caused a monument to be erected to Trenchard's memory (located at Victoria Embankment Gardens, London); and the Air Council has established the Trenchard Memorial Awards to enable outstanding R.A.F. personnel to undertake sporting or adventurous projects while on leave.

years, as Craven and Cate have noted, were the Air Corps effort to establish an independent air force, not achieved until 1947, the development of the doctrine of strategic bombardment, and the search for a heavy bomber by which it could be applied. Moreover, because the senior officers in control refused to issue air service manuals, doctrine was developed in public rather than in secret official conclaves. Mitchell became so much the prophet of airpower that his wartime work has often been overshadowed. His plans for 1919 included airborne landings behind the German lines and the systematic destruction of German cities, starting with Metz.* What also helped the American Air Force in the Second World War was that when President Roosevelt called upon the Army Air Corps in 1934 to carry the mail, the result was such a shambles that navigational training was revamped. But despite the lessons of the Spanish Civil War that bombers needed an escort double their number and of R.A.F. experience in the first years of the war, it was not until 1943 that all of these were driven home and the necessary remedies sought and applied in 1944. Yet in both the American and British Air Forces the normal technological trend to bigness resulted in monster bombers: the six-engined Bristol, whose civilian version was the dismal Brabazon I, and the Consolidated B-36.

The end result of the campaign against Germany was that the West German Federal Office of Statistics reckoned that about 593,000 persons were killed during the bombing of Germany by the Allied Air Forces.† The irony of this lies in the fact that when he addressed the German Air Warfare Academy on its opening in November 1935, Major-General Max Wever, then Chief of Staff of the Luftwaffe, had stated that the objectives were home defence and co-operation with the armies in the field, and to reach these it would be necessary to strike at enemy bombers on their bases and in their factories and to paralyse armaments production so as to provide the surface forces with the chance to overwhelm an opponent.‡

During the war Trenchard wrote a few pamphlets that he published at his own expense.§ His final principles:

* Arnold, *Global Mission*, p. 86.
† *The National Observer*, 8 April 1962.
‡ Emme, *The Impact of Air Power*, pp. 183-185.
§ *The Effect of the Rise of Air Power upon War* (1943), *The Principles of Air Power in War* (1945), and their revised version, *Air Power and National Security* (1946), which is to be found in Emme, pp. 192-200.

1. To obtain mastery of the air, and keep it, which means continuously fighting for it.
2. To destroy the enemy's means of production and his communications in his own country, that is, by strategic bombing force.
3. To maintain the battle without interference by the enemy, which means to enable the commanders to build up colossal supplies and reinforcements necessary for the battle, and to be able to maintain them without interruption by the enemy.
4. To prevent the enemy being able to maintain the battle, that is, to prevent him being able to build up adequate supplies for his armies or navies or air forces.

He recognized after the Second World War that control of the air meant also that some efforts had to be devoted to defence. The danger in his principles, themselves straightforward and sound, lies in their interpretation. Mobile warfare was, the war showed, far less easy to control, while Korea demonstrated that an unorthodox opponent could still function without anything like control of the air. The real danger lies not so much in war as in peacetime preparation for it. This means that the men and material must be available for any kind of war that is likely to develop. Trenchard may have given the R.A.F. the principles, but he did not give it the means.

The long bomber offensive against Germany was fought without obtaining air superiority until almost at the very end. The bomber always did get through, but its losses had only to rise a fraction above 5 per cent for Harris to abandon a particular line of action.* Airborne defence became a critical matter first for the daylight bombers. They did not need air superiority, simply the ability to penetrate to and destroy any chosen target. The Second World War demonstrated that this could be accomplished in two ways: either by heavily escorted mass formations with such concentrated firepower that bomb loads were, in comparison to the effort, small; or by the use of high-speed aircraft, such as the Mosquito, operating on something of a guerrilla technique. These tactics might be described as that of the convoy or of the U-boat. The defence against them was similar to the techniques employed at sea, though the number of targets far exceeded the number of convoys. It was only at the very end of the war that night-fighter technology was developing to the stage where massed airborne defence would have had to be employed if the approach were to continue the use of the heavy

* Actual casualties in terms of aircraft and crews not able to fly the next day reached 25 per cent on occasion.

bomber, a course from which there could be no sudden change. The Battle of Germany became in the end another attritional struggle.

Another factor, often too little taken into account by the airpower theorists, was weather. *The United States Strategic Bombing Survey (Europe)* noted that the Casablanca Directive had called for "the destruction and dislocation of the German military, industrial, and economic system and the undermining of the morale of the German people to the point where their capacity for armed resistance" was fatally weakened, but that the weather over Europe was particularly unsuited to sustained and precise air attack.* Moreover, ever since the Nazis had come to power, the German aircraft industry had been dispersed in buildings especially designed to suffer the least damage from air attack. (An additional weakness of the Allied offensive was the lack of a thorough understanding of German business methods and the development of certain presumptions, based on hopes as at G.H.Q. in France in 1914-18, which seriously impeded an impartial judgement in the selection of targets and the assessment of results.) *The United States Strategic Bombing Survey* came to the conclusion that what defeated the German air force in 1944, despite a tripling of aircraft production, was the massive losses of aircraft from first-line units, the deterioration in quality of German fighter pilots owing to a shortage of gasoline that hampered and restricted training, and attacks on aircraft engine factories, in addition to fundamental weaknesses in organization and planning. (As so often in war, a different philosophy, planning, and development might not have led to an Allied victory.) On a wider scale, in Western Europe airpower was decisive because its ultimate victory in the air was complete, it made major contributions to both the war at sea and on land, ensured the success of the D-Day Invasion, and brought the German economy to the verge of collapse. But it had only succeeded in doing these things in the last two years of the six-year war.† All of these conclusions were expanded in depth and in detail by Webster and Frankland. Their concluding chapter shows only too clearly how the accumulated mistakes of the past resulted in a campaign against Germany that has been likened to the operations on the Western Front a generation earlier. And as they

* *The United States Strategic Bombing Survey (Europe)*, No. 2, p. 3.
† Nine additional lessons are summarized in *ibid.*, pp. 107-108. The war against Japan produced some equally valid conclusions, for which see *ibid.*, (*Pacific*), No. 71A, pp. 61-64.

note, the conception may have been faulty, the weapons inadequate. But was this any reason to deny a campaign medal to those who fought it out, from Marshal of the R.A.F. Sir Arthur Harris down to tail-gunners and ground crews who made it possible? *

Much as the Allied invasion of Europe in 1944 showed in its massive preparations how inadequate was the German planning for an assault on Britain, so the nearly 3 million tons of bombs dropped on Germany during the war indicated how far off the deterrent-strike was from reality in 1939. Not only were the effects upon morale, especially in a police-state society, overrated, but far too much credit was given to the damage that could be done to industrial production. Even the basis of strategic bombing was tuned to the speed of a 1916-18 style war, so that blitzkriegs were over and finished before the negligible effects of attacks on manufacturing were felt at the Front, if felt at all up to 1944. Of the airpower theorists, only Slessor saw oil as the key supply. It seems reasonable to suggest in the circumstances that had the R.A.F. been attuned to the speed of modern war and had it been well supplied with intelligence on the German economy, it should have developed both a tactical air force for direct, expert and effective, army support, and a small, highly skilled force, as large as the budget allowed, designed to strike at the German oil industry. Armed as it was with an umbrella, it should have used it as one, not in futile swings at its opponent's head (will power) or body, to which it could do little damage, but in a thrust at his Adam's apple so as to strike the one vital point at which a small amount of force could disrupt his breathing and render all his power helpless.

Like the *philosophes,* the airpower theorists in a perfectly logical way had created another heavenly city built, this time, upon a solid nineteenth-century Clausewitzian base.

* *The Strategic Air Offensive against Germany,* III, 284-311.
More recently Dr. Frankland has sought to fit the strategic air offensive into the classical pattern of war in which force is met with force and he argues, correctly, that the air weapon appeared to be revolutionary simply because there appeared to be no defence against it. But when asked why the German Army continued to fight when it had lost air superiority, he rather surprisingly said he had no theory to offer. ("Some Reflections on the Strategic Air Offensive, 1939-1945," *JRUSI,* May 1962 [reprint].)

# *Chapter VIII*—The Other Writers on Airpower

It is perhaps not quite fair to include Lanchester and Groves in the first section on airpower and to relegate Marshal of the R.A.F. Sir John Slessor and Air Vice-Marshal E. J. Kingston-McCloughry as they now are to a seemingly lower place, or to put J. M. Spaight at the end of the line. Yet from the point of view of an interwar survey, Slessor and Kingston-McCloughry made lesser contributions to theory, though each was to have an influential role in the Second World War and into the fifties.

Interestingly both served in the Directorate of Planning of the Air Ministry, Slessor as a writer for Trenchard in the latter twenties and later in the mid-thirties as head of the Directorate and Kingston-McCloughry at the end of the thirties and into World War II. Both wrote one book before the war, and both have continued to work in the realm of strategic thought since 1945. Undoubtedly Slessor has been the more directly influential for he became Chief of the Air Staff and was in a position to have his views on the great deterrent enforced. Both of these officers have written their autobiographies; Slessor's *The Central Blue* appearing in 1956, a year after Kingston-McCloughry's more disguised *The Direction of War*. But for an evaluation of thought between the wars, their later works cannot be too exhaustively examined.

## SIR JOHN SLESSOR

Slessor beat Kingston-McCloughry to book publication by only a year, his *Air Power and Armies* appearing in 1936 to be followed by Kingston-McCloughry's *Winged Warfare*. John Cotesworth Slessor was born at Ranikhet, India, in 1897, his father being an officer of the Sherwood Foresters. After going to the noted "public" school,

Haileybury, he joined the Royal Flying Corps in 1915 and served in the anti-Zeppelin defence of London, in France, Egypt, and the Sudan. After the war he spent a few years in India, returning to pass through the R.A.F. Staff College in 1924-25, only two years after it opened. He then had three years in command of No. 4 Army Co-operation Squadron at Aldershot before being posted to the Air Ministry. There he worked directly with Trenchard. From 1931 to 1934 he was an instructor at the Army Staff College at Camberley. His book was the end product of lectures in which he had made a special study of the use of airpower in connection with land warfare in the First World War.

*Air Power and Armies* contained an analysis of the role of the strategic or Independent Air Force. It was a textbook designed to teach those who would conduct tactical air operations the basic structure of such work. As the better military thinkers have done, the author examined real military situations of the past and from them drew lessons for the future. The gist of his arguments was put forward in the plans for the Advanced Air Striking Force (sent to France in 1939) drawn up during the period 1937-41 when he succeeded Group Captain (later Marshal of the R.A.F. Sir) Arthur Harris as Director of Planning at the Air Ministry.

The Introduction contains two items upon which some comment should be made. First, bearing out what was said in Chapter I, it should be noted that Slessor regarded his work, as one would expect of a staff college instructor, as enabling "commanders and staff officers of the future to be wise *before* the event, and to learn not only from the successes, but from the failures of their predecessors." Second, he noted that the Policy of the Balance of Power was out of date in those days of the League of Nations. Nevertheless, if the freedom of the Low Countries had been a cardinal point of British maritime policy, then it was no less vital to Britain in the thirties for reasons of air security. And certainly it was true that at about the time that Slessor went to Air Ministry planning, there was a revived interest in the use of the Low Countries for defensive/offensive purposes on the part of the air strategists. A third point that he noted in passing was the tendency to swing from the one military extreme of presuming that the next war would be just like the last one to assuming that it would be utterly unlike it. In this Slessor represented the moderate school of military thought, which honestly and without prejudice attempted to arrive at solutions that would be in the best national interest despite their own particular Service biases.

The text makes use of passages from the *Field Service Regulations,* II, of 1929, to set the theme for each chapter. Thus the first opens: "The National object in war is to overcome the opponent's will . . . ," with the object of the Army being to defeat the enemy's army in co-operation with the other two Services. And in co-operating with the Army in the field the Air Force was bound to have to tackle the enemy's air force. Slessor correctly noted that as far as the air effort was concerned, the First World War was for the R.A.F. and its ancestors an "Army co-operation" war. This was natural as aeroplanes had little offensive power in themselves, but were extremely valuable for reconnaissance. Thus the primary object of air forces was to obtain local superiority over the battlefield in order that what would later be called P.R.U. (Photographic Reconnaissance Unit) aircraft could take their pictures. In other words, the job of the air commander was to supply an uninterrupted flow of information. But, said Slessor, that was only half the story and the object of *Air Power and Armies* was

> . . . to draw attention to the other aspect of air power in land warfare, namely the positive influence which can be exerted by an air striking force in direct attack upon objectives on the ground. It is this aspect that in the opinion of the writer is still seriously underrated in the British Service to-day, although it may have an influence on the course of a campaign out of all proportion to that which can be exerted by the purely ancillary service of reconnaissance and observation.

The Second World War was to prove this a most prescient statement, for the German blitzkrieg and later Allied tactics in imitation and development of it were to make great use of tactical air forces both for the isolation of the battlefield and as a direct support to the ground forces in dealing with such small objectives as machine guns in Sicilian village church steeples and in such large ones as flank guard to the United States Third Army under Patton in France.

It was in dealing with the object of air superiority that Slessor had to come closest to that delicate subject—the bombing of cities. From the point of view upon which his book was based, the main object in a land campaign would always be the enemy land forces, with their communications and supply systems. But at the same time he recognized that once those forces were defeated, the ultimate reduction of the enemy nation would in all probability be undertaken merely by an air campaign in which the decision would be gained by bombing the vital centres, action against the enemy air force then being merely subsidiary to the prime objective. Moreover, he correctly pointed out, action would have to be taken throughout that land campaign against the logistical base upon which the opposing air force fought, in order both to give operational freedom to the R.A.F. and at the same time to weaken the power that could be brought against British ground forces. (This doctrine had to be severely modified in the high-speed campaigns of World War II, but Harris and others often failed to see this.) But he did not go so far as the absolute theorists in predicting the utter ruin of an army without air cover, for he was a realist and noted that the mere destruction of the enemy's air force would not of itself bring victory. Quietly criticizing the writers of the manuals and other makers of doctrine, he pointed out that if the primary task of the air force in the field was made the creation of a favourable air situation, then, as happened in the First World War, the air commanders would lose sight of the true object of the air striking force and become involved in the daily battle to keep the skies clear over the whole of the Army to the detriment by neglect of more important targets whose destruction would enable the Army to achieve its stated object. In fact, he declared, in many ways the idea of air superiority had become a catchword—in much the same way, he might have added, that Mahanic use of the term "sea power" had at the end of the nineteenth century.

Slessor went on to declare that once warfare went into the third dimension, whether under the sea or in the air, the cubic area of the battlefield became so great that absolute command was hardly ever practicable. (Not long after this, as the Battle of Britain demonstrated, the introduction of radar and of radio-telephone control did in effect reduce the volume of the battlefield to manageable dimensions.) Nevertheless it was true that the surest method of securing freedom of action for one's own aircraft was to destroy the enemy's. As this was not in Slessor's opinion possible, the best that could be hoped for in a war against a first-class enemy was to throw his forces on the defensive and neutralize them, an object achievable only by hard and continuous fighting (how hard and how continuous the 1939-45 war was well to demonstrate). Digressing on this point he noted that the activities of the fighter aircraft in the First World War had been exaggerated out of their true proportion and he went on to quote with approval the section in the American Major W. Sherman's *Air Warfare* (1926) that dealt with pursuit aviation, the fighters, whose only business was to destroy enemy aircraft, whereas all other segments of the air arm had dual roles.

It should be noted in passing that the fighters (meaning both the pilots and their aircraft) in the 1914 war obtained and have retained a distinctive glamour out of proportion to their role, though they were about half of the combat force, for the following reasons: War in the air was comparatively new, and the participants were mostly young quasi-civilians who came from the middle and upper classes. Like all airmen of every age and country, they possessed tremendous enthusiasm, love of their job, and an endless ability to talk shop, which dazzled the earthbound until their own words, with the help of journalists, built up a romantic and glamourous tradition for their sort. They were sportsmen playing a deadly game. They talked in part to keep up their own courage in the face of appalling casualties, as high sometimes as 75 per cent of a squadron a month for the ten months of 1918 in the case Slessor cites of No. 80 Squadron, R.A.F. More than this, fighter pilots caught the public imagination because they were often decorated and because of all those engaged in the war they were performing as individuals, as opposed to the masses, in the muck over which they flew. Their cloth wings sewn on the tunic breast set them apart at once. Who was to know that not every pilot was in command of a fighter?

Slessor went so far as to say that "fighters are an arm of the Service whose influence is entirely indirect and auxiliary." But he agreed with Major Sherman that they were a necessary part of any air force for they would often have to accompany bombers to enable them to beat their way through defensive screens of enemy aircraft in order to gain their objectives. In fact he went so far as to urge that emergency tankage be fitted to fighters to make them more mobile on the Empire reinforcement routes, but never carried this to the logical conclusion of providing drop-tanks as a means of extending their radius of action or time on patrol. That he did not do so may be because he was strongly imbued at the time with the standard belief in the ability of air groups to move through enemy space without interception, since such a force had no flanks and no lines of communication about which to worry. Moreover, such a group could achieve its tactical objective without first having to defeat the opposing air force, and it was not bound for more than a few hours to any particular course of action. Flexibility was its greatest asset.

Enlarging upon this theme, so dear to the hearts of airmen, Slessor proceeded to advance arguments that reflect both the Air Force climate of opinion of his own day and his own experience. Not that some of these concepts do not, in fact, still hold good in these days of the strategic reserve and Army television commercials that proclaim a "here today, Arabia tomorrow, and back on Saturday" conception of air-transportable soldiering. He took up the theme again later in the book. His main point was that airpower was mobile, aerodromes cheap, and that with its rapidity of movement airpower could be at trouble spots about the British Empire quicker than any other force, which thus allowed smaller garrisons to be maintained at distant bases. This was, of course, one of the arguments that Trenchard had used about Singapore.

In Chapter II, "The Main Offensive," Slessor moved closer to the problem of the attack upon vital centres. Examining the Battle of the Somme in the summer of 1916 and taking his cue from the second volume of *The War in the Air*, he proceeded to analyse how the British had achieved local air superiority over that battlefield. Here was the case of first-class powers facing each other in an actual situation. The first of the principles that he felt emerged was that the enemy could be forced by a resolute bombing campaign to go over to the defensive. Judicious selection of objectives would cause the enemy to defend the vital centres that for political or military reasons he could not afford to leave unguarded, and to do this he would concentrate his air force where the attackers could in their turn focus upon destroying it. Thus much depended upon picking the objectives that were most likely to prick the opponent to the quick. This could be done both by fighters operating against his aircraft and by bombers and low-flying fighters attacking his aerodromes. This latter tactic was not particularly favoured by Slessor, who called Churchill to account for deeming it the most important offensive operation in his memorandum of October 1917. Being primarily interested in action in aid of the Army, Slessor pointed to railway junctions as being vital centres that did not have to be destroyed, only disrupted sufficiently to cause the necessary paralysis of the enemy war machine. Yet he recognized that London was a vital centre in the First World War for social and political reasons, even though bombing of it in purely military terms would not have cost the Allies the war. Due to the lack of real evidence on this point, Slessor thought that each side would open the next war with a bombing offensive against the other's vital centres, and that the result would shortly be a deadlock in this sphere, as taking the offensive simply to be on the offensive was not likely to produce any better results in the future than it had in the past. But he did feel that whichever side had the fewer vital points would be in the weaker position, for his opponent would thus be able more easily to select the points upon which to concentrate.

Again Slessor reflected the thought of his day when he talked of the bomber as not being solely a defensive aircraft. Perhaps because of his Army Co-operation background, he regarded the general-purpose aeroplane as the finest and most flexible machine of the time. We must today recognize that from the point of view of Empire defence and of tactical air forces, the two-seater day-bomber/fighters of the Hawker stable had a great deal to be said for them. Nor must these opinions be condemned in view of the failure of the Bristol Blenheim as a fighter and of the Boulton Paul Defiant, for both these types were the first of a new generation of aircraft. The validity of Slessor's argument may be demonstrated with the Beau-fighter and then the versatile de Havilland Mosquito and the later fighter-bombers. Again it was during Slessor's time at the Air Ministry that the shift of emphasis from the bomber force to the home-defence fighter took place, with the conversion of the Blenheim light-bomber into a fighter.

Moreover, he noted, in-the-air defence tended to need to out-number the attackers to be effective, at least that was the lesson of the air raids upon London in 1915-18. And those raids held another lesson also, namely, that the air commander had at his disposal a magnificent power for making diversions so that he could concentrate his forces at the decisive point without much opposition. Though radar went a long way to challenge this freedom, nevertheless, the planning and execution of raids still remained a war of wits, with the commanders-in-chief in the Second World War not much better able to control their forces, once a major operation had started, than were those in the First.

But for the selection of the vital point for any attack, it was vitally necessary that intelligence be properly assessed and co-ordinated. Here Slessor engaged in a brief *obiter dictum* on the tripartite nature of the intelligence organization of the British Services and their abilities to twist the evidence to suit the prevalent doctrine of their own Service. This was a problem that was never entirely satisfactorily settled even during the war and one upon which Kingston-McCloughry was also to comment.

After dealing in his third chapter in quite a straightforward and routine way with the manner in which enemy air forces might be neutralized, Slessor turned at the beginning of the fourth to a discussion of the merits of escort fighters. This was a subject that Trenchard had in 1923 summarily dismissed, yet as Slessor pointed out, during the war it had been British practice to send escort fighters with the bombers and for this work the two-seater with its protected tail had proved a most effective weapon.

But curiously the word "escort" was frowned upon and, although the Americans would readopt it as a type name, the British tended to shy away from the term even in the Second World War and talked instead of providing "fighter cover." Technically what developed was that, after the practice of making some aircraft of the same type fighters and some bombers (so that a homogenous force of attackers and their escort was created) was dropped, the bomber and the fighter became two incompatible types. The load-carrier developed into the lumbering long-range deterrent delivery lorry, while the fighter became a fast-climbing, short-ranged defensive weapon actually unsuited for an offensive role over more than the limited type of battlefield in France and Flanders. The exception was the Mosquito.

Faced with the fact that the defending fighters would concentrate about the likely target, Slessor urged that fighters be scheduled to fly as escort in such a way that they reached the target ahead of the main force and drew off the enemy while bombing was actually in progress. But he recognized that this could be done only when the target was within the single-seater's radius of action. On longer missions the short-ranged fighters would have to be used as inward and outward escorts to the limit of their endurance and for the rest of the raid attempt to provide assistance through an offensive against enemy fighter airfields, as they had upon occasion on the Western Front.

Because of the general paucity of German records, Slessor relied heavily upon lessons from the British side of the line. But he made surprisingly good use of the negative aspects of British operations in the field with his analysis of aerodromes damaged by bombing and the consequent need for dispersal, of the need for quicker methods of getting spares up from better-dispersed stores, of the need to replace men and material, and allied to these the need for rethinking the Empire air reinforcement routes in view of the fact that the capture of a single base could put some of them out of action, notably the route to Singapore.

In the second part of the book Slessor dealt with the selection of objectives, beginning with the thought that the principles of war had been over-codified in the military manuals (after not having been there at all for centuries) and should be reduced to three fundamental rules, which were not principles at all, viz., *concentration, offensive action,* and *security.*

For the land forces the objectives against which air action could be undertaken were divisible into two: fighting troops, and supply. The former included not only the troops in the battle zone, but also their communications, while supply was divisible into production and supply in the field. In the area of supply, therefore, the sources of raw materials were a legitimate target, once again taking the author back into the area considered to belong to the strategic bomber forces. But clearly, he noted, in any major war, attack on production would be the responsibility of the Air Ministry at the direction of the War Cabinet. Yet the results achieved by such operations were likely to have such a vital effect upon the conduct of operations in the field that "a clear appreciation of the relation between attack on production and the more intimate form of co-operation in the land theatre of war is essential to a proper under-standing of strategic air concentration—the fundamental principle on which is based the existence of a centralized autonomous air service." He then again skirted gingerly about the problem of bombardment of cities by referring his readers to J. M. Spaight's *Air Power and the Cities.* He noted in passing the effect of air raid warnings upon production and also observed in a footnote the im-portant point that perhaps a good deal of the rancour between those who had no use for strategic bombing and its rash advocates was the misleading use of the term "independent" coupled with "strategic" to signify operations having nothing to do with the battlefield. On this point he attacked Sir Frederick Sykes and P. R. C. Groves for failing to provide any machinery by which it could be decided that the "necessary uses of aircraft" for the other Services had been achieved, because such agreement was impossible to reach. To this Sykes replied rather unfairly by claiming that Slessor saw the sole object of war as the destruction of the enemy army by direct military action. Sykes objected because he felt this was a critical neglect of his thesis that the Independent Air Force had a role as the destroyer of supply lines.*

Even leaving out the personality factors involved from earlier associations, Slessor's work stands up against such criticism for he was carefully writing about the air striking force attached to the Army, yet he could not neglect making some comments on the way in which this force had to fit into the whole air pattern, or he would have been attacked for neglecting it! Slessor himself noted in *Air Power and Armies* that there would be times when the main bomber force would be called upon to help in tactical operations. This was done after D-Day in 1944. The time, said Slessor, when it should have been thrown into the battlefield was in March 1918, when the Independent Air Force was being formed just as the Germans crashed through the British lines. This was one of the cases when its influence could have been decisive. As a result of that incident, Slessor came to the conclusion that attacks on production should take place only when there is a lull on the battlefield. Yet he also said (and here he may merely have been paying lip service to the doctrine upon which the independent status of the R.A.F. had largely been established) that "although air action against production cannot yet altogether replace active operations on the ground, it can and should limit and reduce them." Certainly it should prevent the senseless battering against unbroken opposition that was such a feature of the 1914 war. "The whole art of air warfare [and, he might have said, of all warfare] is first the capacity to select the correct objective *at the time*, namely, that on which attack is likely to be decisive" and then to concentrate against it the maximum possible force. Thus, in the spring of 1917 the object of Allied air forces should have been the German submarine fleet and its bases.

Turning to the best ways to disrupt supply, he showed himself as well aware, as mechanically minded Air Force officers tended to be, of the power of petrol and its limiting factors. Thus, though he does not say it here,† he was a supporter of mechanized forces able to achieve dispersal and not reliant upon roads or railways, both

---

* Sir Frederick Sykes, *From Many Angles* (1942), pp. 236-237. See also Chapter VI of this book.

† See Chapter II of *The Great Deterrent,* which is his 1936 Prize Essay on this topic.

of which were ideal air targets, especially for fighters once a high degree of air superiority had been established and plenty of machines were available. This certainly was to hold true in the coming war. On the other hand, he also recognized that against first-class troops such action would be hazardous, as trains were likely to be fitted with anti-aircraft weapons. Nevertheless, he saw for tactical aircraft operating close to the troops three important roles. The first was assault action in aid of an attack, the second the turning of a retreat into a rout, and the third defensive action, the balking of an attack. Again here, as in earlier comments, he was to find his conceptions made easier of application by radio, which allowed the development of the "cab-rank" technique for close-support fighters and fighter-bombers.

In analysing Slessor's writing, a large part of *Air Power and Armies* may be neglected, for this contained a perceptive but straightforward analysis of air attack upon communications and an exposition of the Battle of Amiens of 8-11 August 1918. In this he exposed the short-sighted air plans of General L. E. O. Charlton and their failure to appreciate that after the objective had been taken, a counterattack would have to be beaten off if not prevented from developing in the first place. Slessor's purpose in this examination was to show that plans must be made with a wide appreciation of both time and the battlefield. In this battle he saw the lessons of concentration again in terms of the number of aircraft available, maximum efforts by squadrons against the minimum number of targets, and centralization of control so as to achieve the most economical use of the force available. And here again (pages 192-194) as on page 75, Slessor doubted the wisdom of Sir Hugh Trenchard. In the earlier reference he had noted that Trenchard had said that by June 1918 the Anglo-French forces had enough aircraft with which to achieve their objectives in support of the armies and so the Independent Air Force could safely pursue its own programme. At the same time he noted that, despite the lessons of March 1918, Trenchard did not seem to believe very strongly in Army Co-operation work. In these latter pages, Slessor did not name Trenchard, but commented upon the fact that British fighting policy on the ground and in the air was to exert a constant pressure upon the enemy, unlike the French or the German, which believed in resting between efforts. The results, said Slessor, were that there was a strong decline in the fighting efficiency of British squadrons, for their personnel were weary and often untrained. It is also possible to attribute the high casualties suffered by the British air forces to this lack of training and battle fatigue, for weariness is something upon which aviation doctors still keep an eye, even with civil airline pilots.

The last part of *Air Power and Armies* is devoted to a concise analysis of the Third Revolution, as Slessor called the conquest of the air. Other weapons enlarged the battlefield, the air weapon made it likely that ground forces would never even reach the battlefield. But he eschewed such a sweeping claim for his work, which concentrates on how the air arm could serve in a land campaign. As throughout the book, much that he said stood the test of battle and campaign in the Second World War. The intelligence experts did come to study the weak points in enemy transportation systems and did try to lay on air strikes to create difficulties where these did not already exist. But he went further and concluded that the British Army of 1935, still largely a manpower and shellpower organization, was liable to destruction in short order by an enemy with a decent tactical air force, that in any future war no army could afford to be dependent upon a single line of communications as this would be at the mercy of the opposing air force, and third, that future staffs must think wider and use larger maps. In terms of strategical thought, like Liddell Hart and others, Slessor foresaw that the mass army was impossible, for it was wide open in providing enormous possibilities for dislocation and confusion. He also concluded that with the size of the air forces in the late thirties, the concentration of armies in country well served by railways could only be delayed but not disrupted; but the converse was also likely to be true: in a country with but few railways, the enemy's concentration could probably be prevented. (In Korea the Chinese Communists not only showed how hard it was to keep railways knocked out, but also actually moved large forces onto the battlefield without their being detected en route mainly because they moved dispersed as individuals and did not behave like a Western mechanized force but in a primitive manner, which American intelligence failed to comprehend.) Further, the old method of concentrating a huge force before battle would have to be replaced with a Nelsonic (or Napoleonic) system by which the dispersed forces could be concentrated at the decisive place at the correct time. In the case of the invading army, Slessor reckoned that the defender should make use of demolitions in such a way as to create defiles through which the invader would have to pass, for these would then give the defending air force its best chance to stem the advance. Moreover, tank forces would be of great help to the air arm, for fear of tanks would force the enemy to travel in defensive formations rather than dispersed, and this again would make them better targets. Thus the movement forward from the area of concentration would place an army in its most vulnerable formation, especially as its line of communications became attenuated. In addition, railways could no longer because of their liability to interdiction from the air be regarded as an instrument of major tactics. Turning to the use of the Advanced Air Striking Force, he came to his ninth conclusion, namely, that this air group had to seek to isolate the battlefield from enemy reinforcement and supply so that the break-in could be converted to the break-through without loss of impetus caused by enemy counterattacks or stiffening in the rear areas. He also felt, as Churchill so presciently put it in 1917, that army commanders should not make their plans and then turn to the airmen to see how they could help, but should consider how the ground forces could impose a strain upon the enemy so as to give the air campaign a greater chance of success. In conclusion, he suggested that the dream army of the future for Britain would be composed of armoured formations backed by motorized infantry and sappers armed primarily with automatic weapons and anti-tank guns, while overhead would stream the long-range striking force flying past the frontier defences to attack communications behind the enemy's fighting forces or to aid the armoured forces in their counterattack.

The only trouble with the dream was that it became a nightmare four years after *Air Power and Armies* appeared, when the Germans put these ideas into practice and swept across France.

In 1936 Slessor won the Gold Medal Essay contest of the Royal United Service Institution with his "Tactical and Administrative Implications of the Introduction of the Internal Combustion Engine into the British Army, in Relation to Its Capacity to Overcome Modern Defences and Counter the Threat of Air Action." * In it he naturally followed the tack he had taken in his book, while at the same time showing considerable evidence of the influence of other

* This essay was not published in the *JRUSI* until 1947, p. 463 ff.; it is reprinted in Slessor's *The Great Deterrent* as Chapter II.

writers of his day in such phrases as "new-model" Army and the like. The essay also, with its interest in Indian defence, reflects not only a problem that was then of current interest but also the fact that the author was stationed in India at the time as C.O. of No. 3 Wing engaged in the Waziristan operations on the famed Northwest Frontier.

Slessor himself became too busy in the next few years to write any more books. After being Director of Planning, he was Air Officer Commanding No. 5 Group, Bomber Command; Assistant Chief of the Air Staff for a year; and then Air Officer Commanding-in-Chief, Coastal Command, 1943; Commander-in-Chief, R.A.F. Mediterranean and Middle East, 1944-45; Air Member for Personnel, 1945-47; Commandant of the Imperial Defence College; and on 1 January 1950 he became Chief of the Air Staff. After three years as military head of the Royal Air Force he retired from the Service. A year later there appeared his *Strategy for the West*.

In this new work and in the later *What Price Coexistence? A Policy for the Western Alliance*, the former Chief of the Air Staff expanded upon a current political theme in which he found himself considerably involved as one of the Government's principal military advisers. Stemming from various talks given and articles written since the end of the Second World War (some of which are gathered in *The Great Deterrent* [1957]), he faced up to the problem of the role of Britain and the West in the struggle against Russia. This is grand strategy as opposed to the older art of the general. And the impact of his career is to be seen in the much more political slant of these new pieces. But subtly behind them is an interesting return to the old traditional prewar R.A.F. view— that the bomber is the deterrent, especially in the days of the nuclear warhead. Yet this is a more modified, rational, and realistic Service pleading. The atomic bomb has provided the means whereby airpower can do the devastating job if only one bomber gets through to each major target. Thus the deterrent has become a real threat. But at the same time, it has become, Slessor feels, a force for peace, which is again what the airmen have long argued. Put simply, the atomic bomber represented a power that in Trenchardian days was possessed by the R.A.F. only when dealing with desert tribes. Nevertheless, as then, so today, limited wars were more likely than a total conflict.

*The Great Deterrent* is full of provocative little comments upon these matters in the form of essays upon strategy and the Commonwealth, total or limited war, and defence policy in general, to name but a few. *What Price Coexistence?* carries the search for a viable policy into the area of combatting non-warlike Russian expansion. Perhaps it is unkind to classify these new works as yet further Staff appreciations, but in these days of acute concentration upon the subject of Russian relations, they do not stand out clearly as milestones with a long-term viability such as *Air Power and Armies* possesses.

## E. J. Kingston-McCloughry

Air Vice-Marshal E. J. (Edgar James) Kingston-McCloughry was born in 1896 and educated at Adelaide, Australia, and Trinity College, Cambridge, later being graduated from the R.A.F. Staff College in 1929 and from the Army Staff College in 1935. Entering the Engineers in 1914, he transferred to the R.F.C. and served with Trenchard in France in 1918. He rose to be Head Operations Planner, Allied European Air Force Headquarters in 1944 and later Chief Air Defence Officer in the postwar Ministry of Defence. Like a number of the men who served near Trenchard, he was able to write and began entering the Royal United Service Institution contests. In 1927 he won first prize in the Groves Memorial Essay, and in 1942 and 1943 he won the Gordon Sheppard Memorial Prize Essay contests. His first pieces were collected over a decade and in 1937 were published, at the urging of Lord Trenchard, as *Winged Warfare: Air Problems of Peace and War*. This was at a time when the market was being flooded with air volumes as rearmament came increasingly to public notice. It was not until 1947 that the next volume, *War in Three Dimensions*, was completed. After he retired from the Service, *The Direction of War* (1955), *Global Strategy* (1957), *Defence* (1959), and *The Spectrum of Strategy* (1964) were published. A standard run of two thousand copies of each of these volumes was printed. *War in Three Dimensions* was twice reprinted and was translated into Hebrew. The works published in 1955 to 1959 appeared simultaneously in Britain and the United States and have been in several cases translated into Russian, Polish, Rumanian, and Spanish.

*Winged Warfare*, a collection of essays, appears today to be a straightforward, descriptive book with rather little to say. One of the opening essays dealt with the reasons why the Independent Air Force was diverted to morale-breaking, as has been mentioned earlier, while it was only later in the book that there are some more lasting general remarks about air warfare. Viewing the history of air operations as so brief as to be dangerous as a foundation, Kinston-McCloughry called for the creation of a new strategy firmly rooted in land and sea precedents and having as its object the defeat of the enemy's forces by action or restraint. He saw here the role of the Air Force as co-operating with surface forces to defeat the enemy's army, to maintain control of sea communications, and, by directing pressure upon the enemy's life and morale as well as by defeating his air force, providing distant co-operative pressure. The most effective way to use an air force was not necessarily by defeating the enemy's, for it could well be difficult to bring it to battle. It was far better to strike at the enemy's morale, though not necessarily at civilians'. Like most airmen, Kingston-McCloughry believed that the only way to get the enemy's air force away from the front was by bombing some vital point that he would feel compelled to defend. Thus the main British or allied air strength was to be hurled at the enemy's vital points with fighters used only to assist in gaining air superiority. This was still strongly Trenchardian, but influenced by his broadening experience, rather like Slessor's, at the Army Staff College.

In December 1943 he was appointed Chief Operations Planner to Air Chief Marshal Sir Trafford Leigh-Mallory and given the job of preparing the Allied Air Force plans for D-Day. This meant that he had to grapple with the crux of Sir Arthur Tedder's air problem, explored in such depth in Webster and Frankland—how to utilize the same bomber forces for immediate support of surface operations and for the strategic air offensive against Germany (as in 1918). This was inter-Service and inter-Allied planning with a vengeance, with personality conflicts at high levels thrown into the bargain. Looking back on this in May 1962, Air Vice-Marshal Kingston-McCloughry said that he believed the plans for Overlord were his most influential contribution to military thought and affairs, for these plans were conceived in such a way that they had wide influence upon ideas of Allied command, especially in both the practical planning ramifications and repercussions over the years and in the inter-Service relations and chains of command.* Moreover, it was this experience that placed him in touch with Sir Solly Zuckerman, a brilliant and perceptive scientist, Chief Scientific Adviser to the Ministry of Defence in 1961. Kingston-McCloughry admits that Sir Solly opened his eyes to non-military tools for strategic research, especially the scientific. At the same time this experience with the Allied planners led to two books, of which *War in Three Dimensions* was the first.

Starting with the classical concept of war, a theme that he repeated in condensed form in *Global Strategy* a decade later, Kingston-McCloughry took the Clausewitzian assumption that the only way to defeat the enemy was in battle, noting, however, that in naval warfare a fleet that could not be brought to battle might be neutralized. With the Second World War there really developed long-range bombardment of a new sort, which laid bare the whole of an opponent's war-making power. After noting that ballistic missiles were the most economical war weapons if trained personnel handled them, he made the valid observation that a familiar carrier and a novel weapon tend at first to introduce panic. What he had in mind was, of course, the idea of mating the familiar German V-2 rocket with the American atomic warhead. Carrying the old Air Force arguments about the volume of space into outer space, he showed how the power of penetration of enemy territory was quite different from that of surface forces. (It was not until the early sixties that anti-missile missiles have begun to become practical, emphasizing that to every challenge there is a technological, as well as a human, response if enough money is spent to stimulate it. A parallel impact was that of radar upon the freedom of aeroplanes in the late thirties and early war years.) Kingston-McCloughry further argued that long-range bombardment was always an offensive force seeking the enemy, but that when not employed it had no positive effect in war, though in peacetime it might act as a deterrent, for in war it could have but a vague reprisal value.

When one considers the proportion of the British defence effort in two wars that was absorbed in preparing to counter this deterrent (and possible invasion)—what Kingston-McCloughry calls the limited fleet-in-being, a Mahanic missile force—it must be wondered

* Letter of 8 May 1962 in reply to my queries.

if he is correct. It would perhaps be fairest to say that the effect of the fleet-in-being threat is greatest when the weapons-system is newest and least known to the potential victim, and that this psychological force decreases as knowledge and countertechnique is developed until a point is reached at which the public and its political leadership accept the risk as a normal one.

In 1947 it was possible to argue that missiles could destroy the enemy's ability to make war without destroying his armed forces or breaking his will to war. At the same time, Kingston-McCloughry added the significant rider that this could be so only if the enemy could not—and, one might add, does not—devote time and resources to dispersion of, and the means of recovery for, his vitals. But if the new missiles raised again the question of concentration of force, they also raised once again the problem of the economy of force as well. Thus there was a vital need for the creation of a three-dimensional intelligence service, one of his favourite points,* which would in peacetime know all about the enemy, the degree of vulnerability and the relative importance of possible targets in his homeland.

In discussing the secondary functions of air forces in his fourth chapter, Kingston-McCloughry, like Slessor in *Air Power and Armies*, cried out against the miscategorization of aircraft into "tactical" and "strategical." The role that an air-striking force plays, like that of the missile, depends upon *"the object with which the target is selected at that particular time."*

At times it seems that Kingston-McCloughry's vision is too parochial. This appears in such remarks as that in which he says that airborne forces can be used only when the forces dropped will be relieved by surface forces in a short time, a memory of Arnheim and an ignorance of Burma, and as when he predicates so much of his strategic idea upon the assumption that the war will come only between industrialized states of the European pattern. This is reminiscent of Marx's work, which made no allowance for his utopia being tried *en masse* in such a backward area as early twentieth century Russia. Nor did Marx any more than many military pundits think in terms of the response to the challenge he created and how to meet that reaction.

* It has also been one of Slessor's. In July 1935 Lord Strabolgi (J. M. Kenworthy), another intelligence man, wrote "National Defence: The Need of a Combined General Staff," *Fortnightly Review*, pp. 31-40.

Looking into the future in Chapter VIII of *War in Three Dimensions*, Kingston-McCloughry felt that the emphasis would be upon developments above and below the earth's surface, and in this he was at variance with Liddell Hart, who has steadfastly maintained that armoured forces still are potent, but have never really been tried. But apart from that, time has supported Kingston-McCloughry, for the emphasis has been shifted from the surface forces to atomic submarines and to nuclear aircraft-carriers at sea, while in the air not only has the speed at which men could fly been quadrupled in the two decades since 1945, but man has now rocketted himself into outer space. The concentration of public thought has been upon atomic developments, but as he pointed out, gas and bacteriological warfare have not been neglected entirely. Nevertheless, the most important part of *War in Three Dimensions* was devoted to an analysis of atomic problems.

Modern nuclear warfare is costly. Thus, says Kingston-McCloughry, the need is even more than in the Second World War for accuracy in delivery. Yet at the same time, the economics of warfare makes the number of possible targets much smaller than they were before and, therefore, the defence is placed in an easier position, for it has fewer vital areas to protect. Fortunately the balance of fear has been on the side of peace, and as a result time has been allowed for the development of counterweapons. Harking back in thought to Lanchester, Kingston-McCloughry saw in 1947 that time was of the essence and that even a short loss of control could prove decisive to such an extent that a superior power might be upset by even a minor setback, which created a moral factor not to be overlooked or underestimated. The author rightly foresaw that the period of American dominance would be only the opening phase of the atomic age and that this would end as soon as any other power had the capability of bombing the United States or any other opponent. At the same time, the decision-makers would find themselves faced with the age-old military problem once again in trying to assess what the opponent could do, thus presenting themselves with a supreme and frightful opportunity for self-delusion and disaster.

In the case of the United States in the monopoly period of atomic weaponry, he foresaw that American policy-makers would have to face first the decision whether or not to use the atomic weapon in order to obtain a quick and cheap victory (a better word might be "stoppage") if war broke out, and second the political one of whether to profit by their omnipotent power once a stockpile had been accumulated. But, he noted, the crux of the question in these cases was whether or not the consequences would ultimately be more damaging to the user. This was what Liddell Hart and others had been trying to point out in the interwar years, that war is not an end in itself, but only the means to an objective.

For the United States he saw two conditions as of paramount importance in making the atomic bomb the centre of her strategy in or after the monopoly position: that the reliance upon one weapon assumes the unconditional determination to use it, regardless of the circumstances, to produce a decisive result, and that the monopoly period is limited and that once it has passed new factors arise, especially the doubt as to the easy decisiveness of the weapon. It was, he said, suicide to base the whole of a defence policy upon a strategy that was provisional and easily nullifiable. For some time, and somewhat lagging behind the realities of developments in Russian atomic technology, American policy did centre about the great deterrent, despite these wise words and those of Sir John Slessor. Kingston-McCloughry then proceeded to make the entirely sensible point that, if this were not so, then "the diplomatic effect of its possession, like the diplomatic effect of any other disparity of weapons or military force, is no greater than the practical possibilities." In the postmonopoly period, then, the overriding factor would become once again the fear of reprisals; then this in its turn would revive conventional military power. In fact, as far as the distinguished air vice-marshal was concerned, the atomic weapon was and would remain a burden until small and selective nuclear weapons were operational.

Much of what he said in 1947 might have been written of the R.A.F. and the British in the interwar years, though with one significant difference: in the years before 1944 the British did not in fact possess a war-stopping weapon.

Returning to the concepts of three-dimensional warfare, he noted that at sea in the future the defence of convoys and fleets would increasingly be undertaken by aircraft carriers specially equipped for anti-submarine warfare, a development from the Second World War where on both land and sea, as well as in the air, there had been an inadequate appraisal of the requirements for waging war in three dimensions. As he saw it, "the duty of a government is to ensure that current defence preparations shall so correspond with current appreciation that there is a minimum both of risk and of waste." Thus, in peacetime a nation had to assess the force it would need upon the outbreak of war and for its continuation. Peacetime preparations had then to be based upon these ideas while at the same time considering how these actions might prevent or defer the wars assumed. After considering these ideas in relation to Imperial defence, he made the point that for effective defence the policy-makers had to determine, just as a company commander had, the line of maximum penetration beyond which the enemy cannot be allowed to pass. The vital hinterland enclosed by this line was, in Imperial terms, quite similar to the mercantilist's in terms of raw materials' sources and the like. How far the people would allow outposts to be erected in advance of the maximum line was a matter governed by public opinion and the very nature of a country. The smaller its area and resources, the greater it was affected by new developments in military technology. In this respect he concluded that there was, in fact, in 1938 little likelihood of an opening air blow against England for until after the defeat of Poland, Germany herself was too vulnerable to this type of action, which would have delayed the speedy conclusion of her land campaigns and have lessened any chance of British acquiescence in her actions. It must be suggested that Kingston-McCloughry was here, despite his general prescience or because he was a serving officer, still reflecting the general R.A.F. prewar view that Britain had a strategic bombing deterrent force that Germany respected. Perhaps in 1935 Hitler did have some fear of it at a time when the Luftwaffe was still weak and when its Chief of Staff, Oberst Wever, was still alive and pushing the need for a strategic force. But after his death in 1936 the German Air Force was increasingly dominated by Göring's World War fighter companions who thought strictly in terms of a tactical air force. Thus a combination of events shifted the German glance elsewhere, leaving the British alone scared of the great mythical deterrent they had created. Operations during the Spanish Civil War dispelled no illusions for the Germans because the Condor Legion possessed superior equipment to that of the Loyalists, so neither the protection of fast bombers nor the limited range of the escorting fighters needed remedying. It was not until 1940-41 that both the Germans and the British were disillusioned.

Turning in Chapter X to a summary of the principles upon which defence policy in peacetime is made, Kingston-McCloughry came to the conclusion, reflecting again his own experience, that the gravest difficulty was perhaps the determination of how much fore-warning of war there would be. This, he felt, could be shortened by a steep curve of expansion of the armed forces and by an extension of the zone of partial resistance. But again, a lot depended upon the quality of the intelligence available. The wise leader, in other words, trades space for time. This gives him protection against surprise and freedom to mount a counterstroke, rather than embroiling him in the opening confusion that accompanies first contact with the enemy.

That this book shows that Kingston-McCloughry was more mature in thought than before the war must be attributed to the fact that he went through a tempering by experience in the Second World War. In contrast to the experience of officers in the First World War, this was at a much more sophisticated and intellectual level in a more refined and industrialized war.

The second of the postwar books, *The Direction of War,* is the most interesting of all his books for it is autobiographical. In it he not only deals with the making of war and plans for war but also with the conflicts of personality and how these affected operations. And while this is in many respects his best book, it is also the most easily examined for much that he says in certain chapters he or somebody else has already said. The sections dealing with former concepts of the political direction and high command of war, the First World War, the beginnings of air warfare, and on the developments between the wars, are straightforward for anyone with a knowledge of English history and political development, though for a foreigner a number of the references and assumptions might not be entirely clear. Basically the point being driven home is that the political side must be aware of the military factors that affect advice and that the military must give up their old parochial habits and pull together for national strength through the Ministry of Defence. In addition, those civilians, like the Scientific Adviser, who are appointed to such bodies as the Chiefs of Staff Committee, must also take their responsibilities seriously. And even here the personality factor must be taken into account, as for instance in the difference between Britain's greatest wartime Prime Minister, Churchill, and his immediate peacetime predecessors. It is notable that in these first five opening chapters he is much more willing to admit the failure of R.A.F. policy, equipment, and vision before and during the Second World War. And as he himself might well admit, this new freedom has come from no longer being a career man.

Kingston-McCloughry said in the Introduction that certain fundamentally changed conditions affected Britain's position. These were that she was after 1945, if not after 1919, a marginal power incapable of starting or stopping a major war on her own, that she had become vulnerable to mortal blows herself, and that the cost of rearmament and of the protection of civilians and their property had become overwhelming, just at the time when the people themselves were no longer willing to tolerate even the kind of casualties that Bomber Command had suffered in the 1939-45 war.

In passing it may be mentioned that the double distinction of the High Direction and the High Command might well be combined under one term, the most suitable perhaps being "the Higher Direction." Under this can be included the political, diplomatic, economic, military, social, and psychological aspects of the direction of war and peace along with their auxiliary and ancillary formations in terms of those that advise and supply the information and the means for taking decisions and carrying them into action.

In dealing with the operation of the High Command of the Air Force, Kingston-McCloughry was in a position to observe well, yet just enough below the top not to be swept out of office each time there was a change of command. His was, in fact, then, one of those backbone positions from which emanates a subtle power that permeates the bureaucratic side of any organization. As he himself points out, in those days—and still—there was a natural human tendency on the part of intelligence officers to accept only that evidence that suited their own or their Service's view. The pressure of actual war soon dislocated the joint planning organization. Moreover, the war also glaringly revealed the lack of knowledge on the part of many officers of the differences between a political and a military leader's approach to war. Kingston-McCloughry was closer to the political than to the Service people at times and so is more aware of this problem than fellow officers who did not serve in such a privileged position. As the officer responsible in the early days of the war and through the French disaster for the assignment of air transport available to the military, Kingston-McCloughry very quickly began to experience political pressure brought to bear upon the military to override his reasonable decision against doing something. It was apparently an eye-opener for him. In this vein then he goes on to examine the setting up of the American Political Direction under Franklin Roosevelt, the conversion of this into the Higher Direction and its integration also with the Allied Combined Chiefs of Staff that was emulated at theatre-command levels all over the world. Yet here, also, the political aspects dominated and inter-Service and inter-Allied prestige and desires became factors that influenced the decision-makers. When the invasion of northern France, known as Overlord, was being planned, Kingston-Mc Cloughry had a ringside seat, or really that of a handler, as the head air operations planner at SHAEF, the Allied combined headquarters. Here he saw all the dangers of lack of decision and responsibility in and for planning, and it appears to have imprinted an indelible memory upon his brain. And it was here that personalities were most in force. On the part of his own Service, he was caught in the middle of the battles between Sir Arthur Harris of Bomber Command, Chief of the Air Staff Lord Portal, Eisenhower's Deputy Supreme Commander Lord Tedder, and the Air Commander-in-Chief designate of the Allied air forces for the invasion, Air Chief Marshal Sir Trafford Leigh-Mallory. Added to this was the appointment of Air Marshal Coningham of the Desert Air Force to command the British Tactical Air Force. But all these personalities with their private abrasions were reflecting only a basic strategic issue—could the bomber offensive win the war alone, or was an invasion necessary?

The critical battleground became the Transportation Plan under which the beachhead had to be isolated to prevent the Germans from winning the reinforcement race. In the course of examining this Plan, which involved the destruction of the major French and Belgian rail centres, Kingston-McCloughry came into contact with Sir Solly Zuckerman. Zuckerman's examination of operations in Italy reached much the same conclusions that Slessor had in *Air Power and Armies,* that isolation could be achieved through the destruction or disruption of the rail network that fed into the beachhead area. Opposed to this view were the so-called "Bomber Barons," Harris and Spaatz, who were determined to hamstring Overlord so that it could never be mounted. These were honest differences of opinion, but the Zuckerman Plan depended upon their resolution in favour of army co-operation. Compelled to acquiesce, Harris became a supporter when he found that his bombers could achieve something useful. Space does not permit a full examination of Kingston-McCloughry's chapters here on these and subsequent operations, but readers will find themselves well rewarded if they study them.

As I already overstepped the bounds prescribed in dealing with *The Direction of War* at some length, for it is really a postwar book, it must suffice merely to mention *Global Strategy*. In this volume and its successor, *Defence*, Kingston-McCloughry streamlines his thought into a simple, but provocative, textbook in which both the professional and the layman can trace quickly one interpretation of the evolution of strategy and how it should be made in the modern world. The danger into which these later works fall is that they appear thin because of their very simplicity. What is needed is more historical background, more examples and reinterpretations of past, especially aeronautical, history. *The Spectrum of Strategy* (1964), although valuable as an outline of the basis on which British defence White Papers should be written, is similarly weak on historical examples.

## J. M. SPAIGHT

No survey of the British airpower theorists of the interwar years would be complete without some mention of Trenchard's good friend James Molony Spaight. Born in Ireland in 1877, the younger son of a justice of the peace, J. M. Spaight was educated at Trinity College, Dublin, through which he passed as first a scholar and then as a student of law, emerging in 1905 with both a Bachelor and a Doctor of Laws. Meanwhile, in 1901 he had entered the Civil Service. After a number of appointments, he moved to the Air Ministry, where in 1930 he became Director of Accounts and in 1934 Principal Assistant Secretary until his retirement in 1937. Long before this he had begun to make a name for himself as a writer upon the legal aspects of warfare. In 1911 he produced *War Rights on Land* and followed this three years later with *Aircraft in War*, parts of which appeared in *The Army Review* in April 1914. Only the first chapter of this work was not a legal treatise. In it he set out the uses of aircraft pretty much as they were seen by the airmen of the day, including bomb-dropping and leaflet raids. But he did add, "It is unlikely that civilized nations will ever wreck one another's purely residential and commercial cities." But any city that had any defences could expect to be bombed. And he quoted in support Col. Louis Jackson's remarks at a contemporary Royal United Service Institution lecture that great centres of population would be bombed, to which Colonel David Henderson, who had the Chair, retorted that such an action would be militarily unethical.* Nevertheless, as in so many ethical matters, history nastily backed up the immoral.

As soon as the war was over, Spaight, who seems to have had a keen eye for the trends of public interest, published *Aircraft in Peace and the Law* (1919), followed in 1924 by *Air Power and War Rights.* This legal and historical handbook to such things as the shooting of men on parachutes and the like is a mine of information arranged in tidy legal form. It was reissued in 1934, and a revised and enlarged edition appeared after the Second World War. In 1926 came *Aircraft and Commerce in War,* in part considering the role of airpower at sea, and in the next year a handbook, *The Beginnings of Organized Air Power,* a text on the constitutional more than the historical aspects of the establishment of the Air Ministry and of the duties of the higher officials in it. In *Pseudo-Security* (1928) he attacked the League of Nations concept of peace and security through combined force that was lulling Europe in the post-Locarno years, putting what he called the jurist's other side of the case. In 1930 he returned to the theme of Chapters VII to XI of *Air Power and War Rights* by making a study of the naval bombardments of the nineteenth century and then using them as a precedent for air bombardments. "Air power," he said, "is essentially a moral[e]-breaking force. As such it has enormous possibilities. It will demand freedom to exploit them to the full." Acceptance of the principle that bombing was merely an extension of naval bombardment to inland areas would ensure that the action of airpower was not "diverted from the primary end of all war-like endeavour— the breaking of the enemy's armed strength." A moral as well as a military overthrow was the objective. Therefore,

> Disarmament assumes in the philosophy of air power thus outlined a place of prime importance. Air power is envisaged as a disarming, a preventive, a war-breaking rather than a war-making force.

* *JRUSI*, 1914, p. 701.

As Spaight saw it, airpower was the ideal instrument for use in the "sanction wars" of the future for it was "the hose pipe of the international fire-brigade." And it must be recalled that he, a Trenchardite, was writing this on the eve of the Disarmament Conference finally held at Geneva from 1932 to 1934, in which the abolition of bombing and the internationalization of civil aviation were serious proposals. In concluding this particular work he spoke for many when he talked about the "Dreams of Air Power," the dreams that aviation could bring peace to the world through the deterrent power that it possessed. And this was, also, a thought much in the minds of airmen then and since. Spaight used it to justify the quick aerial bombardment of cities as being far better than the mass slaughter of the nation's youth in bloody ground-bound battles. This was again of the times, nor must it be forgotten that Spaight was at this time a senior civil servant in the Air Ministry.

In 1932 he published a standard piece on *An International Air Force*, which provided again something of a legal brief. Six years later he wrote a useful survey of aeronautical thought of the day in *Air Power in the Next War*, one of the volumes in the series (edited by Liddell Hart) on a future conflict. Like many of the writings of the period in which rearmament was at last under way, the books in the "Next War" series tried to present a rational picture, especially in the light of what had happened in China, Abyssinia, and was still emerging from the Spanish Civil War. In a chapter aptly entitled "Flights of Fancy, and the Facts," Spaight tried to steer a clean path between not only the airpower enthusiasts with their predictions of catastrophe reaching out to every whitewashed cottage in the nation, who were aided by the Government's rather extraordinary approach to the whole business of Air Raid Precautions, which tended to put fear before precaution, but also the experts who said nothing could be done. What he pointed out was that an air blow might well be struck at London and other cities, but that it was simply impossible for an enemy to find the aircraft to be everywhere at once, or even to destroy all of the nation piece by piece. He put forward a well-prepared brief, but it was all perforce based upon what was already in print. This is not to say that it was not a learned synthesis and a necessary book for the day, but rather that it did not contain any such material as would make it regarded as a classic. It is a museum piece, reflecting its day—quite safe in its assumptions based upon the conception that airpower would be important, not decisive in the next war, but that its greatest contribution would be to prevent the next war in the first place.

During the war he produced *The Sky's the Limit* (1940), *The Battle of Britain* (1941), *Volcano Island* (1943), and *Bombing Vindicated* (1944), none of which can be ranked as other than wartime grist of the same sort that Admiral Richmond also wrote. By the end of the war he was sixty-eight years old, yet in 1948 he published two more books in addition to the third edition of *Air Power and War Rights*. These were *The Atomic Problem* and *Air Power Can Disarm*. The latter was a sequel to *Air Power and the Cities* (1930) in which he had raised a series of questions, and he now sought to see what answers the Second World War had produced. Not unnaturally, in view of the balanced stand that he had taken in 1938, he was able to show that airpower had helped to disarm the enemy, carried the battle to the roots of his fighting power, destroyed the material element of his armed strength, been able to push the bombers through, and been able to destroy targets within cities.

There were some points upon which, equally naturally, he had not been right, though the truth of this was not apparent until after Webster and Frankland wrote in 1961. Certainly airpower had hardly proved decisive as a deterrent, nor could it really be claimed for it that it had got the job done very fast, for the great air offensive against Germany, as we now know, did not really begin to have much effect until after the middle of 1944, nearly five years after the war had begun. Airpower did not then prove to be the weapon of disarmament, despite Spaight's claim. Nor did it prove possible for it to strike only at industrial targets, though to cover this point he postulated that war workers were not civilians. And it might also be, perhaps unfairly, pointed out, that with airpower so slow to make itself felt, it was possible that ground forces could destroy the base from which it operated, and that was a gamble that was taken in 1940 against Britain—and nearly succeeded.

## IN CONCLUSION

Certain remarks upon the airpower theorists must wait till the final chapter. In looking back upon the men whose works have been noticed here, certain patterns emerge:

First, these writers tended to deal with their work in the early stages as though it was a mere extension of the older arms. In this they were correct as far as the broad principles of war, and even of tactics, were concerned; but they failed to recognize the special advantages and limitations of the new weapon, and, perhaps unconsciously to ease their own burdens, they tended to hope for standardization and so simplification at far too early a date technologically and technically. On the other hand, they were also guilty of being visionary and of making sweeping statements upon occasion. Yet of the men actually examined here, it may be said that almost none of them was wildly off the mark. What can be held against them is that they were guilty of giving their Service powers that it did not possess the means to implement. This was much less true of the second generation like Slessor and Kingston-McCloughry than of the first.

Second, it may also be noted that the two theorists who became Chiefs of the Air Staff were both advocates of the deterrent strike force. But Slessor, in whose day the R.A.F. actually did possess a knockout power, was far more cautious and realistic than Trenchard, whose force possessed none of it. But here again, training, background, and environment are inescapable. Trenchard belonged to the nineteenth century British Army, Slessor to the twentieth century Air Force.

Third, the influence of environment, experience, and training is undeniable. Spaight was legal-minded throughout. Trenchard was hardly more of a modernist than Haig, nor was Sykes far removed from his military background or his own character. Groves, ironically, simply secured Trenchard's position by his onslaught, though his line of thought was more original. Douhet, too, was influenced by his environment, but he had little influence in England until after 1933. With the two later theorists, Slessor and Kingston-McCloughry, the more balanced view appears. Neither of them accepted fully either the Trenchard *dicta* or the view that the Air Force alone could win all wars. Their experience as instructor and pupil, respectively, at the Army Staff College broadened their horizons and made them realize the need for co-operation between the Services in order to achieve the common goal. The problem for all these men was to harmonize air strategy and tactics with both the traditional arms and with the technical possibilities of their Service's weapon. Their job was not unlike that of the proponents of armoured and mechanized warfare, their success about the same.

*Book Three*

# Comments and Conclusions

# *Chapter IX*—Comments and Conclusions

In their various ways the theorists of the interwar years were seeking either to justify the course of action they were taking or, and more often, to try to lead their nation and their Service away from the point of no return that military doctrine and action had reached by the middle of the First World War. Like the *philosophes* of the Enlightenment, yet with more originality, the pundits were attempting to educate mankind, for they wrote not merely for the military mind but also for the civilian. What does a study of these men and their works reveal?

Though it might seem valid to suggest that the lower a man's rank or the quicker he left the Service, the more he produced, this is really not so. Whether or not a writer or a man of action obtains tangible results depends to a very great extent on the inner drive that he possesses. It is extremely difficult for a man in the Services to write much. Tradition is against it. It is liable to censorship. It must be non-controversial or anonymous.* If it is to be the latter, it may not bring either personal satisfaction or advancement. If it is the former, it has to balance delicately between the little bit of dissent that is mistaken for brilliance and the radicalism that can blight a career. Essentially it must exhibit clarity of thought and style to gain official approval while being upon a safe subject. It is perfectly true that there were exceptions. Fuller and Richmond, it may be argued, reached flag rank. But both were retired without being appointed to eminent posts. Slessor did not do the bulk of his writing until after he retired, while Trenchard worked solely from the inside and at the top. In fact, Trenchard became virtually impregnable by chance and the force of his own personality.

* This is less true today than it was in the interwar years, especially in the American forces.

To achieve a measure of immortality, a writer must publish books. Articles die away in the dusty bound volumes of periodicals or become the first things thrown away on moving or on death. Preeminent in the game of preserving the best of the articles was Liddell Hart. But Slessor and Kingston-McCloughry also collected and reissued their better pieces. And who can blame them? Other writers do it. It is an intellectual habit and a justifiable one.

It is notable that while other intellectuals, such as poets, novelists, artists, and musicians, not to mention historians, have been rewarded with honours, the military intellectuals have been largely ignored. When they have received an accolade, it has usually been in some other capacity. The long delay in conferring honorary degrees and knighthood upon Liddell Hart has been noted. Nor has Fuller or Kingston-McCloughry been so honoured. Trenchard was knighted for his work in the field and ennobled upon retirement as Chief of the Air Staff. Richmond was knighted and became a Professor at Cambridge. These men have had few of the rewards in a society where such a system exists. Yet their work came closer to affecting the life of the nation than perhaps any other intellectual group, barring only scientists, politicians, and military commanders. Moreover, not infrequently their influence outside of the country exceeded their power in it. Liddell Hart and Fuller exercised considerable influence over the German, Russian, and American armies. It is only the airpower people who had a disproportionate voice at home, and they largely succeeded in scaring the country not into creating a credible deterrent but into believing that they would be the victims of a knockout blow.

It is generally acknowledged that one of the functions of intellectuals is to search for the truth; another, to expose the weaknesses and faults of society. These the military intellectuals attempted to do. They explored the past in order to find the eternal truths that could be applied to the present and the future. A glance at their bibliographies reveals this quite clearly in the cases of Liddell Hart, Fuller, and Richmond. They pointed to the weaknesses of their society. They noted the disparity between the *modus vivendi* and *operandi* of the Services as compared to the way of the modern nation. They drew attention to the age and mental shortcomings of both the commanders in the First World War and of their successors. They looked at the way History was made and showed how the Muse was corrupted in the womb by falsified documents, tainted interpretations, and deliberate fabrication. But their most important work was in attempting to show the errors of the past and the way to Heaven in the future. Yet they were generally realists, though their outlook upon reality depended to a certain extent upon their education and the age in which they were born.

Trenchard and Richmond were of the nineteenth century. Trenchard had a less than brilliant school career and a traditional Army training thereafter. Haig, the cavalryman, the solid, honest British soldier, was Trenchard's idol; and he intended to maintain the offensive in that tradition. He had the Army mind that sought to obtain the perfect weapon, to train men to use it with precision on the parade ground, while neglecting that rather more important business of developing a well-balanced conception of its use in war. For despite his emphasis upon training, he bequeathed to Churchill the Prime Minister, his former master, a weapon hardly ready for war even in 1940.

Richmond was even more of the Victorian military age than Trenchard in certain respects. He was trained in the old naval manner through the school ships and a steady career in men-of-war with an occasional spell at the Admiralty. And though he came from a Service whose technical knowledge was well rated, he lacked the ability to see what the newer weapons might do. He was still a battleshipman with the Navy's traditional disdain for the submarine, the aircraft carrier, and for aeroplanes.

Fuller, the non-conformist, was a man of the later nineteenth and early twentieth century. An agnostic who loved machinery, he applied science to the problems of the battlefield. He saw much as discipline or control. Thus his view of the way to save the nation in what he feared would be the aerial onslaught was through discipline. Fuller's self-education gave him some of the insulation of the martyr, the strength to say what had to be said, knowing that he would not be popular for doing so. But it also led him into the difficulty that his works, except for the purely orthodox military treatises, have become controversial politically. To be unorthodox, to make others think was from the early years of the century part of his character.

It is interesting that, of the theorists, Liddell Hart, Slessor, and Kingston-McCloughry were students at Cambridge University and Richmond later a professor there. Lord Tedder, who produced a standard historical work on naval warfare shortly after coming down, was also a student at Cambridge. The three Air Force men entered their Service in the days before it established its own college. It is curious that, though Oxford had a chair of military history, the Chichele, it did not in the interwar years produce a military prophet.

In all three Services or areas of martial affairs, the new thinkers were in varying degrees concerned over the harmony of the armed forces with the society that they protected. The Navy moved perhaps no more slowly to accept the facts of the Industrial Revolution than did the Army, while the Air Force was by no means a clear leader in technology. There is much, in explaining the reason for this, in Sir Giffard Martel's comment that most officers did not know how to draw up a specification for industrial production. In fact, few of them had any training in industry or much knowledge of its practices. Naval officers were better off in this than those of the other Services. And this lack of technological knowledge is to be seen in the writings of the theorists. They were not above being caught in the same difficulties themselves. They had a tendency to seek simple solutions that neglected likely developments that did not suit their theoretical conceptions. They occasionally sought to go against the flow, as Captain Ackworth, R.N., did with the coal-burning revivals, or conversely were caught in the toils of tradition, as in the long refusal of the Air Staff, official theorists in this sense, to accept monoplanes or escort fighters or big bombs. The pundits reflected their society and their Service's mind in their inability to see or to accept what appear now to have been perfectly logical developments or extensions of the manner in which war and society were travelling. Examples of this are Richmond's oft-mentioned failure to see the defensive role of aircraft carriers against shore-based aircraft, Fuller's overwhelming belief in the opening air strike, and Trenchard's failure to train an all-weather air force as the logical outcome of the deterrent doctrine. Yet in many respects the military intellectuals were ahead of their countrymen in attempting a realistic analysis not only of the conduct of war but also of why it might start. Most of them were or are political scientists with a strong interest in the interrelationship of politics and the conduct of war. This is especially to be seen in Richmond's *Statesmen and Sea Power* and his unfinished enlargement of this theme, and in the works of Sir Frederick Maurice the younger. Liddell

Hart, Fuller, and Kingston-McCloughry have all engaged in exploring the effects of character upon decision-making, in the study of psychology, and in operational analysis.

The military intellectuals also present the timeless intellectual problem of the origin of ideas. Obviously there have been in their cases three sources of stimulation: mechanical, military, and mental. First, they sought to apply mechanics to military problems with the aim of providing generally greater mobility, defence, or striking power, while at the same time lightening the physical loads of ordinary men. This is most notable in Fuller and Liddell Hart and much less so, perhaps because their familiarity with it made them overlook technology, in the cases of Trenchard and Richmond. Second, these people were determined to avert another war like the last one. It is the instinct of self-preservation plus the dislike of inefficiency that compels some persons to seek solutions to the ills of the world. It is the force of perfectionism, the power that keeps saying, "There must be a better way." Third, they were stimulated by what they read and heard and saw, but how much and by what?

On the whole, cross-pollination of ideas, such as the influence of Douhet, is not nearly such a simple knot to unravel as some scholars would like to assume. First, there has to be proof that a man has read a particular writer or a certain book, article, manual, etc. Second, it has to be shown that his ideas actually are plagiarized from someone else. Third, can he be made to admit that he owes a debt to another? The solution to the first is largely a mechanical problem and, therefore, merely a matter of tedious examination of particular volumes or files to discover if, in fact, the thinker did read, not just own, a particular volume. Sometimes the answer is simple. Perhaps he wrote a book review, or an article, or a diary, or a letter. But what if he did not? On the other hand, it may be possible to show that he must have read the volume, but when confronted with this evidence, the subject will deny that he was influenced by it. Men tend not to care to acknowledge their debt to the dead, unless such an association is to their advantage. Now, on the second point, it is perhaps a little harsh to suggest that ideas have been plagiarized when in many cases it may be a completely unconscious borrowing, or none at all. It is quite likely that men working on the same materials with much the same background, or at least with the same objectives, will reach the same conclusions or the same solutions. But to take the other side yet again, it is also possible to show that certain dominant intellectuals have had a decisive influence. This is particularly true of the military intellectuals, who have at times had a captive audience. Liddell Hart and Walser wrote official manuals; Fuller, Grenfell, and Slessor produced basic treatises. Moreover, as in the case of most messiahs, the military intellectuals have found grouped about them their disciples. The greater the influence of the pundits, the more difficult it has become to probe behind them and find the sources of their ideas. The third point relating to the admission of ideas has already been covered in part. Still it is perhaps worth noting that whether or not the idea was spontaneous or borrowed, after a time the theorist will adopt it for his own and a lie-detector test will not contradict his belief in his own originality.

A few practical examples may be cited in support of the above remarks, presented largely to justify the reason for not making an elaborate attempt to assign origins to the thoughts and ideas of the military intellectuals. Both Liddell Hart and Fuller read Henderson, but neither today admits Henderson's influence, though Fuller mentions him in *Grant and Lee*. Richmond read Mahan, but he served under Lord Fisher at the Admiralty, and Fisher had no use for Mahan at all. Yet due to the very paucity of naval writings, we can assume that Mahan did affect Sir Herbert's mind. In the case of the airmen, who influenced whom? Did Spaight or others influence Lanchester? Did Lanchester inspire Trenchard, or was it Henderson or du Peuty or Haig or just the war itself? Or was it Foch and Balfour and Hankey? Certainly Trenchard influenced the R.A.F. and equally certain his group affected Fuller. But between Trenchard and Liddell Hart there was an interplay, at first as friends, but after the mid-thirties they went their separate ways and what had been an acceleration towards a common objective became a sharpening of divergences in opposition.

The problems with which these military intellectuals were dealing and their influence in terms both of solutions and of human failings also deserve some comments in conclusion.

First, there is the oft-mentioned failing of the military mind to consider that its own ideas or weapons may not be invincible and the enemy's unavailing. This idea of impregnability was expressed in a failure to see the merits of other arms, as in the case of Richmond, or other weapons, in the case of Trenchard. Another aspect of the same delusion was the lack of foresight in regard to what the enemy might do to counter certain developments and what, in consequence, their own Service would have to do to parry this action. If faced with a deterrent striking force, the obvious solution was dispersion before the firing started. This in its turn required the attacker to develop better means of target location and destruction. But was it done? The evidence of the Second World War is quite plain that it was not. But by no means did they all fall into this trap, and Liddell Hart's *Strategy* in particular sought to avert this folly.

Second, there is the fact that on the whole these writers were aware that what was good for one was not good for all. This was the argument that Richmond used in naval affairs, that the more moderate airpower writers conveyed, and that Fuller and to a greater extent Liddell Hart tried to propagate. Most notable in this respect was Liddell Hart's attempt to show Britain that she should fight wars in her traditional way and not become embroiled in Continental struggles, though the possibility of her remaining aloof was lessened by the coming of airpower. On a lower level this is reflected in the demands for balanced forces, while the old military mind is seen in the Air Force's gradual concentration upon the general-purpose aircraft and the *offensive à outrance* of Bomber Command, two incompatibles.

The most interesting and alarming phenomenon that emerges from this study is that of mass misdirection and delusion when logic was carried to its inevitable extreme. The knockout-blow scare had two sources and travelled along parallel paths to disenchantment.

In the beginning there were those who said that the logical way to attack the enemy was to move back from the battlefield, where no one could obtain a decisive advantage, to the railway junctions through which the enemy's supplies came. But when they came there, they were already manufactured. So hit the factories. The factories were manned by workers, but in an industrial war they were combatants. Thus the worker became a legitimate target. And as he was also a democrat, then he could be held responsible for his government's action. So could his wife and his adult relatives. Taken as a group, it was their will that had then to be broken in order to make the Government stop the soldier at the Front. This was the indirect approach that became mixed with retaliation in the cauldron of the First World War. From this simple logical view compounded by politics emerged the idea, which supported both the deterrent and airpower bombers, that the will of the enemy nation was the true target. Owing to the novelty of air bombardment in the 1914 war, the psychological effect of it upon civilians was exaggerated. If the old saw is that familiarity breeds contempt, its corollary is that the unknown produces awe. Thus the scene was set for the confidence man.

The preachers of the gospel of airpower were perfectly logical and credible and were even aided by their opponents, who took such a violently reactionary view that they did themselves more harm than good. So the prophets gained the moral ascendancy. Added to this, they were the purveyors of statistics. In fact, they were given a monopoly. Anyone who wished to challenge their assumptions was in the analogous position of one challenging the authority of the Church. Yet, in fact, there were other sources of information, other ways of analysing the material available. The problem of those who undertook this augean task was that they had themselves to be simon-pure. Second, they had to have irrefutable evidence, clearly set out. And, third, they had to attract an influential audience.

As has since become patent, the airpower disciples were taking Britain on the road to potential disaster. Their statistical evidence was based upon far too small a sampling; they made no allowance for probability; and they had not prepared to carry out the role in which they had cast themselves. Nor had they undertaken a psychological analysis of the likely effect of bombing on populations with a strong core of veterans of World War I trench warfare barrages. But for this they may be excused, since they had not tested their bombs either. In other words, the knockout air strike demonstrates the dangers of the lack of intellectual challenge and the ease with which the public and the Government can be trapped in a logical canyon. They were corralled by the materialists riding their hobbyhorses. Just because a man may be gifted in one field, it by no means ensures that he is rational and respectable in all. Lord Cherwell is one example, Trenchard another. Scientific and professional opinion may not always be helpful. But how else are such ideas to be measured, challenged, and evaluated? This is an eternal question. But there is an answer.

Time itself, given about fifteen years, will provide a revelation in terms of new interpretations, new evidence, and a change in the public attitude. New international tensions will cause a reappraisal. Yet the soundest prophet may be damned when what he has foretold happens before his advice has been implemented. And in the final victory others more self-seeking and publicity-conscious may gain the fame. Many intellectuals have died in poverty only to be discovered and acclaimed by another generation.

The Second World War both justified and exposed the military intellectuals in a way that seldom happens to those whose grappling with eternal truths is all imaginary.

The new war, for which some have called World War I a rehearsal, was a conflict of mobility. The blitzkrieg made astute use of mechanization, armour, airpower, and psychology, as well as of industrial capacity. Armies plunged ahead so fast, as compared to 1914-18, that lines rarely formed except where, as at Cassino, natural features made it possible to dig in and hold. Even the defensive battles were mobile. At sea the historic idea of convoy was readopted, but with new features as new weapons became available. And as sufficient escorts were commissioned to do more than merely guard the merchantmen, hunter-killer groups ranged the oceans to turn the tables on the stalker while overhead the even greater mobility of the aeroplane gave the U-boat no safety. In the air the bomber did get through, but small losses (some as low as five per cent) caused his transfer to other targets or other duties. The oft-scorned defensive fighter and the much-debated escort fighter had to be used. Everywhere there was evidence of the indirect approach. It was to be seen in the fields of France, in paratroop operations in Norway and Crete, in the operations in the Western Desert, and in the air battle of Germany, not to mention operations in the Pacific. It was a war in which psychology was employed in everything from whistling bombs on the battlefield to leaflets and loudspeakers, to the relation of food to news, to the myth of the invincible Aryans. More than this, the Second World War was a technological war not merely of industrial production, but also one in which "boffins" (operational scientists) and operational research became vital tools that commanders had to learn to understand and evaluate. And finally, the 1939 war raised once again the question that always comes to dog the materialists— what is the best operational size for any weapon? Economy of force was dominant here, too. It was not always the biggest that was the best. Neither the battleship, nor the super-tank nor the heaviest bomber proved to be the cheapest or more efficient weapons. Those that won the war were medium-sized, mobile, and operable by former civilians in pursuit of their commander's plans based as often as not upon the ideas of the British military intellectuals.

This book started by suggesting that several factors affected the way the military intellectuals wrote. Perhaps not least was their feeling that Britain had not won the First World War. It had not been for them an exhilarating military experience. It had lacked the glamour of the Boer War or the Indian frontier with their mobile operations. It had degenerated into an amateur affair fought by civilians, in which politicians and not generals were in control. The military intellectuals wanted to know why. And they believed that they had found out. It was an industrial war that required managers, and so the pundits became planners and management consultants. They saw their job as producing victories. But not just military successes, not simply a clearing of the bottlenecks, but rather a re-establishment of a profitable equilibrium, which we call peace. And like good consultants, their aim was largely to avoid a breakdown in the first place. Thus, the environment in which they lived very much affected their outlook and their writings, from the right-wing views of Fuller to the concepts of dynamic defence of Liddell Hart. The airpower theorists lived in an industrial age, and they created a theory that was designed to restrain an industrial competitor. But they failed to see that industrial society is very complex and that, to be successful, businessmen have to be nimble, so their industrial reflexes are quick. A failure in one plant, in one salient, brings out the staff and the reserves. They respond to the challenge. It took a good deal of the 1939 war for this plain truth to be brought home to the ordinary military mind, and even to some of the politicians.

The military intellectuals have a role and a place in society. They are the nation's testers and tasters. They provide the skilled knowledge and independent judgement by which official actions may be judged. Like many intellectuals they usually are genuine patriots who want the best for their country. But even they must not be allowed to presume that they alone know what this should be. It has increasingly become recognized that the pundits should be consulted. In the interwar years they did exercise some influence upon the Higher Direction through interviews, memoranda, and special consultation, and through Members of Parliament. It is ironic that they are now apparently being consulted more as Britain's position in the world declines.*

The military intellectuals in the interwar years provided the policy and strategy-makers in Britain with a different point of view. If any policy was debatable, they could be counted upon to have some opinion. If it was widely at variance with that espoused in Government circles, the Minister who wanted to oppose this policy, or who wanted support for yet another idea, could probably obtain some assistance from these outsiders. In the notable case of Richmond and MacDonald, Liddell Hart and Hore-Belisha, they obtained it. In the case of Trenchard as Chief of Staff, they failed. For it was not until after he had left office that Liddell Hart swung to a defensive policy matched to Britain's military necessity of the day. It was not until after Inskip became Minister for the Co-ordination of Defence that an influential politician called for outside advice on the air defence of Britain. And at the time of Munich the power of the new defence was too weak to stop a German air strike against London, actually a figment of Air Ministry imagination, while the R.A.F. itself could not strike Germany. Chamberlain was thus caught defenceless and powerless in the middle of a debate between two influential schools of thought.

In a search for truth it is perhaps appropriate to end with a comment upon historians. No more than the military intellectuals are they free from the prejudices and pressures of environment. Owing to the fact that official histories tend to be thought of as gospel, they can be the most misleading of all. This is particularly dangerous and unfortunate when much of the writing on war has (of necessity for the wars within the last fifty years) to be based upon their evidence. We now know that they have been distorted either subtly or deliberately. Though exactly how much effect this has had remains to be seen. But there is the problem that many lessons of a recent war must await the appearance and analysis of the Government volumes. Yet properly trained scholars, analysts,

* Lawrence W. Martin, "The Market for Strategic Ideas in Britain," *The American Political Science Review,* LVI (March 1962), 23-41.

and military intellectuals can piece together a large part of the story and draw the necessary fresh lessons from what appeared during and shortly after the conflict. It remains one of the most important roles of the military intellectual to digest and expound upon this knowledge, enriched by his own observations.*

* Just as this work goes to the printers, two items of interest have appeared: Colonel Russell V. Ritchey, "The Military Profession as a Competitive Environment," *Air University Review,* September-October, 1965, pp. 2-9; and Robert E. Futrell, "Airpower Lessons of World War II," *Air Force/Space Digest,* September 1965, pp. 42-50, 53.

# Appendixes

# Appendix A—F. W. Lanchester, *Aircraft in Warfare* (January 1916, pp. 130-131)

**88. *The Command of the Air.*** It is probable that in the future the employment of aircraft in large numbers, tactically in a combative capacity, may, in effect, still further deepen the fighting-line. Without attempting to predict exactly what *rôle* the aeroplane will take in this regard, it is safe to say that if, during a battle, it is found practicable to conduct air raids and air attacks systematically over a considerable belt of territory in the rear of an enemy's lines, this belt will require to be defended, and (if the air forces employed are of numerical strength comparable to the other Arms) the belt will actually become a measure of the depth of front. The permanent defeat of the enemy's air fleet and, as we may express it, the *capture of his air* will then become the first and most important duty of the Aeronautical Arm. It is difficult to gauge what the total consequence of defeating the enemy in the air will be. It is unlikely that it will entirely prevent his aerial reconnaissance; his scouts will doubtless manage to run the gauntlet and continue to keep him sufficiently informed. On the other hand, he will be deprived of all those uses of the Aeronautical Arm in which some more direct and definite purpose is involved, such as the direction of gun-fire, defence of stores, protection of cavalry, etc. He will require to submit to aeroplane attack without possibility of effective counter; he will be subjected to long-range gun-fire (directed by aeroplane) without means of returning it: his cavalry will be continually harassed by machine-gun fire and explosive grenades, and will cease to be of service; his railways, convoys, and mechanical transport will be nowhere safe; and he will need to expend an undue proportion of his resources in patrolling his lines of communication and guarding points of strategic importance. The command of the air opens up possibilities in the direction of raiding of a kind and with a scope not hitherto known in warfare. To what extent it will be found possible for aircraft to detach themselves from their base, and execute

*251*

extended raids in territory held by the enemy, only the future can determine. It would certainly appear that if the inhabitants are friendly, and the enemy's aircraft are no more a force to be reckoned with, tactics of this kind may be quite feasible.

Once again the author would point out that the experience of the present war is no guide; the Aeronautical Arm *quâ* Arm cannot at present be said to exist. The Flying Corps, excellent though it be, is scarcely more than necessary to constitute an armed reconnaissance service.

89. *Total Defeat in the Air an Irreparable Disaster*. From the foregoing it would appear to be at least doubtful whether in future warfare an army which has been deprived of its aircraft, or has to admit the air supremacy of an enemy, will find itself in a position to carry on a campaign. It is, in any case, certain that it will only be able to do so at a very grave disadvantage. It is the author's opinion that the time will come when the total and irretrievable loss of the command of the air to an enemy will be regarded as a disaster of an altogether irreparable and decisive kind, and although there may be a great deal of fighting still before the end, nothing less than an overwhelming superiority in the other arms will save an army deprived of its air service from ultimate defeat. We are thus led to the consideration of a branch of the subject of extreme importance—namely, *aeroplane tactics*.

# *Appendix B* — Major-General Trenchard's Order, 22 September 1916

Since the beginning of the recent operations the fighting in the air has taken place over the enemy's line, and visits of hostile aeroplanes over our lines have been rare. It is to be hoped that this state of things may continue, but as one can never be certain of anything in war, it is perhaps an opportune moment to consider what policy should be adopted were this state of affairs to change, and were the enemy to become more enterprising and more aggressive.

It is sometimes argued that our aeroplanes should be able to prevent hostile aeroplanes from crossing the line, and this idea leads to a demand for defensive measures and a defensive policy. Now is the time to consider whether such a policy would be possible, desirable and successful.

It is the deliberate opinion of all those most competent to judge that this is not the case, and that an aeroplane is an offensive and not a defensive weapon. Owing to the unlimited space in the air, the difficulty one machine has in seeing another, the accidents of wind and cloud, it is impossible for aeroplanes, however skilful and vigilant their pilots, however numerous their formations, to prevent hostile aircraft from crossing the line if they have the initiative and determination to do so.

The aeroplane is not a defence against the aeroplane. But the opinion of those most competent to judge is that the aeroplane, as a weapon of attack, cannot be too highly estimated.

A signal instance of this fact is offered to us by the operations which took place in the air at Verdun.

When the operations at Verdun began, the French had few machines on the spot. A rapid concentration was made, and a vigorous offensive was adopted. The result was that superiority in the air was obtained immediately, and the machines detailed for artillery co-operation and photography were enabled to carry out their work unmolested, but as new units were put into the line which had less experience of working with aeroplanes, a demand arose in some quarters for machines of protection, and these demands were for a time complied with. The result was that the enemy took the offensive, and the French machines were unable to prevent the hostile raids which the enemy, no longer being attacked, was now able to make. The mistake was at once realised and promptly rectified. A policy of general offensive was once more resumed, and the enemy at once ceased to make hostile raids, all his time being taken up in fighting the machines which were attacking him. Superiority in the air was thus once more regained.

On the British front, during the operations which began with the battle of the Somme, we know that, although the enemy has concentrated the greater part of his available forces in the air on this front, the work actually accomplished by their aeroplanes stands, compared with the work done by us, in the proportion of about 4 to 100. From the accounts of prisoners, we gather that the enemy's aeroplanes have received orders not to cross the lines over the French or British front unless the day is cloudy and a surprise attack can be made, presumably in order to avoid unnecessary casualties. On the other hand, British aviation has been guided by a policy of relentless and incessant offensive. Our machines have continually attacked the enemy on his side of the line, bombed his aerodromes, besides carrying out attacks on places of importance far behind the lines. It would seem probable that this has had the effect so far on the enemy of compelling him to keep back or to detail portions of his forces in the air for defensive purposes.

When Lille station was attacked from the air for the first time no hostile aeroplanes were encountered. The second time, this place was attacked our machines encountered a squadron of Fokkers, which were there for defensive purposes. This is only one instance among many.

The question which arises is this: Supposing the enemy, under the influence of some drastic reformer or some energetic leader, were now to change his policy and follow the example of the English and the French, and were to cease using his aeroplanes as a weapon of defence and to start a vigorous offensive and attack as many places as far behind our lines as he could, what would be the sound policy to follow in such a case? Should we abandon our offensive, bring back our Squadrons behind the line to defend places like Boulogne, St. Omer, Amiens and Abbeville, and protect our artillery and photographic machines with defensive escorts, or should we continue our offensive more vigorously than before? Up to now the work done by the Germans compared with that done by our aeroplanes stands, as we have seen, in the proportion of 4 to 100, but let us suppose that the enemy initiated a partial offensive in the air, and that his work increased, compared with ours, to a proportion of 30 or 50 to 100, it is then quite certain that a demand for protective measures would arise for protective Squadrons and machines for defensive patrols.

One of the causes of such demands is the moral effect produced by a hostile aeroplane, which is out of all proportion to the damage which it can inflict.

The mere presence of a hostile machine in the air inspires those on the ground with exaggerated forebodings with regard to what the machine is capable of doing. For instance, at one time on one part of the front whenever a hostile machine, or what was thought to be a hostile machine, was reported, whistles were blown and men hid in the trenches.

In such cases the machines were at far too great a height to observe the presence of men on the ground at all, and even if the presence of men was observed it would not lead to a catastrophe. Again, a machine which was reported in one place would certainly, since it was flying rapidly, be shortly afterwards observed in another part of the lines and reported again, but the result of these reports was often that for every time the machine was sighted a separate machine was reported, leading at the end of the day to a magnified and exaggerated total.

The sound policy, then, which should guide all warfare in the air would seem to be this: to exploit this moral effect of the aeroplane on the enemy, but not to let him exploit it on ourselves. Now this can only be done by attacking and by continuing to attack.

It has been our experience in the past that at a time when the Germans were doing only half the work done by our machines that their mere presence over our lines produced an insistent and continuous demand for protective and defensive measures.

If the Germans were once more to increase the degree of their activity even up to what constitutes half the degree of our activity, it is certain that such demands would be made again.

On the other hand, it is equally certain that, were such measures to be adopted, they would prove ineffectual. As long as a battle is being fought, any machine at the front has five times the value that the same machine would have far behind the lines.

If the enemy were aware of the presence of a defensive force in one particular spot he would leave that spot alone and attack another, and we should not have enough machines to protect all the places which could possibly be attacked behind our lines, and at the same time continue the indispensable work on the front.

But supposing we had enough machines both for offensive and for defensive purposes. Supposing we had an unlimited number of machines for defensive purposes, it would still be impossible to prevent hostile machines from crossing the line if they were determined to do so, simply because the sky is too large to defend. We know from experience how difficult it is to prevent a hostile vessel, and still more a hostile submarine, from breaking a blockade, when the blockade extends over a large area. But in the air the difficulty of defence is practically unlimited, and because the aeroplane is fighting in three dimensions.

The sound policy would seem to be that if the enemy changes his tactics and pursues a more vigorous offensive, to increase our offensive, to go further afield, and to force the enemy to do what he would gladly have us do now. If, on the other hand, we were to adopt a purely defensive policy, or a partially offensive policy, we should be doing what the French have learnt by experience to be a failure, and what the rank and file of the enemy, by their own accounts, point to as being one of the main causes of their recent reverses.

Moreover, in adopting such a policy it appears probable that the Germans are guided by necessity rather than by choice, owing to the many fronts on which they now have to fight, and owing also to the quality and the quantity of machines they have to face on the Western Front alone. Nevertheless, one cannot repeat too often that in war nothing is certain, and that the Germans may, either owing to the pressure of public opinion, or the construction of new types of machines, or the rise of a new leader, change their policy at any moment for a more aggressive one.

September 22nd, 1916

Source: Maurice Baring, *R.F.C., H.Q.,* pp. 180-184; *The War in the Air,* II, 472-475.

# *Appendix C*—The Place of Douhet

Bernard Brodie in his *Strategy for the Missile Age* (Princeton, 1959, 71 ff.) furthers the myth that Douhet was mainly responsible for the growth of British and American airpower theory by calling his section "The Heritage of Douhet." A careful search of publishers' lists, *Books in Print,* back to its inception in 1928, of the *English Book Catalogue, The International Index to Periodicals,* as well as queries to British aeronautical libraries, reveals no evidence of the existence of Douhet's works in Britain until the middle to late thirties. The earliest British edition of *The Command of the Air* is a 1943 reprint of the 1942 American translation by Dino Ferrari of the 1927 edition. The first recorded English translation of any of Douhet's writings has long been thought to be the 1933 United States Army Air Corps Tactical School one of "Une novelle doctrine de guerre: l'oevre du général Douhet" by General Tulasne in *Revue Des Deux Mondes* (15 May 1932, pages 282-303). Since then Major Alfred Hurley, U.S.A.F., in doing the research for *Billy Mitchell, Crusader for Air Power* (New York, 1964), has found Douhet's ideas set out by Lt/Col. A. Guidoni, an early Italian aerial torpedo expert and at the time Italian air attaché in Washington, as "The Problems of the Independent Air Force," *Aviation* (New York, XIII, 20 November 1922, 687). (This magazine is now *Aviation Week.*) The first promulgation in England did not come until the *Royal Air Force Quarterly* of April 1936 (pages 152-159). Sometimes this has been ascribed to Lt/Col. H. de Watteville's "Armies of the Air" in *The Nineteenth Century and After* (October 1934, pages 353-368), but this overlooks the long English background already described. The first complete exposition in English was Louis Sigaud's *Douhet and Aerial Warfare* (New York, 1941). But though General of the Army H. H. ("Hap") Arnold notes correctly in his *Global Mission* (pp. 131-132) that Douhet's ideas confirmed what the United States Army Air Corps had already worked out for itself, Roger Burlingame in *General Billy Mitchell* (New York, 1956, pp. 54-83) furthers the myth by referring to the likely influence of Douhet on Mitchell. At the same time Burlingame badly overrates Trenchard's interest in an independent air force *in 1917*, a mistake that Arnold also makes (*Global Mission*, pp. 78, 160).

Douhet tells us that he wrote a piece called *La Preparazione* in 1909, but it is not clear from either the Dino Ferrari translation or from the research being done by Frank Cappelluti of Rutgers, who visited the Caproni Museum in 1963, whether or not this was merely a collection of newspaper articles similar to those being written or to lectures being given by others at the same time. In their day many of these verged on science-fiction in their predictions of the future use of airpower. Some recent work by writers in *The Airpower Historian* (J. L. Boone Atkinson, July 1957, pp. 141-149); Colonel Edgar S. Gorrell's Memorandum (reprinted in the April 1958 issue, pp. 102-117, and based on Admiral Mark Kerr's) suggests that Douhet was the mouthpiece of Count Caproni, the Italian bomber designer and manufacturer. This is a point that it is to be hoped Cappelluti's dissertation will clarify. Douhet's *Command of the Air* did not appear until 1921, at which time the aircraft manufacturers were desperately trying to persuade their governments to give them orders in order to stay alive. The 1921 edition was published by the Italian Air Ministry, which was shortly, after Mussolini came to power, to become the administrator of a highly independent air force. The 1927 edition was put out by the Fascist Ministry of Culture at a time when Italians were becoming quite air-conscious.

After what has been said in Chapter VI, it seems quite clear that Douhet had no influence in the forming of British airpower theory. Those airmen who read his works—and there cannot have been many who read Italian—liked his writings for the very human reason that he agreed with what they were saying. On the whole the Douhet myth appears to have arisen largely during the Second World War. No doubt it grew fastest in America where the United States Army Air Force, Alexandre P. de Seversky, and academicians swung enthusiastically into the business of indoctrinating the nation with a martial background, and where Billy Mitchell's name was no certain light. That the British got less than their proper credit for creating the theory of deterrents was due to their own reluctance to engage in the production of manuals and to a paucity of serious non-Service students of airpower, not to mention the way in which *The War in the Air* helped to confuse the picture. The one Englishman who gave some credit to Douhet prewar was J. M. Spaight in *Air Power in the Next War* (1938). Liddell Hart in *The Revolution in Warfare* (New Haven, 1947, p. 10) supports the view that the R.A.F. developed its own doctrine, as does Marshal of the R.A.F. Sir John Slessor, once in the Trenchard brains trust, in *The*

*Central Blue* (1959, p. 39). It is opposed by Air Marshal Sir Robert Saundby in "Prophet of Air Power," *The Aeroplane* (4 May 1956, pp. 342-343). On the general development of air doctrine, see Eugene Emme's compilation, *The Impact of Air Power* (New York, 1959); Thomas H. Greer, *The Development of Air Doctrine in the [U.S.] Army Air Arm* (Maxwell A.F.B., Ala., 1955), and E. M. Earle, *The Makers of Modern Strategy* (Princeton, 1952), which must be used with care as it was written in 1942.

Since the above was written, my article, "The Dangerously Neglected," has appeared (*Military Affairs*, XXIX, No. 2, Summer 1965), 73-87. Comments have been made by both Bernard Brodie and Eugene Emme in their letters to me. We continue to disagree as to the prevalence of Douhet's influence in Britain. The logical conclusion would seem to be that here is another case similar to that of Newton and Leibnitz, of Darwin and Wallace. Faced with the same challenge, various people developed the same responses. Who got the credit has depended upon who was in the best position to publicize his work and to maintain his position. The British approach was the more silent, perhaps because there was no Congress to convince. But there can probably never be a definitive answer to the question raised. The best that can be hoped for is a serious study of official and personal papers in all three countries (Britain, the United States, and Italy). Dr. Noble Frankland has written me that none of his research on the background for *The Strategic Air Offensive against Germany* revealed any mention of Douhet's name.

# *Appendix D*—A Checklist of British Military and Other Periodicals in which the Military Writers Published, 1918-1940

Paul A. Spence and Helen J. Hopewell
*Union List of Foreign Military Periodicals*
Air University Library, Maxwell A.F.B., Ala., 1957
Very useful in the United States

*The Army Quarterly*
London, October 1920-

*Army, Navy and Air Force Gazette*
London, 1922-1936
Superseded by *The United Services Review*, 1860-1939

*British Legion Journal*
London, July 1921-

*Cadet Journal and Gazette*
Army Cadet Force Association
London, 1920-

*Cavalry Journal*
London, 1906-1942 (suspended 1914-1918)
Now *The Royal Armoured Corps Journal*
London, July 1946-

*The English Review*
London, 1844-1853, 1908-1937

*The Fortnightly Review*
London, 1865-

*The Globe and Laurel:* Journal of the Royal Marines
Southsea, Hants, 1892-    ; bimonthly

*The Gunner:* Official organ of the Royal Artillery Association
Woolwich, 1919-    ; monthly

*The Naval Review*
London, 1911-
Confidential for twelve years from date of publication

*Navy*
The Navy League
London, 1895-    ; monthly

*The Nineteenth Century and After*
London, 1877-
*The Twentieth Century* as of 1951

*Journal of the Royal Air Force College*
Cranwell, 1920-    ; three numbers yearly

*The Royal Air Force Quarterly*
London, 1920-
Not to be confused with *The Royal Air Force Review,* 1946-

*Royal Army Ordnance Corps Gazette*
R.A.O.C. Association
Aldershot, 1906-1919, N.S. 1920-

*Journal of the Royal Artillery*
Royal Artillery Institution
Woolwich, 1858-    ; quarterly

*Royal Engineers Journal*
Institution of the Royal Engineers
Chatham, 1870-1904, N.S. 1905-    ; quarterly

*Journal of the Royal United Service Institution*
London, 1857-    ; quarterly at first but long since monthly
There is now *The Consolidated Author and Subject Index to the JRUSI*
   (ed. Robin Higham)
Ann Arbor, Mich., 1965

*Journal of the United Service Institution of India*
New Delhi, 1871-    ; quarterly

*Tank:* Journal of the Royal Tank Regiment
London, 1919-    ; monthly

*United Service Magazine*
London, 1829-1920

*United Services and Home Defence Review*
Croydon, 1860-    ; bimonthly

*The Army and Navy Gazette*
London, 1860-1921
*The Army, Navy, and Air Force Gazette,* 1922-1936
*The United Services Review,* 1936-1939

*Waggoner:* Journal of the Royal Army Service Corps
Aldershot, 1955-
*Royal Army Service Corps Journal,* 1891-1954

*Wire*
Royal Corps of Signals
London, 1924-    ; monthly

See also the footnotes and Bibliography in my *Armed Forces in Peacetime: Britain, 1918-1939.*

# Index

# Index

(*See also* Table of Contents)

# About the Author

During World War II Robin Higham was a pilot in the RAF. After the war he attended and graduated from Harvard College. He secured his master's degree from Claremont Graduate School and his Ph.D. at Harvard University. He has taught at the University of Massachusetts, University of North Carolina, and is currently the specialist in modern British history, technology and war, in the history department of Kansas State University. This book developed from work done on a National Security Policy Research Fellowship from the Social Science Research Council.

The typeface used for the composition of both the text and display of this book was Baskerville. It was printed by letterpress on 60# Mead Imperial Antique and bound in Columbia's Bayside Vellum, BSV-033. Manufactured by Quinn & Boden Company, Inc., Rahway, New Jersey.